D1596725

PHILOSOPHY OF
GERMAN IDEALISM

The German Library: Volume 23
Volkmar Sander, General Editor

PHILOSOPHY OF GERMAN IDEALISM

Edited by Ernst Behler

CONTINUUM • NEW YORK

1987

The Continuum Publishing Company
370 Lexington Avenue, New York, NY 10017

The German Library
is published in cooperation with Deutsches Haus,
New York University.
This volume has been supported by a grant
from Robert Bosch GmbH.

Printed in the United States of America

Library of Congress Cataloging in Publication Data

Philosophy of German idealism.

(The German library ; v. 23)
1. Philosophy, German—18th century. 2. Philosophy,
German—19th century. 3. Idealism, German. I. Behler,
Ernst, 1928–   II. Series.
B2745.P45 1987   141'.0943   86-29082
ISBN 0-8264-0306-9
ISBN 0-8264-0307-7 (pbk.)

ACKNOWLEDGMENTS
We gratefully acknowledge permission to reprint "Deduction of a Universal Organ of
Philosophy, or Main Propositions of the Philosophy of Art According to Principles of
Transcendental Idealism," by F. W. J. Schelling, from *Philosophies of Art and Beauty*:
Selected Readings in Aesthetics from Plato to Heidegger, edited by Albert Hofstadter
and Richard Kuhns. © 1964 by The University of Chicago Press. All rights reserved.

Contents

Introduction

The texts of this volume constitute highlights in the movement called transcendental idealism and ought to be seen together with those selected in Volume 13 on Kant and Volume 27 on Hegel. They are mainly taken from Fichte, Schelling, and Jacobi, who are much lesser known in the English-speaking world than the founder of transcendental idealism, Kant, and the philosopher in whom this movement supposedly found its culmination, Hegel. We even notice a certain value judgment and a teleological conception in the notion of transcendental idealism inaugurated by Hegel and strongly maintained by his followers. According to this conception, the movement proceeded in progressive phases, in ascending stages, leaving behind previous positions as preliminary preformations, as mere stepping stones, and coming to full fruition only in Hegel. This view is obvious in phrases like "from Kant to Hegel" or "the accomplishment of idealistic thought in Hegel." We have to keep in mind, however, that this is a retrospective judgment and not at all shared by the early representatives of this movement, even doing severe injustice to them.

The entire movement certainly originated with Kant and the tensions implied in his philosophy. He was perceived not only as the "all-crushing" Kant, however, but as a philosopher who, although envisioning a new metaphysical system, had not yet pursued this task himself, remaining instead preoccupied with preparing the critical foundations of it. Karl Leonhard Reinhold was the first Kantian to attempt such a metaphysical system from Kant's critical principles.[1] Fichte and Schelling clearly saw themselves as carrying out this task, whereas Jacobi remains more of a stranger in this group of speculative idealists. Because of his insistence on a type of reason which transcends the realm of philosophical speculation, however, his unrelenting critique of absolutized reason, and his pronounced dislike of what he called a "purely logical enthusiasm," Jacobi accompanies this movement as its most vociferous challenger.

Besides transcendental speculation and self-determination of reason, some of the most frequently used terms in these texts are system and systematic. The attempt to philosophize in a strictly systematic fashion is noticeable in almost every piece of this volume. Hegel formulated this tendency in a writing of 1803 when he stated: "That philosophizing which does not construct itself as a system is a permanent escape from limitations, is more of a struggling of reason for freedom than a pure self-recognition of freedom which is certain and conscious of itself."[2] Yet one look at the development of the movement itself as it is mirrored in the texts of this volume soon reveals that a final system of "absolute knowledge" did not materialize and remained in a state of constant becoming and reformulation. This does not only apply to the movement as a whole, but also to its individual representatives who like Fichte, continuously revised their philosophy or like Schelling, went through the most profound changes of basic philosophical positions throughout their lifetime.

The time-span covered in this volume comprises the years from 1794 to 1809. In 1794, Fichte formulated in the first introduction to his philosophy the goal of transcendental idealism, i.e., accomplished self-recognition of reason in programmatic terms. In 1809, Schelling with his *Philosophical Investigations into the Essence of Human Freedom* engaged in speculations which progressively led him to his philosophy of mythology and philosophy of revelation. These speculations can be seen as an abandonment of the principles of transcendental idealism for the sake of a different type of philosophy, that of the will, which became predominant during the following decades of the nineteenth century.

1. See *Philosophie aus einem Prinzip. Karl Leonhard Reinhold*, ed. Reinhard Lauth (Bonn, 1974).
2. In his *Difference Between Fichte's and Schelling's Systems of Philosophy* of 1801, referring to the thought process inaugurated by Fichte.

I

Johann Gottlieb Fichte (1762–1814) emerged as a leading figure of the new philosophical movement when in 1792, influenced by Kant, he anonymously published his *Attempt at a Critique of All Revelation*. Because of its Kantian thrust, the public received the text as a writing by Kant, and when Kant revealed the name of its real author, Fichte's philosophical fortune was made. At that time Fichte also presented himself as a strongly politically motivated author who vigorously defended the principles of the French Revolution against Edmund Burke and Burke's German followers in his *Contribution to a Correction of the Public's Judgments on the French Revolution* of 1793 and his *Reclamation of Freedom of Thought, to the Princes of Europe* of 1794. In May 1794, Fichte accepted a chair of philosophy at Jena and through the power of his thought and rhetoric made this university the so-called "strong-hold of German idealism." Of particular importance was his influence upon the romantic generation in Germany, upon the Schlegel brothers and Novalis, but also upon Wilhelm von Humboldt and Schiller. On August 17, 1795, Friedrich Schlegel wrote to his brother about Fichte: "The greatest metaphysical thinker now living is a most popular writer [. . .] He is one after whom Hamlet yearned in vain: every feature of his public life seems to say: this is a man."

The most basic feature in Fichte's philosophy can be seen in the attempt to overcome the split of reality into being on the one hand, and consciousness on the other—a split which had dominated Western thought throughout its tradition. In order to formulate this point of view in more "transcendental" terms, we would have to say that we have contact with being only in the medium of consciousness and that conversely, the object of knowledge is given only in the act of our knowing the object. Being and consciousness therefore simply cannot be separated from each other.[3] As a matter of fact, in the Introduction to the second edition of his *Critique of Pure Reason*, Kant had already stated: "I call transcendental all knowledge which is not so much occupied with objects as with the mode of our

---

3. Reinhard Lauth, "Die Bedeutung der Fichteschen Philosophie für die Gegenwart," *Philosophisches Jahrbuch* 70 (1963), 253–254. See also *Der transzendentale Gedanke. Die gegenwärtige Darstellung der Philosophie Fichtes*, ed. Klaus Hammacher (Hamburg, 1981).

cognition of objects [. . .]." Transcendental, in this conception, simply designates an approach which no longer, as in traditional philosophizing, focuses on the pregiven reality of objects, but views them in their interrelationship with the knowing subject. In this sense, Fichte wrote to P. J. Appia on June 23, 1804: "All philosophizing up to Kant had being as its object. Because of a lack of attention, all [philosophers preceding Kant] overlooked the fact that there is no being except in a consciousness and, conversely, no consciousness except in relation to a being; that therefore the proper *As Such*, as the object of philosophy, can be neither being, as in all pre-Kantian philosophy, nor consciousness—which, however, has not even been attempted—but only the absolute unity of the two beyond their separateness."

In a radical manner, transcendental philosophizing thereby turns upon itself, becomes a reflection of itself, and constitutes itself as a "science of science" or a philosophy of philosophy. If the subject matter is representation, this type of philosophy does not deal with representation in the manner of "common human understanding," but as a reflection upon the representing of representation, just as perception turns into a self-contemplation of perception. This is "speculative" thinking in the true sense of the word, i.e., the identity of subject and object. All idealistic philosophers agree that it was Kant who introduced this speculative or transcendental point of view when in the "Transcendental Analytics" of his *Critique of Pure Reason*, he deduced the categories as conditions *a priori* of reason by means of pure reasoning, by reasoning upon reason itself. Fichte's position of transcendental philosophy, however, went one decisive step beyond that of Kant. By assuming the unknowable "thing in itself" as the ultimate source of all knowledge, Kant maintained a sphere of reality outside of ourselves and accomplished what was considered a merely "formal" synthesis of subject and object, of consciousness and being. This "thing in itself," however, Fichte would argue, owes its existence only to the fact that I don't reflect sufficiently upon it. Indeed, it exists only as long as I do not reflect upon it. For as soon as I focus my reflection upon this thing in itself, it loses the basic quality of "in itself" and becomes something for the ego and therefore by the ego. For Fichte there is indeed no being without consciousness, just as there is no consciousness without being. In Fichte's words, the foundations of ideality and reality reside within the ego.[4]

This absolute principle, prior to its division into being and consciousness, is the Archimedean point from which Fichte's philosophy evolves. In his early period he called this principle the ego in the sense of a general, absolute spiritual principle. Negating an independent reality outside of ourselves, which through affections could cause sensations within ourselves, this philosophy has the ego itself as its principle object and realizes itself in progressive steps of self-recognition. Consciousness is not a pregiven fact that could be represented, but an action that has to be acquired. The inseparableness of the duality of consciousness and being results in living interaction. Fichte's absolute principle cannot be considered as factual or existing, but is essentially living and agile, a doing rather than a deed. In his *Foundation of the Entire Science of Knowledge* of 1794, he attempted to unfold before the eyes of the reader or listener this process in ascending syntheses as a transcendental history of consciousness. In its desire to be entirely by itself and with itself, that is, to be completely free, the ego constantly encounters barriers and finds itself in otherness and alienation. After having overcome one barrier, the ego is confronted with yet another, and so the transcendental thought process moves on toward the goal of absolute self-consciousness and self-determination. This alternation of affirmation and negation, of emerging from and returning to the self, of expansion and contraction in an ascending and progressive development, is the basic model of Fichte's philosophical reflection and became the stimulus for such seemingly disparate issues as revolutionary dialectics and romantic irony.

Wissenschaftslehre, science of knowledge as a whole, then is that which founds, deduces, and completes absolute knowledge in its principles—independent of whether Fichte during the course of his development, calls the first principle the ego, the absolute, or God.[5] With regard to their positions in the entirety of his philosophy, we should take each text precisely by its title. *On the Concept of the*

4. See his *Foundation of the Entire Science of Knowledge* of 1794.
5. Reinhard Lauth, *Zur Idee der Transzendentalphilosophie* (München-Salzburg, 1965), 98–99.

Science of Knowledge is nothing but a programmatic introduction to the new type of philosophizing which Fichte was proposing. The *Foundation of the Entire Science of Knowledge* is nothing but a foundation of the new philosophy and not yet this philosophy itself. Indeed, the *Foundation* is followed by the system of the entire science of knowledge which Fichte presented in various series of lectures beginning in 1804. Another important aspect of Fichte's philosophy is that it not only contains the principles for a deduction of the particular disciplines of philosophy, but also the different spheres of life. Fichte himself attempted practical applications of his philosophy to life in his more popular writings such as *The Closed Commercial State, Addresses to the German Nation*, or *The Way Toward the Blessed Life*. It was one of Fichte's most profound convictions that his philosophy would interact with the life at his time and produce an entirely new epoch in the history of humanity. As he entitled another text of his popular writings *The Vocation of Man*, we can retranslate this title into the more rigorously philosophical language of "self-determination of a rational being" and come to another version of the term "science of knowlege."[6] A comment on the special position of Fichte's *Lectures on the Vocation of the Scholar* can be found in the "Note on the Texts" of this volume.

II

Although on good personal terms with Fichte, Friedrich Heinrich Jacobi (1743–1819) was nevertheless the most severe critic of Fichte's systematic tendency and his attempt to construct a completed system of reason. Absolute reason, in the last analysis, was nothing but atheism for Jacobi, and the endeavor of Fichte's science of knowledge was so alien and repugnant to him that a conflict between the two philosophers was unavoidable. Whereas this controversy was conducted in the manner of a mutually respectful dissent, however, Hegel's excessive polemics led to the result that the entirety of transcendental idealism fell under the indictment of "nihilism," and Jacobi's formerly more technical usage of the term assumed the caustic and aggressive nuance which it has since kept.

6. Reinhard Lauth, "J. G. Fichtes Gesamtidee der Philosophie," *Philosophisches Jahrbuch* 71 (1964), 255–256.

Jacobi's philosophical beginnings go back to far beyond the inception of Fichte's philosophy and coincide with Kant's critical foundation of transcendental idealism. His point of departure, however, was by no means idealistic, but had a definite sensualistic thrust. In his *On the Doctrine of Spinoza, in Letters to Mendelssohn* of 1785 as well as in *David Hume on Faith, or Idealism and Realism* of 1787, and in all of his subsequent writings, Jacobi pursued one central idea, i.e., that philosophical speculation alone arrives merely at a monotonous necessity suppressing such spontaneous and immediate phenomena as freedom, intelligence, personality, moral judgment, but foremost the idea of a personal God. Anticipating a basic thought of Kierkegaard, Jacobi maintained that only a leap could help get away from this dull necessity and that the spring coil lifting us from it would be this dull necessity itself if one only stepped hard enough upon it.[7] In his conversations with Lessing, Jacobi was urbane and self-critical enough to call his philosophy of the leap a *salto mortale*,[8] and it was Friedrich Schlegel who in an essay of 1796 first used this term to stigmatize what he at that time considered a surrendering of philosophy to blind faith. Indeed, it was basic to Jacobi's thought to establish an either/or between necessity and freedom, Spinozism and theism, nothingness and God, and to overcome what he stigmatized as a one-sided dominion of reason. However, whereas Spinoza had provided the model for absolutized reason in Jacobi's early writings, Fichte gave him a much more intensified example of systematic speculation; and it was indeed in his open letter to Fichte of 1799 that the term nihilism made its entrance into philosophical discussion.[9]

The foundation of Jacobi's critique of Fichte and his concept of nihilism has been characterized as epistemological, but can be seen more precisely as an attempt to demonstrate the irreconcilable conflict between idealistic speculation and the needs of human life.[10] We comprehend a thing, Jacobi would argue, only by constructing it, letting it arise in our thoughts, objectifying it, and precisely thereby

---

7. *Friedrich Heinrich Jacobis Werke*, 6 vols. (Leipzig, 1812–1824), IV, I, XL.
8. *Friedrich Heinrich Jacobis Werke*, IV, 59, 74.
9. See below, pp. 119–41.
10. Michael Brüggen, "Jacobi, Schelling und Hegel," *Friedrich Heinrich Jacobi. Philosoph und Literat der Goethezeit*, ed. Klaus Hammacher (Frankfurt, 1971), 287.

suspending it in thought, annihilating it, and making it subjectively our own creation and a mere scheme.[11] To comprehend freedom and God leads, in the last analysis, to an annihilation of freedom and God. The scientific discourse about God results in the death of God, a purely "logical enthusiasm,"[12] and has no other consequence but nihilism. Inverting the real into the ideal, the basic action of reason, marks the beginning of the "philosophy of absolute nothingness," and the idea of an absolute centrifugal and centripetal movement as practiced by Fichte suggested to Jacobi only a movement out of nothing, to nothing, for nothing, and into nothing.[13] In his urbane manner, however, he assured his "dear Fichte" that he would not mind it if Fichte considered as "chimeric" what Jacobi opposed to idealism and scolded as nihilism.[14]

According to many contemporaries, especially Schelling and Hegel, Fichte had provided only a partial and one-sided solution to the task of uniting consciousness and being, subject and object, by placing the center of gravity into the ego's activity and degrading the object to a mere occasion for the subject's self-realization—to a non-ego. When Schelling in his *Ideas on a Philosophy of Nature* (1797), and more systematically in his *System of Transcendental Idealism* (1800), presented nature as the corresponding and complementary pole in an interaction of spirit and nature, he was on his way toward what was considered at that time the philosophy of identity of an accomplished ideal-realism, the completed synthesis of subject and object or, in short, absolute idealism. Now, according to Schelling's famous dictum, nature appeared as visible spirit and spirit as invisible nature.[15] The lightning flash of the idea had struck into the real and expanded as nature. It therefore no longer mattered whether in the philosophy of nature we started out with nature or in transcendental philosophy with spirit. One pole of the duality eventually would lead to the other and, as Hegel put it in his *Lectures on the History of Philosophy*: "Nature thus drives toward spirit, just as spirit drives toward nature."

This philosophy of identity constituted a much greater challenge

11. See below, p. 127.
12. See below, p. 129.
13. See below, p. 133.
14. See below, p. 136.
15. See below, p. 167.

to Jacobi, however, than Fichte's thought. Jacobi believed he was able to unravel the latter philosopher's transcendental idealism like a knitted sock into the single thread from which it had been woven. By deducing freedom, consciousness, and intelligence from their opposite, however, namely nature, Schelling developed a much tighter system of necessity and required a much greater effort on the part of Jacobi to maintain his dualism of necessity and freedom, of immanent and transcendent nature, and to resist the assumed identity of the two realms. On several occasions, he called Schelling's synthesizing of spirit and nature, freedom and necessity, Plato and Spinoza a deception with language which appeals to reason but is misleading about the absolute irreconcilibility of the two systems.[16] Instead of attacking the system of identity directly, however, Jacobi published in 1801 the more conciliatory text *On the Attempt of Criticism to Bring Reason to Understanding*. Schelling surmised Jacobi to be the author of a review very hostile to his *System of Transcendental Idealism* and insisted on a more principal attack on his opponent. It was Hegel who carried out this task in his *Faith and Knowledge or the Reflective Philosophy of Subjectivity in the Complete Range of its Forms as Kantian, Jacobian, and Fichtean Philosophy* of 1802.

At that time Hegel and Schelling were co-editors of the *Critical Journal of Philosophy*. Hegel took a Schellingian position in this controversy by adopting the philosophy of identity. The essay, as has been claimed, could very well have been written by Schelling, although Jacobi recognized its true author by the poor style of the presentation. The section on Jacobi was particularly polemical. Hegel attacked Jacobi not so much from the metaphysical position of an identity of nature and freedom but from the practical and moral consequences of this doctrine. Whereas Jacobi had insisted upon the voice of the human heart as the source of the good action, Hegel, in his conformism of freedom and nature, theory and practice, reproached Jacobi for disdaining the "objective" form and manifestation of morality, namely, morals and laws as they are alive and recognized among a people.

Schelling's philosophy of identity aroused sharp controversies in 1803 which resulted in the appearance of several most polemical

16. Michael Brüggen, "Jacobi, Schelling und Hegel," 213, 218, 220.

books.[17] One of them, by Jacobi's friend Friedrich Köppen, maligned Schelling's doctrine as the "philosophy of absolute nothingness"—a claim certainly derived from Jacobi's term nihilism: a philosophy which lays claim on all and everything, like Schelling's system of identity, necessarily results in absolute nihilism. When Jacobi offered his response to Hegel's attack in three open letters to Köppen, and Köppen included them as an appendix in his book, Jacobi certainly contributed to the eschatological nuance in the term nihilism noticeable throughout the nineteenth century and culminating in Nietzsche.[18]

III

The title "The Oldest Systematic Program of German Idealism" was of course formulated retrospectively when Franz Rosenzweig edited the manuscript for the first time in 1917. It consisted of only one page in the handwriting of Hegel. The bold and amazing content of this manuscript has made critics wonder about the time this text originated and who could possibly have been its author. The most obvious assumption, Hegel, seemed to be excluded because the entire thrust of the argument—calling for a withering away of the state, considering the highest act of reason an aesthetic one, claiming for poetry the supremacy in the intellectual world, and demanding a new mythology—appeared to be in flagrant contradiction with fundamental issues of Hegel's philosophy. Critics were therefore inclined to attribute the text to Schelling who toward the end of the eighteenth century indeed took this "aesthetic" turn. Even Hölderlin was considered as a possible author because as with other representatives of the romantic generation, such ideas were natural to him. Yet one soon realized that Hölderlin at best could have inspired the author of the text.

17. E.g., Johann Friedrich Fries, *Reinhold, Fichte, Schelling* (Leipzig, 1803); Cajetan von Weiller, *Der Geist der allerneuesten Philosophie der HH. Schelling, Hegel, und Kompanie. Eine Übersetzung aus der Schulsprache in die Sprache der Welt*, 2 Parts (München, 1803–1805); Friedrich Köppen, *Schellings Lehre oder das Ganze der Philosophie des absoluten Nichts. Nebst drei Briefen verwandten Inhalts von Friedrich Heinrich Jacobi* (Hamburg, 1803).

18. See on this topic *Der Nihilismus als Phänomen der Geistesgeschichte in der wissenschaftlichen Diskussion unseres Jahrhunderts*, ed. Dieter Arndt (Darmstadt, 1974).

New discoveries about Hegel's philosophical beginnings, however, and recent investigations into the "romantic" character of his early phase have made it quite possible that Hegel could have been the author of this document and that it was he who envisioned an idea which, as the author muses, "has never occurred to anyone's mind."[19] Since the dispute is far from being resolved, however, the text has been listed as the product of an "anonymous author," assuming of course that it was either Hegel or Schelling who wrote it.

In its grandiose transition from a completed metaphysical system of morality (Kant) and the derivation of the entire world from a free and self-conscious being (Fichte) to the idea of beauty as the center of truth and goodness and the philosophy of the spirit as an aesthetic philosophy, the text introduces us to the phase of transcendental idealism most powerfully represented by Schelling. With its "aesthetic" trend as well as with its view of poetry and the new mythology, the program simultaneously corresponds to ideas formulated by Schiller and Friedrich Schlegel.[20] The year of its conception appears to be 1797.

IV

Friedrich Wilhelm Joseph Schelling (1775–1854) took his philosophical starting point from Fichte and wrote on February 5, 1795, to Hegel: "For me the highest principle of all philosophy is the pure, absolute ego, that is, an ego as mere ego, not yet determined by objects, but *posited* through freedom." Yet Schelling's philosophy soon revealed trends which not only made him depart from Fichte, but eventually led him to a questioning of the basic idealistic trust in absolute reason and freedom. This already becomes obvious in what has been called Schelling's first philosophical dispute with Fichte in his *Philosophical Letters on Dogmatism and Criticism* of 1796. In these letters, Schelling envisions two basic trends of reason, one toward criticism and the other toward dogmatism, one

19. Otto Pöggeler, "Hegel, der Verfasser des ältesten Systemprogramms des deutschen Idealismus," *Hegel-Studien* (Beiheft 4), 17–32; Otto Pöggeler, "Hölderlin, Hegel und das älteste Systemprogramm," *Das älteste Systemprogramm. Studien zur Frühgeschichte des Idealismus*, ed. Rüdiger Bubner (Bonn, 1973), 211–259.

20. For Schlegel on mythology, see *German Romantic Criticism*, Volume 21 in The German Library, pp. 95–133.

striving toward an absolute identity of the subject and the other of the object, and thereby calling for an eventual synthesis (or identity) of the two.[21] Schelling seems to intimate already that the philosophical system of transcendental idealism cannot be limited to the rational, conscious, and free dimensions of the ego, but requires complementation from another sphere.

We are here at the origin of Schelling's first decisive contribution to idealistic philosophy, his *Naturphilosophie* (philosophy of nature), which between 1797 and 1800 manifested itself in a number of writings and enjoyed the most favorable receptions, not only among the romantics and Goethe, but also among the scientists of the time. The basic idea can be formulated the following way: When I recognize nature as a reasonable phenomenon of order, I cannot attribute this merely to myself, but have to admit that nature must have reason and order in itself and thereby *analoga* to my own spirit.[22] Nature and spirit appear as two corresponding spheres of a universal process in which the absolute manifests itself. Nature remains the basis of all spiritual phenomena which, conversely, tend to nature. This universal process is an artistic one uniting, in its emanation from the absolute, unconscious and conscious phases. Schelling saw natural preformations of the spirit not only in light, gravity, magnetism, and electricity, but especially in the organism (organization) and its self-forming unity pervading unconsciously all subordinate parts.

It is obvious that Schelling's second philosophical dispute with Fichte had to occur when he developed the philosophy of identity and presented philosophy of nature as the equivalent to transcendental philosophy, as he did in the Introduction of his *System of Transcendental Idealism* of 1800.[23] The prime principle of philosophy no longer was the pure, absolute ego, undetermined by any object, but the absolute as the identity of nature and spirit and the

21. Reinhard Lauth, "Die erste philosophische Auseinandersetzung zwischen Fichte und Schelling 1795–1797," *Zeitschrift für philosophische Forschung* 21(1967), 341–367.

22. See Walter Schulz, "Freiheit und Geschichte in Schellings Philosophie," *F. W. J. Schelling, Philosophische Untersuchungen über das Wesen der menschlichen Freiheit* (Frankfurt, 1975), 11–12.

23. Reinhard Lauth, "Die zweite philosophische Auseinandersetzung zwischen Fichte und Schelling über die Naturphilosophie und die Transzendentalphilosophie und ihr Verhältnis zueinander (Herbst 1800-Frühjahr 1801)," *Kant-Studien* 65 (1974), 397–435.

indifference of unconscious and conscious activity. This philosophy of identity certainly was Schelling's most important contribution to the development of transcendental idealism and the philosophy of art, naturally evolving from this new system, his most original accomplishment. Art appeared as an exemplification of the world-process and symbolizes creation on the part of the absolute or absolute creation. Art demontrates the identity or the indifference of unconscious and conscious activity. Art represents an infinity in finite shape, and that precisely is Schelling's definition of beauty. We have to be careful, however, not to understand these speculations as a plea for mere aestheticism. The emphasis in Schelling's philosophy of art is on philosophy and not on art. In other words, what mattered for him was not so much art itself, but the absolute in the form and in the shape of art. This was conceivable for him because, according to his principle of identity, art just like the universe, was grounded in the absolute.

Schelling's *Philosophical Investigations into the Essence of Human Freedom* of 1809 lead to a basic questioning not only of the conception of freedom in Kant's and Fichte's sense of autonomous self-determination, but also of his own idealism as a movement from nature toward spirit, freedom, and art. In this most crucial text, Schelling actually comes to the realization that idealistic philosophy is unable to demonstrate the specifics of human freedom, that essential realms of reality do not permit rational explanation, and that man no longer is the means for a comprehension of the world.[24] Of course Schelling does not declare world and nature as unreasonable or irrational because it is man who bears the last responsibility. More precisely and according to the technical language of this text, human freedom is a "capability for good and for evil," it is a "living, positive capability for good and evil," that is, for maintaining the order of nature and spirit or for reversing and upsetting it by turning nature loose and perverting its interaction with spirit. Yet it is obvious that this writing constitutes the decisive turning point in Schelling and brings the history of transcendental idealism, the theme of this volume, to its closure.

E.B.

24. Walter Schulz, "Freiheit und Geschichte in Schellings Philosophie," 17.

Note on the Texts

The following anthology attempts to provide representative texts of transcendental idealism and presents in the first section writings by Fichte which introduce the core of his philosophy, his *Wissenschaftslehre*. The most literal translation of this untranslatable term would be doctrine of science, but this would not at all render the meaning of an investigation into the essence and nature of knowledge essential to *Wissenschaftslehre*. Other translations such as science of knowledge or theory of scientific knowledge come closer to this meaning and have been given preference in this volume. Fichte published the first introduction to his science of knowledge, *Concerning the Concept of the Theory of Scientific Knowledge, or of So-Called Philosophy*, as a guide for his students in 1794 at Weimar. A later one, the *Crystal Clear Report to the General Public Concerning the Actual Essence of the Newest Philosophy*, appeared in 1801 in Berlin. It avoids the terms transcendental idealism and system of the science of knowledge because of their unpopular character and substitutes for them "newest philosophy." Because of its greater accessibility, this later text has been chosen as an introduction to the science of knowledge and, because of chronological reasons, placed second. It should be noted, however, that this text is introductory and outlines only the contours of the new philosophy, whereas the content of the science of knowledge itself has to be studied in Fichte's *Foundations of the Entire Science of Knowledge* of 1794 as well as in his later lectures on this subject. *The Crystal Clear Report* is also of importance for Fichte's philosophy of language and its relationship to the romantic theory of language—a topic which has gained increasing importance in recent research.[1] This text is furthermore a document of the controversy between Fichte and Schelling and contains Fichte's polemics against Schelling's recognition of the philosophy of nature as a second and equivalent branch of transcendental idealism.

Fichte's *Some Lectures Concerning the Scholar's Vocation* of Jena, 1794, occupies a key position in the exposition of his philosophy,[2] as it is the task of the "scholar" to promote the ultimate goal of the science of knowledge, the perfectibility of man, by communicating in nontechnical language with the public. Fichte's interaction of philosophy and life, theory and practice is best illustrated by these lectures and their particular diction. They were delivered on Sunday and pursued the purpose of a "formation of the heart to virtue." To provide space for other texts in this volume, we have omitted the Fifth Lecture—an argument against Rousseau, who had denied a beneficial influence of the arts and the sciences upon the perfectibility of the human race.

Aside from their individual editions, the German originals of all of these texts have appeared in Fichte's collected works edited by his son J. H. Fichte (*Johann Gottlieb Fichte's Sämmtliche Werke*, Berlin, 1856). The German original of the first text of this section has also been edited in the critical Fichte edition sponsored by the Bavarian Academy of Sciences and edited by Reinhard Lauth and Hans Jacob. The German text of the *Crystal Clear Report* will appear in the next volume of *Werke* in that edition. Although previous English translations were available, for the sake of accuracy all Fichte translations in this volume are newly done. With permission of the Cornell University Press, we have reproduced Daniel Breazeale's translation of *Some Lectures Concerning the Scholar's Vocation* from his Fichte anthology. John Botterman and William Rasch translated the text of *A Crystal Clear Report* for this volume.

Jacobi's open letter to Fichte (*Jacobi an Fichte*) appeared in the fall of 1799 in Hamburg and became part of the third volume of Jacobi's collected works (*Friedrich Heinrich Jacobis Werke*), published in 1816 in Leipzig. The three letters in which Jacobi responded to

---

1. See Kurt Müller-Vollmer, "Fichte und die romantische Sprachtheorie," *Der transzendentale Gedanke*, ed. Klaus Hammacher (Hamburg, 1981), 442–59.
2. Reinhard Lauth, "J. G. Fichtes Gesamtidee der Philosophie," 75.

Hegel's polemics formed the appendix to Friedrich Köppen, *Schellings Lehre oder das Ganze der Philosophie des Absoluten Nichts. Nebst drei Briefen verwandten Inhalts von Friedrich Heinrich Jacobi* (Hamburg, 1803). Our anthology brings the first of these three letters. There are no previous English translations of these texts by Jacobi. Diana I. Behler translated them for this volume.

The "Oldest Systematic Program of German Idealism" appeared in 1917[3] for the first time and has since been republished in several editions. The first edition was based on a sheet of paper in Hegel's handwriting which was preserved at the Königliche Bibliothek in Berlin and was lost during the Second World War. A photograph of the manuscript is preserved in the estate of Martin Buber. The brief text had been translated into English for different anthologies. Diana I. Behler produced a new translation for the present volume.

The translation of Schelling's *Ideas on a Philosophy of Nature* follows the second edition of 1803 without considering the variants in the first edition of 1797. The *Deduction of a Universal Organ of Philosophy* forms the concluding section of Schelling's *System of Transcendental Idealism* of 1800. The translation of Schelling's *Philosophical Investigations into the Essence of Human Freedom* brings the complete text of the edition of 1809. Aside from their individual editions, the German original of each of these texts had appeared in Schelling's collected works edited by his son K. F. A. Schelling (Stuttgart-Augsburg, 1859). Priscilla Hayden-Roy produced the translations of *Ideas on a Philosophy of Nature* and *Philosophical Investigations into the Essence of Human Freedom* for this volume. The *Deduction of a Universal Organ of Philosophy* follows Albert Hofstadter's translation in the book *Philosophies of Art and Beauty: Selected Readings in Aesthetics from Plato to Heidegger*, edited by Albert Hofstadter and Richard Kuhns (Random House, Modern Library, 1964).

I should like to thank Professor Reinhard Lauth from the University of Munich and Professor Otto Pöggeler from the University of Bochum who were so kind as to advise me when I selected the texts for this volume. The publication of this volume was supported by a grant from the Graduate School of the University of Washington.

3. Franz Rosenzweig, *Das älteste Systemprogramm des deutschen Idealismus. Sitzungsberichte der Heidelberger Akademie der Wissenschaften. Philos.-Histor. Klasse* 5 (Heidelberg, 1917).

JOHANN GOTTLIEB FICHTE

Some Lectures Concerning the Scholar's Vocation

Written and Delivered, Summer 1794
Published, 1794

Preface

These lectures were delivered this past summer semester before a considerable number of our students. They provide entry into a whole which the author wishes to complete and to lay before the public at the proper time. External circumstances, which can contribute nothing to the correct evaluation or understanding of these pages, have induced me to have these first five lectures printed separately and, moreover, to have them printed exactly in the form in which they were first delivered, without altering one single word. This may excuse several careless expressions. Owing to my other work, I was not able from the beginning to polish them in the way I would have liked. Declamation can be used to assist an oral delivery, but revising them for publication would have conflicted with my secondary aim in publishing them.

Several expressions found in these lectures will not please every reader, but for this the author should not be blamed. In pursuing my inquiries I did not ask whether something would meet with approval or not, but rather whether it might be true, and what, according to the best of my knowledge, I considered to be true I expressed as well as I could.

In addition, however, to those readers who have their own reasons to be displeased by what is said here, there may be others for whom what is said here will seem to be useless, because it is something which cannot be achieved and which fails to correspond to anything in the real world as it now exists. Indeed, I am afraid that the majority of otherwise upright, respectable, and sober persons will judge these lectures in this way. For although the number of persons capable of lifting themselves to the level of ideas has always been a minority in every age, this number (for reasons which I can certainly leave unmentioned) has never been smaller than it is right now. It may be true that, within that area to which ordinary experience assigns us, people have never thought for themselves more widely nor judged more correctly than they do now; however, just as soon as they are supposed to go any distance beyond this familiar area, most persons are completely lost and blind. If it is not possible to rekindle the higher genius in such persons once it has been extinguished, then we must permit them to remain peacefully within the circle of ordinary experience. And insofar as they are useful and indispensable within this circle, we must grant them their undiminished value in and for this area. They are, however, guilty of a great injustice if they try to pull down to their own level everything which they cannot themselves reach, if, e.g., they demand that everything which is published should be as easy to use as a cookbook or an arithmetic book or a book of rules and regulations, and if they decry everything which cannot be employed in such a manner.

That ideals cannot be depicted within the real world is something that we others know just as well as such persons do—perhaps we know this better than they. All we maintain is that reality must be judged in accordance with ideals and must be modified by those who feel themselves able to do so. Supposing that such persons cannot be convinced that this is true, still, since they are what they are, they lose very little by not being convinced, and mankind loses nothing. It merely becomes clear from this that they cannot be counted on to contribute anything to the project of improving mankind. Mankind will undoubtedly continue on its way. May a kindly nature reign over such persons, may it bestow upon them rain and sunshine at the proper time, wholesome food and undisturbed circulation, and in addition—intelligent thoughts!

Jena, Michaelmas 1794

FIRST LECTURE
Concerning the Vocation of Man as Such

You are already somewhat acquainted with the purpose of the series of lectures which I am beginning today. I would like to answer—or rather, I would like to prompt you to answer—the following questions: What is the scholar's vocation? What is his relationship to mankind as a whole, as well as to the individual classes of men? What are his surest means of fulfilling his lofty vocation?

The scholar is a scholar only insofar as he is distinguished from other men who are not scholars. The concept of the scholar arises by comparison and by reference to society (by which is understood here not merely the state, but any aggregate whatsoever of rational men, living alongside each other and thus joined in mutual relations).

It follows that the scholar's vocation is only conceivable within society. The answer to the question "What is the scholar's vocation?" thus presupposes an answer to another question: "What is the vocation of man within society?"

The answer to this latter question presupposes, in turn, an answer to yet another, higher one: "What is the vocation of man as such?" That is to say, what is the vocation of man considered simply *qua* man, merely according to the concept of man as such—man isolated and considered apart from all the associations which are not necessarily included in the concept of man?[1]

If I may assert something without proof, something which has undoubtably already been demonstrated to many of you for a long

---

1. [Note to the Danish edition.] One should be careful not to extend this proposition too far. The concept of man *in general*, disregarding the empirical conditions of his *actual existence*, certainly does not contain the property of being associated with other men. When we are talking about the vocation of man as such we undeniably must disregard these empirical conditions. But a *real* person, a person taken along with all of his specific characteristics, can only be conceived of as an individual, which is to say that he can only be conscious of himself as an individual. But the concept of an individual is an entirely reciprocal concept: "I am such and such," which is to say, "I am *not* some particular other thing," and the former means no more than the latter. Furthermore, real men are possible only insofar as they are associated with others like themselves. No man exists in isolation. The concept of an individual postulates the concept of his species. In my book, *Foundations of Natural Right* (Jena, 1796), I have deduced this conclusion from transcendental principles.

time and something which others among you feel obscurely, but no less strongly on that account: All philosophy, all human thinking and teaching, all of your studies, and, in particular, everything which I will ever be able to present to you can have no purpose other than answering the questions just raised, and especially the last and highest question: What is the vocation of man as such, and what are his surest means for fulfilling it?

For a clear, distinct, and complete insight into this vocation (though not, of course, for a feeling of it) philosophy in its entirety — and moreover a thorough and exhaustive philosophy — is presupposed. Yet the vocation of man as such is the subject of my lecture for today. You can see that unless I intend to treat philosophy in its entirety within this hour, I will be unable to deduce what I have to say on this topic completely and from its foundations. What I can do is to build upon your feelings. At the same time you can see that the *ultimate* task of all philosophical inquiry is to answer that question which I wish to answer in these public lectures: "What is the vocation of the scholar?" or (which amounts to the same thing, as will become evident later), "What is the vocation of the highest and truest man?" And you can see as well that the *first* task of all philosophical inquiry is to answer the question: "What is the vocation of man as such?" I intend to establish the answer to this latter question in my private lectures. All I wish to do today is to indicate briefly the answer to this question — to which I now turn.

The question concerning what the genuinely spiritual element in man, the pure I, might be like, considered simply in itself, isolated and apart from any relation to anything outside of itself, is an unanswerable question, and taken precisely it includes a self-contradiction. It is certainly not true that the pure I is a product of the not-I (which is my name for everything which is thought to exist outside of the I, everything which is distinguished from the I and opposed to it). The assertion that the pure I is a product of the not-I expresses a transcendental materialism which is completely contrary to reason. However, it certainly is true (and, at the appropriate place, will be strictly demonstrated) that the I is never conscious of itself nor able to become conscious of itself, except as something empirically determined — which necessarily presupposes something outside of the I. Even a person's body (which he calls "his" body) is something apart from the I. Yet apart from this connection with a body he would not be a person at all, but would be something quite inconceivable (if one can still refer to a thing which is not even conceivable as "something"). Thus neither here nor anywhere else does the expression "man considered in himself and in isolation" mean: man considered as a pure I and apart from all relationship to anything at all apart from his pure I. Instead, this expression means merely: man conceived of apart from all relationship to rational beings like himself.

What is man's vocation when he is conceived of in this manner? What is there in the concept of man which pertains to him but not to the nonhumans among those beings with which we are acquainted? What distinguishes man from all those beings with which we are acquainted but which we do not designate as human?

I must begin with something positive, and since I cannot begin here with what is absolutely positive, i.e., with the proposition "I am," I will have to propose an hypothetical proposition, one which is indelibly etched in human feeling—a proposition which is at the same time the result of all philosophy, a proposition which can be strictly demonstrated and which will be demonstrated in my private lectures. The proposition in question is the following: Just as certainly as man is rational, he is his own end; i.e., he does not exist because something else is supposed to exist. Rather, he exists simply because *he* is supposed to exist. His mere existence is the ultimate purpose of his existence; or (which amounts to the same thing), it is contradictory to inquire concerning the purpose of man's existence: he is *because* he is. This quality of absolute being, of being for his own sake, is the characteristic feature, the determination or vocation of man, insofar as he is considered merely and solely as a rational being.

But mere absolute being, being purely and simply, is not all that pertains to man. Other, particular determinations of this absolute being also pertain to him. It is not simply that *he is, he also is something*. He does not say merely "I am," he adds "I am this or that." He is a rational being insofar as he is at all. But what is he insofar as he is something or other? This is the question we have to answer now.

Man is not first of all *that which* he is because *he* exists, but rather because *something other than he exists*. As we have already said above and will demonstrate in the proper place, empirical self-consciousness, i.e., the consciousness of any specific determination or vocation within ourselves at all, is impossible apart from the presupposition of a not-I. This not-I must affect man's passive faculty, which we call "sensuousness." Thus, to the extent that man is something [definite] he is a sensuous being. But according to what we have already said, man is a rational being at the same time, and his reason should not be cancelled by his sensuousness. Reason and sensuousness are supposed to coexist alongside each other. In this context the proposition "man is because he is" is transformed into the following: "*man is supposed to be what he is simply because he is.*" In other words, all that a person is should be related to his pure I, his mere being as an I. He is supposed to be all that he is simply because he is an I, and what he cannot be because he is an I, he is not supposed to be at all. This formula, which remains obscure, will become clear at once.

The pure I can be represented only negatively, as the opposite of the not-I. The characteristic feature of the latter is multiplicity, and thus the characteristic feature of the former is complete and absolute unity. The pure I is always one and the same and is never anything different. Thus we may express the above formula as follows: Man is always supposed to be at one with himself; he should never contradict himself. For the pure I cannot contradict itself, since it contains no diversity but is instead always one and the same. However, the empirical I, which is determined and determinable by external things, can contradict itself. And if the empirical I contradicts itself, this is a sure sign that it is not determined in accordance with the form of the pure I, and thus that it is not determined by itself but rather by external things. But since man is his own end, the empirical I should not be determined in this external manner. Man is supposed to determine himself and not permit himself to be determined by something foreign. He is supposed to be what he is because this is what he wants and is supposed to want to be. The empirical I is supposed to be determined in a manner in which it could be eternally determined. Therefore, I would express the principle of morality in the formula (which I mention only in passing and for the purpose of illustration): "Act so that you could consider the maxims of your willing as eternal laws for yourself."

The ultimate characteristic feature of all rational beings is, accordingly, absolute unity, constant self-identity, complete agreement with oneself. This absolute identity is the form of the pure I and is its only true form, or rather, in the conceivability of identity we *recognize* the expression of the purer form of the I. Any determination which can be conceived to endure forever is in accordance with the pure form of the I. This should not be understood only half-way and one-sidedly. It is not simply that the will should always be one with itself (though this is all that moral theory is concerned with), but rather that all of man's powers, which in themselves constitute but one power and are distinguished from each other merely in their application to different objects, should coincide in a complete identity and should harmonize with each other.

At least for the most part, however, the empirical determinations of our I do not depend upon us, but upon something external to us. The will is of course free within its own domain, i.e., in the realm of objects to which, once man has become acquainted with them, it can be related. This will be demonstrated at the proper time. But feeling, as well as the representation which presupposes feeling, is not something free, but depends instead upon things external to the I — things whose characteristic feature is not identity at all, but rather multiplicity. If the I is, nevertheless, always supposed to be one with itself in this respect [i.e., with respect to external things], then it must strive to act directly upon those very things upon which human feeling and representation depend. Man must try to modify these things. He must attempt to bring them into harmony with the pure form of the I, in order that the representation of these things, to the extent that it depends upon the properties of the things, may harmonize with the form of the pure I. But it is not possible to modify things in accordance with our necessary concepts of how they should be purely by means of the will alone. A certain skill is also needed, a skill acquired and sharpened by practice.

Furthermore, and even more important, the unhindered influence of things upon the empirically determinable I, an influence to which we naturally entrust ourselves so long as our reason has not yet been awakened, gives a particular bent to our empirically determinable I. And since this bent is derived from things outside of us, it is impossible for it to be in harmony with the form of our pure I. Mere will is not sufficient for removing these distortions and restoring the original pure shape of our I; we require, in addition, that skill which we acquire and sharpen through practice.

The skill in question is in part the skill to suppress and erradicate those erroneous inclinations which originate in us prior to the awakening of our reason and the sense of our own spontaneity, and in part it is the skill to modify and alter external things in accordance with our concepts. The acquisition of this skill is called "culture," as is the particular degree of this skill which is acquired. Culture differs only in degree, but is susceptible of infinitely many gradations. It is man's ultimate and highest means toward his final end *qua* rational and sensuous creature: toward complete harmony with himself. When man is considered merely as a sensuous creature, then culture is itself his final end. Sensuousness should be cultivated: that is the highest and ultimate thing which one can propose to do with it.

The net result of all that has been said is the following: Man's ultimate and supreme goal is complete harmony with himself and — so that he can be in harmony with himself — the harmony of all external things with his own necessary, practical concepts of them (i.e., with those concepts which determine how things *ought to* be). Employing the terminology of the Critical Philosophy, this agreement is what Kant calls "the highest good."[2] From what has already been said it follows that this "highest good" is by no means constituted of two parts, but is completely unitary: the highest good is the *complete harmony of a rational being with himself*. In the case of a rational being dependent upon things outside of himself, the highest

2. [Note to the Danish edition:] Expressed more clearly, it does not follow that something is a good thing for us simply because it makes us happy. Quite the reverse, something makes us happy because it was a good thing prior to us and our feeling of happiness. The chief mistake of the Eudaimonean system and the most important reason why one cannot get the defenders of Eudaimonism to accept the opposite view is that they completely reverse the relationship between the faculties of desire and knowledge. Since Eudaimoneans are generally transcendent dogmatists who think that everything which appears in the I is determined by things outside the I, they have to begin [their account of] the entire efficacy of rational beings with the impression that an [external] thing makes upon us and with our awareness of this. Whether they clearly say so or whether it remains concealed at the basis of their argument, they think that the faculty of knowledge gives us, above all, an object. And part of their concept of this object is that it is supposed to provide a certain sort of pleasure. (They would escape from their error at once if they would only ask themselves how such knowledge [i.e., knowledge that a particular object will provide a particular pleasure] is possible.) They contend that an impulse towards an object arises only as a result of this theoretical understanding. They conclude that something is good because we have been convinced that it will make us happy.

This, however, is not the way it works, but just the reverse. Impulse or drive is first and foremost in man. And impulse demands its object in advance of any kind of knowledge and in advance of the object's existence. It simply demands something, even if what it demands does not exist at all. What can and will make us happy is determined in advance by impulse. We are happy over something we receive, because

good may be conceived as twofold: as harmony between *the willing* [of such a being] and the idea of an eternally valid willing (i.e., good as *ethical goodness*), or as the harmony of our willing (it should go without saying that I am here speaking of our rational willing) with external things (i.e., good as *happiness*). And thus we may note in passing that it is not true that the desire for happiness destines man for ethical goodness. It is rather the case that the concept of happiness itself and the desire for happiness first arise from man's moral nature. Not "what makes us happy is good," but rather, "only what is good makes us happy." No happiness is possible apart from morality. Of course, *pleasant* feelings are possible without morality and even in opposition to it, and in the proper place we will see why this is so. But pleasant feelings are not happiness; indeed, they often even contradict happiness.

Man's final end is to subordinate to himself all that is irrational, to master it freely and according to his own laws. This is a final end which is completely inachievable and must always remain so—so long, that is, as man is to remain man and is not supposed to become God. It is part of the concept of man that his ultimate goal be unobtainable and that his path thereto be infinitely long. Thus it is not man's vocation to reach this goal. But he can and he should draw nearer to it, and his true vocation *qua man*, i.e., insofar as he is rational but finite, a sensuous but free being, lies in *endless approximation toward this goal*. Now if, as we surely can, we call this total harmony with oneself "perfection," in the highest sense of the word, then *perfection* is man's highest and unattainable goal. His vocation, however, is to *perfect himself without end*. He exists in order to become constantly better in an ethical sense, in order to make all that surrounds him better *sensuously* and—insofar as we consider him in relation to society—*ethically* as well, and thereby to make himself ever happier.

---

it was a good thing for us [as determined by our impulses or drives] before we received it. This is how all human drives, physical as well as moral, operate. I do not enjoy food and drink because I have found them to taste good on a few occasions—why should they have tasted good to me? But rather, I desire to nourish myself in a particular manner irrespective of food and drink, and this is why they taste good to me. Similarly I can be satisfied with myself if I have told the truth, but I do not tell the truth because it provides me with this pleasure. The reverse is the case: truth is the only thing that provides this sort of satisfaction because the moral drive demands truth in advance of any experience.

Such is man's vocation, insofar as we consider him in isolation, i.e., apart from any relation to rational beings like himself. We do not, however, exist in isolation, and though I cannot turn today to a consideration of the general connection between rational beings, I must, nevertheless, cast a glance upon that particular association with you which I enter upon today. What I would like to help many aspiring young men to grasp clearly is that lofty vocation which I have indicated briefly to you today. It is this vocation which I would like for you to make the most deliberate aim and the most constant guide of your lives: you young men who are in turn destined to affect mankind in the strongest manner, and whose destiny it is, through teaching, action, or both, in narrower or wider circles, to pass on that education which you have received and on every side to raise our fellow men to a higher level of culture. When I teach you I am most probably teaching unborn millions. Some among you may be well enough disposed toward me to imagine that I sense the dignity of my own special vocation, that the highest aim of my reflections and my teaching will be to contribute toward advancing culture and elevating humanity in you and in all those with whom you come into contact, and that I consider all philosophy and science which do not aim at this goal to be worthless. If this is how you judge me, then allow me to say that you are right about my intentions. Whether or not I have the power to live up to this wish is not entirely up to me. It depends in part on circumstances beyond our control; it depends in part upon you as well—upon your attentiveness, which I hereby request; upon your own efforts, which I cheerfully count upon with complete confidence; and upon your confidence in me, to which I commend myself and will seek by my actions to commend to you.

SECOND LECTURE
Concerning Man's Vocation Within Society

Before it can become a science and a theory of scientific knowledge, philosophy must answer a number of questions, questions the dogmatists, who decide everything, have forgotten to ask and which the sceptics have dared to raise only at the risk of being accused of irrationality or wickedness—or both at once.

I have no desire to be superficial and to treat shallowly a subject concerning which I believe myself to possess better-founded knowledge. Nor do I wish to conceal and pass over in silence difficulties which I see clearly. Yet it remains my fate in these public lectures to have to just touch upon several of these still almost entirely untouched questions and to touch upon them without being able to exhaust them fully. At the risk of being misunderstood or misinterpreted I will be able to provide nothing but *hints* for further reflection and *directions* toward further information concerning matters I would prefer to have treated fundamentally and exhaustively. If I suspected that among you there were many of those "popular philosophers" who solve every difficulty easily and without any effort or reflection, merely with the aid of what they call their own "healthy common sense"—if this is what I thought, then I would seldom stand here before you without quailing.

Among the questions which philosophy has to answer we find the following two in particular, which have to be answered before, among other things, a well-founded [theory of] natural rights is possible. First of all, by what right does a man call a particular portion of the physical world "*his* body"? How does he come to consider this to be his body, something which belongs to his I, since it is nevertheless something completely opposed to his I? And then the second question: How does man come to assume that there are rational beings like himself apart from him and how does he come to recognize them, since they are certainly not immediately present to his pure self-consciousness?[3]

What I have to do today is to establish what the vocation of man within society is, and before this task can be achieved the preceding questions have to be answered. By "society" I mean the relationship in which rational beings stand to each other. The concept of society presupposes that there actually are rational beings apart from oneself. It also presupposes the existence of some characteristic features which permit us to distinguish these beings from all of those who are not rational and thus are not members of society. How do we

3. [Note to the Danish edition.] The author has since answered both of these questions in his previously mentioned book on natural right.

arrive at this presupposition, and what are these characteristic features of rational beings? This is the initial question which I have to answer.

Persons still unaccustomed to strict philosophical inquiry might well answer my question as follows: "Our knowledge that rational beings like ourselves exist apart from us and our knowledge of the signs which distinguish rational beings from non-rational ones have both been derived from experience." But such an answer would be superficial and unsatisfying. It would be no answer at all to *our* question, but would pertain to an altogether different one. Egoists also have these experiences to which appeal is being made, and they have still not been thoroughly refuted on that account. All that experience teaches us is that our consciousness contains the idea or *representation* of rational beings outside of ourselves. No one disputes this and no egoist has ever denied it. What is in question is whether there is anything *beyond the representation* which corresponds to it, i.e., whether rational beings exist independently of our representations of them and would exist even if we had no such representations. And in regard to this question we can learn nothing from experience, just as certainly as experience is experience, i.e., the system of our representations.

The most that experience can teach is that there are effects which resemble the effects of rational causes. It cannot, however, teach us that the causes in question actually exist as rational beings in themselves. For a being in itself is no object of experience.

We ourselves first introduce such beings into experience. It is *we* who explain certain experiences by appealing to the existence of rational beings outside of ourselves. But *with what right* do we offer this explanation? The *justification* needs to be better demonstrated before we can use this explanation, for its validity depends upon such a justification and cannot be based simply upon the fact that we actually make use of such explanations. Our investigation would therefore not be advanced a single step [by appealing to experience in the manner just indicated]. We are left facing the question previously raised: How do we come to assume that there are rational beings outside of us and how do we recognize them?

The thorough investigations of the Critical Philosophers have unquestionably exhausted the theoretical realm of philosophy. All remaining questions must be answered on the basis of practical principles (a point which I mention merely for its historical interest). We must now see whether the proposed question can actually be answered from practical principles.

According to our last lecture, man's highest drive is the drive toward identity, toward complete harmony with himself, and — as a means for staying constantly in harmony with himself — toward the harmony of all external things with his own necessary concepts of them. It is not enough that his concepts not be *contradicted* (in which case he could be indifferent to the existence or non-existence of objects *corresponding* to his concepts); but rather [in order to achieve the harmony desired] there really should be something corresponding to these concepts. All of the concepts found within the I should have an expression or counterpart in the not-I. This is the specific character of man's highest drive.

Man also has the concepts of reason and of rational action and thought. He necessarily wishes, not merely to realize these concepts within himself, but to see them realized outside of him as well. One of the things that man needs is for rational beings like himself to exist outside of him.

Man cannot bring any such beings into existence, yet the concept of such beings underlies his observation of the not-I, and he expects to encounter something corresponding to this concept. The first, though merely negative, distinguishing characteristic of rationality, or at least the first one that suggests itself, is efficacy governed by concepts, i.e., purposeful activity. What bears the distinguishing features of purposefulness may have a rational author, whereas that to which the concept purposefulness is entirely inapplicable certainly has no rational author. Yet this feature is ambiguous. The distinguishing characteristic of purposefulness is the harmony of multiplicity in a unity. But many types of such harmony are explicable merely by natural laws — not *mechanical* laws, but *organic* ones certainly. In order, therefore, to be able to infer convincingly from a particular experience to its rational cause we require some feature in addition [to purposefulness]. Even in those cases where it operates purposefully, nature operates in accordance with *necessary laws*. Reason always operates *freely*. The freely achieved harmony of multiplicity in a unity would thus be a certain and non-deceptive distinguishing feature of rationality within appearances. The only question is how one can tell the difference between an effect one has experienced which occurs necessarily and one which occurs freely.

I can by no means be directly conscious of a freedom [i.e., a free subject] outside of myself. I cannot even become conscious of a freedom within me; i.e., I cannot become conscious of my own freedom. For freedom in itself is the ultimate explanatory basis for all consciousness, and thus freedom itself cannot belong to the realm of consciousness. What I can become conscious of, however, is that I am conscious of no cause for a certain voluntary determination of my empirical I other than my will itself. As long as one has explained oneself properly in advance, one might well say that this very lack of any consciousness of a cause is itself a consciousness of freedom — and we wish to call it such here. *In this sense* then, one can be conscious of one's own free action.

Suppose now that the manner of behavior of that substance which is presented to us through appearance is altered, altered by *our* free action (of which we are conscious in the sense just indicated), and altered so that it no longer remains explicable by *that* law in accordance with which it operated previously, but can only be explained by that law upon which *we* have based *our own* free action — a law which is quite opposed to the previous law. The only way in which we could account for the alteration in this case is by assuming that the cause of the effect in question was also rational and free. Thus there arises, to use the Kantian terminology, an *interaction governed by concepts*, a purposeful community. And this is what I mean by "society" — the concept of which is now specified completely.

One of man's fundamental drives is to be permitted to assume that rational beings like himself exist outside of him. He can assume this only on the condition that he enter into society (in the sense just specified) with these beings. Consequently, the social drive is one of man's fundamental drives. It is man's *destiny* to live in society; he *should* live in society. One who lives in isolation is no complete human being. He contradicts his own self.

You can see how important it is not to confuse society as such with that particular, empirically conditioned type of society which we call "the state." Despite what a very great man has said, life in the state is not one of man's absolute aims. The state is, instead, only a *means for establishing a perfect society*, a means which exists only under specific circumstances. Like all those human institutions which are mere means, the state aims at abolishing itself. *The goal of all government is to make government superfluous*. Though the time has certainly not yet come, nor do I know how many myriads or myriads of myriads of years it may take (here we are not at all concerned with applicability in life, but only with justifying a speculative proposition), there will certainly be a point in the *a priori* foreordained career of the human species when all civic bonds will become superfluous. This is that point when reason, rather than strength or cunning, will be universally recognized as the highest court of appeal. I say "be recognized," because even then men will still make mistakes and injure their fellow men thereby. All they have to have is the good will to allow themselves to be convinced that they have erred,[4] and, as they are convinced of this, to recant their errors and make amends for the damages. Until we have reached this point we are, in general, not even true men.

According to what we have said, the positive distinguishing feature of society is *free interaction*. This interaction is its own end, and it operates *purely and simply* in order to operate. But when we maintain that society is its own end we are not by any means denying that the manner in which it operates might be governed by an additional, more specific law, which establishes a more specific goal for the operation of society.

The fundamental drive was the drive to discover rational beings like ourselves, i.e., *men*. The concept of man is an idealistic concept, because man's end *qua* man is something unachievable. Every

---

4. [Note to the Danish edition.] But if it is now impossible for either party to be convinced — which is something which may easily occur, despite the sincere intentions of each — then what is right remains in dispute, and one of the parties suffers a wrong. But what is right should never remain in dispute, for there should be no wrong. Beyond this [appeal to reason via the path of mutual argument] there must also be an infallible and supreme judge to whom one would be duty-bound to submit oneself. And there must be positive laws, since judgment can only be passed according to law. And there must be a constitution, since this supreme judge could not be appointed except in accordance with a rule. Thus, to the extent that the state is related to human fallibility and is, in the final instance, that which puts an end to human quarreling over questions of right, then the state is completely necessary and can never cease to exist.

But to the extent that the state is related to the evil will, to the extent that it is a compulsory power, then its final aim is undoubtedly to make itself superfluous, i.e., to make all compulsion unnecessary. This is an aim which can be achieved even if good will and the confidence in it do not become universal. For if everyone knows on the basis of long experience that every act of injustice will surely bring misfortune and that every crime will surely be discovered and punished, then one may expect that from prudence alone they will not exert themselves in vain, that they will not willfully and knowingly bring harm upon themselves.

individual has his own particular ideal of man as such. Though all of these ideals have the same content, they nevertheless differ in degree. Everyone uses his own ideal to judge those whom he recognizes as men. Owing to the fundamental human drive, everyone wishes to find that everyone else resembles this ideal. We experiment and observe the other person from every side, and when we discover him to lie *below* our ideal of man, we try to raise him to this ideal. The winner in this spiritual struggle is always the one who is the higher and the better man. Thus the *improvement of the species* has its origin within society, and thus at the same time we have discovered the vocation of all society as such. Should it appear as if the higher and better person has no influence upon the lower and uneducated person, this is partly because our own judgment deceives us: for we frequently expect fruit at once, before the seed has been able to germinate and develop. And perhaps it is partly because the better person stands upon a level which is so much higher than that of the uneducated person that the two do not have enough points of mutual contact and are unable to have sufficient effect upon each other—a situation which retards culture unbelievably and the remedy for which will be indicated at the proper time. But on the whole the better person will certainly be victorious, and this is a source of reassurance and solace for the friend of mankind and truth when he witnesses the open war between light and darkness. The light will certainly win in the end. Admittedly, we cannot say how long this will take, but when darkness is forced to engage in public battle this is already a guarantee of the approaching victory [of light]. For darkness loves obscurity. When it is forced to reveal itself it has already lost.

Thus the following is the result of all of our deliberations so far: Man is destined for society. *Sociability* is one of those skills which man should perfect within himself in accordance with his vocation as a man, as this was developed in the previous lecture.

However much man's vocation for society as such may originate from the innermost and purest part of his nature, it is, nevertheless, merely a drive and as such it is subordinate to the supreme law of self-harmony, i.e., the ethical law. Thus the social drive must be further determined by the ethical law and brought under a fixed rule. By discovering what this rule is we discover what *man's* vocation within *society* is—which is the object of our present inquiry and of all our reflections so far.

To begin with, the law of absolute self-harmony determines the social drive *negatively*: this drive must not contradict itself. The social drive aims at *interaction, reciprocal* influence, *mutual* give and take, mutual passivity and activity. It does not aim at mere causality, at the sort of mere activity to which the other person would have to be related merely passively. It strives to discover *free, rational* beings outside of ourselves and to enter into community with them. It does not strive for the *subordination* characteristic of the physical world, but rather for *coordination*. If one does not allow the rational beings he seeks outside of himself to be free, then he is only taking their *theoretical ability* into account, but not their free practical rationality. Such a person does not wish to enter into society with these other free beings, but rather to master them as one masters talented beasts, and thus he places his social drive into contradiction with itself. Indeed, rather than saying that such a person places his social drive into contradiction with itself, it is far more true to say that he does not possess such a higher drive at all, that mankind has not yet developed that far in him, that it is he himself who still stands on the lower level of the half-human, the level of slavery. He is not yet mature enough to have developed his own sense of freedom and spontaneity, for if he had then he would necessarily have to wish to see around him free beings like himself. Such a person is a slave and wishes to have slaves. Rousseau has said that many a person who considers himself to be the master of others is actually more of a slave than they are. He might have said, with even more accuracy, that everyone who considers himself to be a master of others is himself a slave. If such a person is not a slave in fact, it is still certain that he has a slavish soul and that he will grovel on his knees before the first strong man who subjugates him. The only person who is himself free is that person who wishes to liberate everyone around him and who—by means of a certain influence whose cause has not always been remarked—really does so. We breathe more freely under the eyes of such a person. We feel that nothing constrains, restrains, or confines us, and we feel an unaccustomed inclination to be and to do everything which is not forbidden by our own self-respect.

Man may employ mindless things as means for his ends, but not rational beings. One may not even employ rational beings as means for their own ends. One may not work upon them as one works upon dead matter or animals, i.e., simply using them as a means for accomplishing one's ends without taking their freedom into account. One may not make any rational being virtuous, wise, or happy against his own will. Quite apart from the fact that the attempt to do so would be in vain and that no one can become virtuous, wise, or happy except through his own labor and effort — even apart from this fact, one should not even wish to do so even if it were possible or if one believed that it were; for it is wrong, and it places one into contradiction with oneself.

The law of complete, formal self-harmony also determines the social drive *positively*, and from this we obtain the actual vocation of man within society. All of the individuals who belong to the human race differ among themselves. There is only one thing in which they are in complete agreement: their ultimate goal — perfection. Perfection is determined in only one respect: it is totally self-identical. If all men could be perfect, if they could all achieve their highest and final goal, then they would be totally equal to each other. They would constitute but one single subject. In society, however, everyone strives to improve the others (at least according to ones own concept [of "improvement"]) and to raise them to the ideal which one has formed of man. Accordingly, the ultimate and highest goal of society is the complete unity and unanimity of all of its members. But the achievement of this goal presupposes the achievement of the vocation of man as such, the achievement of absolute perfection; thus the former is just as inachievable as the latter, and it remains inachievable so long as man is not supposed to cease to be man and to become God. The *final goal* of man within society is thus the complete unity of all individuals, but this is not the *vocation* of man within society.

Man can and should approximate endlessly to this goal. Such approximation to total unity and unanimity may be termed "association." The true vocation of man within society is, accordingly, association — association which constantly gains in internal strength and expands its perimeter. But since the only thing on which men are or can be in agreement is their ultimate vocation, this association is only possible through the search for perfection. We could, therefore, just as well say that our social vocation consists in the process of communal perfection, i.e., perfecting our self by freely making use of the effect which others have on us and perfecting others by acting in turn upon them as upon free beings.

In order to fulfill this vocation and to do so ever more adequately, we require a skill that is acquired and increased only through culture. This skill has two aspects: the skill of *giving*, or affecting others as free beings, and the capacity for *receiving*, or for making the most of the effect which others have upon us. We will specifically discuss both of these skills at the proper place. One must make a particular effort to maintain the latter [i.e., the capacity to receive] alongside a high degree of the former, for otherwise one remains stationary and thus regresses. Rarely is anyone so perfect that he cannot learn from almost anyone at least in some respect—one perhaps that seems unimportant to him or that he has overlooked.

I am acquainted with few ideas more lofty than this idea of the way the human species works upon itself—this ceaseless living and striving, this lively contest of give and take, which is the noblest thing in which man can participate, this universal intermeshing of countless wheels whose common driving force is freedom, and the beautiful harmony which grows from this. Everyone can say: "Whoever you may be, because you bear a human face, you are still a member of this great community. No matter how countlessly many intermediaries may be involved in the transmission, I nevertheless have an effect upon you, and you have an effect upon me. No one whose face bears the stamp of reason, no matter how crude, exists for me in vain. But I am unacquainted with you, as you are with me! Still, just as it is certain that we share a common calling—to be good and to become better and better—it is equally certain that there will come a time (it may take millions or trillions of years—what is time!) when I will draw you into my sphere of influence, a time when I will benefit you too and receive benefit from you, a time when my heart will be joined with yours by the loveliest bond of all—the bond of free, mutual give and take."

THIRD LECTURE
Concerning the Difference Between Classes Within Society

We have now presented man's vocation *qua* man as well as his vocation within society. The scholar exists as a scholar only within the context of society. Accordingly, we could now turn to an investigation of the particular vocation within society of the scholar. However, the scholar is not merely a member of society; he is at the same time a member of a particular class within society. At least one speaks of "the learned class." Whether such talk is justified will be seen at the proper time.

Thus our main inquiry concerning the scholar's vocation presupposes, not only the two inquiries we have just completed, but also a third, an investigation of the following important question: How does the difference between the various classes of men arise in the first place? Or, what is the origin of inequality among men? Even without any preliminary investigation we understand by the word "class," not something which originated accidentally and without any help from us, but rather something determined and arranged by free choice and for a purpose. Nature may be responsible for that *physical inequality* which arises accidentally and without our assistance, but the *inequality of classes* appears to be a moral inequality. Concerning this moral inequality the following question naturally arises: What is the justification for the existence of different classes?

Many attempts have already been made to answer this question. Some persons, proceeding from first principles derived from experience, have seized upon and rhapsodically enumerated the various purposes which are served by the difference between classes and the many advantages we derive from this. By this means, however, we would sooner answer any other question whatsoever than the one just raised. The *advantage* which someone derives from a particular arrangement does nothing to *justify* it. The question raised was by no means the historical question concerning the purposes which may have led to this arrangement [viz., the difference between classes], but rather the moral question concerning the permissibility of making such an arrangement, whatever purposes it might have had. This question has to be answered on the basis of principles of pure reason, indeed, on the basis of principles of pure practical reason. So far as I know, no one has ever even attempted to provide such an answer. I must preface my own attempt with a few general principles from the Theory of Scientific Knowledge.

All laws of reason have their foundation in the nature of our mind, but we first become empirically conscious of these laws through an experience to which they are applicable. The more often we have occasion to apply them, the more intimately they become interwoven with our own consciousness. This is how it is with *all* laws of reason, and specifically, with the laws of practical reason—

laws which, unlike those of theoretical reason, do not aim at a mere *judgment*, but rather at external efficacy. These practical laws are present to consciousness in the form of *drives*. All drives have their foundation in our nature — but no more than their foundation. Every drive has to be *awakened* by experience before we can become conscious of it. Furthermore, in order for a drive to become an *inclination* and for its satisfaction to become a *need*, the drive in question has to be developed through frequently repeated experiences of the same type. Experience, however, is not dependent upon us; neither, therefore, is the awakening and the development of our own drives at all dependent upon us.

The independent not-I, considered as the basis of experience, i.e., *nature*, is something manifold. Not one of its parts is totally identical to any other part (a proposition which is also affirmed by the Kantian philosophy and can be strictly demonstrated within that philosophy). From this it follows that nature affects the human mind in a variety of very different ways and never develops the mind's capacities and aptitudes in the same way twice. What we call "individuals," as well as their particular empirical individual nature is determined by the different ways in which nature acts upon them. Thus we can say, in respect to his awakened and developed abilities, that no individual is completely the same as anyone else. From this there arises a physical inequality to which we have contributed nothing and which we are also unable to remove by the exercise of our freedom. For before we can freely resist nature's influence upon us, we must have become conscious of our freedom and able to use it. This state, however, can be attained in no other manner except by the awakening and development of our drives — something which does not depend upon us.

The highest law of mankind and of all rational beings is the law of total self-harmony or absolute identity. But to the extent that this law becomes something positive and obtains some content by being applied to nature, it demands that all of an individual's talents should be developed equally and that all of his abilities should be cultivated to the highest possible degree of perfection. This demand cannot be fulfilled by the mere law alone, because, according to what has just been said, its fulfillment does not depend merely upon the law, nor upon *our will* (which is, of course, determinable by the law), but rather depends upon *the free operation of nature*.

If we assume that there are several rational beings and relate this law [of self-harmony] to society, then the demand that *every person* should cultivate all of his talents equally contains at the same time the demand *that all of the various rational beings should be cultivated or educated equally.* Since all talents are based merely upon pure reason, they are all equal in themselves; therefore, they should all be cultivated to the same extent—which is what is required by this demand. Equal results must always follow from the equal cultivation of equal talents. And thus here we arrive by another route at the conclusion established in our last lecture: the final aim of all society is *the complete equality of all of its members.*

We have already shown in the previous lecture and by another route that the mere law can no more fulfill this demand [for the complete equality of all the members of society] than it can fulfill the above demand upon which this lecture is based [i.e., the demand for the equal cultivation of all of ones talents, as well as the equal cultivation of all of the members of society]. Nevertheless, the free will *should* and *can* strive for an ever closer approximation to this end.

This is where the efficacy of the social drive enters in. For the social drive aims at this same end and will provide the means for the endless approximation which has been demanded. Included within the social drive, or the drive to interact with other free, rational beings and to interact with them *qua* free, rational beings, are the following two drives: *the drive to communicate*, i.e., the drive to cultivate in other persons that aspect of personality in which *we* ourselves are especially strong and, insofar as it is possible, to make everyone else equal to our own better self; *the drive to receive*, i.e., the drive to allow others to cultivate in us that aspect in which they are especially strong and we are especially weak. Nature's mistakes are in this way corrected by reason and freedom, and that one-sided development which nature has furnished each individual becomes the common property of the entire species. In return, the entire species cultivates the individual. On the supposition that all of the individuals who are possible under a specific set of natural conditions actually do exist, then the species will provide the individual with all the education which is possible in such circumstances. Nature develops everyone one-sidedly, but it does so at every point in which it comes into contact with any rational being. What reason does is to unite these points, thus presenting a solid and extended front to nature. In this manner reason compels nature to cultivate every talent in the species at least, since it did not wish to do so in the individual. Through these drives [viz., the drive to communicate and the drive to receive] *reason* itself sees to the equitable distribution of the desired education among the individual members of society. And *reason* will continue to see to this, since the realm of nature does not extend this far.

Reason will see to it that every individual obtains *indirectly from the hands of society* that complete education which he could not obtain *directly* from nature. Thus from the advantages possessed by each individual society will accumulate a common store for the free use of everyone, thereby multiplying the advantages by the number of individuals. Reason will make the individual's deficiencies into a common burden and will thus infinitely reduce them. Expressed differently and in a manner which more easily lends itself to some applications: the aim of all cultivation of skill is the subordination of nature (in the sense specified) to reason and the agreement of experience (to the extent that it is independent of the laws of our faculty of representation) with our necessary practical concepts of experience. Reason is, accordingly, engaged in a constant struggle with nature, a war that can never end—so long as we are not supposed to become gods. However, nature's influence should and can become weaker and weaker, whereas reason's dominion should and can become stronger and stronger. Reason ought to gain one victory after another over nature. Perhaps an individual may struggle successfully against nature at that particular point where he comes into contact with it, although in every other aspect he is governed by nature. But society now joins together and assumes joint responsibility: what the individual could not accomplish by himself can be accomplished by the united strength of all. Of course, everyone struggles alone, but all of us share in the weakening of nature through the common struggle and in that victory over nature separately achieved by each person in his own field. Hence physical inequality even serves to strengthen that bond that unites all men in one [social] body. The compulsion of our needs and the much sweeter compulsion to satisfy these needs binds us even more closely together. In seeking to weaken the power of reason, nature succeeds only in strengthening it.

So far everything has proceeded naturally: we have shown that there are a great variety of different *personal characters*, in accordance with the various types and levels of development, but we have not yet shown that there are any distinct *classes*. We have not yet shown this, because we have been unable so far to indicate *any particular free determination*, i.e., any voluntary choice of a particular sort of education. One should not misunderstand or only partially understand the claim that we have been unable so far to indicate any particular free determination. The social drive as such certainly does involve freedom: it merely urges; it does not compel. One may resist and suppress this drive. Out of misanthropic egoism one can isolate himself completely and can refuse to accept anything from society, in order not to have to render anything to it. Out of crude animality one can overlook the freedom of society and can consider it to be subordinate to his mere caprice, because he thinks of himself as subordinate to the caprice of nature. But this is not what we are here concerned with. If we are responsive to the social drive at all, then this drive requires us to share the good that we possess with those who need it and to receive what we lack from those who have it. For this no special new determination or modification of the social drive is required—which is all that I meant to say.

The characteristic difference [between the distinction between persons and the distinction between classes, i.e., between natural and social inequality] is as follows: *Under the circumstances which have been set forth so far*, I, as an individual, surrender myself to nature for the development of any particular talent which I may have. I do so *because I must*. I do not have any choice in the matter, but involuntarily follow the guidance of nature. I accept all that nature provides, but I cannot accept what she does not wish to provide. Though I neglect no opportunity to cultivate as many aspects of my personality as possible, I create no such opportunities at all, because I cannot do so. But if, *on the other hand*, as linguistic usage indicates, a class is something which is supposed to be freely chosen, then before *I can choose a class*—if I am to do so—I must have *previously* surrendered myself to nature. For in order to make such a choice various drives have to have been awakened within me, and I have to have become conscious of various talents. Nevertheless, *in the choice itself* I resolve that from now on I will pay no heed to certain opportunities which nature may provide, and I will do so in order to be able to devote all of my strength and natural gifts *exclusively to developing one or more specific skills.* My class is determined by the particular skill to the development of which I freely dedicate myself.

The question arises: *Ought* I to select a particular class, or, if I am not morally *obliged* to do so, *may* I dedicate myself solely to one particular class, i.e., to cultivating only one aspect of myself? If, as a matter of unconditional duty, I ought to choose some specific class, then it must be possible to derive from the supreme law of reason [viz., the law of self-harmony] a drive which has as its object this choice of a class—in the same way in which it is possible to derive from this law a drive whose object is society as such [viz., the social drive derived in the Second Lecture]. If I am merely permitted to choose a class, then no such drive can be derived from the law of reason, and all that can be so derived is the permission to make such a choice. In this latter case it must be possible to indicate some empirical datum which determines the will to make the actual choice which the law merely permits. Such an empirical datum would specify a mere prudential rule, but not a law. We will see how this works in the course of our investigation.

The law commands: "Cultivate all of your talents completely and equally, insofar as you are able to do so." But the law does not specify whether I should exercise these talents directly upon nature, or indirectly through community with others. This choice, accordingly, is left entirely to my own discretion. The law commands: "Subordinate nature to your aims." But the law does not say that if I discover that nature has already been sufficiently molded by others for some of my purposes, then I ought to mold it further for all possible human purposes. Thus the law does not prohibit me from choosing a particular class, though neither am I enjoined by it to make such a choice, simply because I am not forbidden to do so. Here I find myself in the realm of free choice. I may choose a class, and in order to decide whether or not I should do so (though not in order to decide which particular class to choose—something which I will discuss on another occasion), I have to base my decision upon quite different grounds than those which can be immediately derived from the law.

As matters now stand, man is born into society. He no longer encounters nature in its native state; instead, he finds it already prepared in various ways for his possible purposes. He discovers a multitude of men in various branches [of knowledge and activity] busily cultivating nature for the use of rational beings in all their various aspects. He discovers that many things which he would otherwise have to do for himself have already been accomplished. He may be able to lead a very comfortable life without directly applying his own strength to nature at all, and perhaps he could attain a certain sort of perfection merely by enjoying what society has already achieved, in particular, by enjoying what society has contributed to his own cultivation. But this is not permissible. He must at least try to pay his own debt to society. He must take his place. He must at least strive in some way to improve society, which has done so much for him.

There are two ways in which one may attempt to do this: On the one hand, he can try to cultivate every aspect of nature by himself. But then it might take him his entire lifetime—and, if he had them, several lifetimes—to learn what had already been accomplished by those who preceded him and what still remained to be done. Such an effort would be superfluous, and thus from the standpoint of the human species his entire life would be lost, certainly not through the fault of his evil will, but rather because of his lack of good sense. Or, on the other hand, one can seize upon some particular speciality—perhaps the one which for the time being he is most interested in completely exhausting and for whose cultivation he is already best prepared by nature and society—and dedicate himself exclusively to it. The cultivation of his other talents he leaves up to society, while at the same time he intends, strives, and wishes to contribute to the cultivation of society within his own speciality. With this he has chosen a class, and this choice, considered in itself, is perfectly legitimate. Yet, like all free acts, this one too is subject to the ethical law, insofar as the ethical law regulates our behavior. I.e., this act is subject to the categorical imperative, which I express as follows: "never will things which contradict each other." So expressed, this is a law which everyone can obey satisfactorily, since what we will depends not in the least upon nature, but only upon us.

The choice of a class is a free choice. Thus we may not compel any person to join any particular class, nor may we deny him admission to any class. Every individual action, as well as every general institution which aims at such compulsion is illegitimate. This is so quite apart from the fact that it is stupid to compel a man to join a particular class or to bar him from another, since nobody can be totally acquainted with anyone else's special talents. A member of society who is assigned to the wrong place in this manner is often totally lost for society. Apart from this, such compulsion is wrong in itself, because it places our own action in contradiction with our practical concept of it. We desired a *member* of society, and we produce a *tool* of society. We desired a *free fellow-worker* on our great project, and we produce a *coerced, passive instrument* of the same. Thus, as far as we were able, we have killed the man within the person we have treated in this manner; we have wronged him, and we have wronged society.

We selected a particular class as well as a specific talent for further cultivation, *because we wanted to be able to repay society for all that it has done for us.* Consequently, everyone is bound actually to apply his education for the benefit of society. No one has the right to work merely for his own private enjoyment, to shut himself off from his fellow men and to make his education useless to them; for it is precisely the labor of society which has put him in a position to acquire this education for himself. In a certain sense education is itself the product and the property of society, and thus the man who does not want to benefit society robs it of its property. Everyone has the duty, not only to want to be generally useful to society, but also the duty, according to the best of his knowledge, to bend all of his efforts toward society's final end: the constant improvement of the human species, liberating it ever more from natural compulsion, and making it ever more independent and autonomous. And thus from this new inequality [i.e., the inequality of classes] there arises a new equality: the equitable advancement of culture in every individual.

I am not claiming that things are always actually as I have just described them. But according to our practical concepts of society and the different social classes, this is how things ought to be, and we can and should work to make them so. At the proper time we shall see how vigorously the scholarly class in particular can work toward this end and how many means to this end it has in its power.

If we only contemplate the idea just presented, even apart from all relation to ourselves, we can at least catch a glimpse beyond ourselves of an association in which one cannot work for himself without working at the same time for everyone, nor work for others without working for himself; for the successful progress of any member [of this association] is the successful progress of them all, and one person's misfortune is everyone's misfortune. Simply through the harmony which it reveals in the most diverse things, this spectacle pleases us sincerely and exalts our spirit mightily.

Our interest in this spectacle only increases when we take ourselves into account and consider ourselves as members of this great and intimate association. Our sense of our own dignity and power increases when we say to ourselves that which every one of us can say: "My existence is not vain and purposeless. I am a necessary link in that great chain which began at that moment when man first became fully conscious of his own existence and stretches into eternity. All these people have labored for my sake: all that were ever great, wise, or noble—those benefactors of the human race whose names I find recorded in world history, as well as the many more whose services have survived their names. I have reaped their harvest. Upon the earth on which they lived, I tread in their footsteps, which bring blessings upon all who follow them. As soon I wish, I can assume that lofty task which they had set for themselves: the task of making our fellow men ever wiser and happier. Where they had to stop, I can build further. I can bring nearer to completion that noble temple that they had to leave unfinished."

"But," someone may say, "I will have to stop too, just like they did." Yes! and this is the loftiest thought of all: Once I assume this lofty task I will never have completed it. Therefore, just as surely as it is my vocation to assume this task, I can never cease *to act* and thus I can never cease *to be*. That which is called "death" cannot interrupt my work; for my work must be completed, and it can never be completed in any amount of time. Consequently, my existence has no temporal limits: I am eternal. When I assumed this great task I laid hold of eternity at the same time. I lift my head boldly to the threatening stony heights, to the roaring cataract, and to the crashing clouds in their fire-red sea. "I am eternal!" I shout to them, "I defy your power! Rain everything down upon me! You earth, and you, heaven, mingle all of your elements in wild tumult. Foam and roar, and in savage combat pulverize the last dust-mote of that body which I call my own. Along with its own unyielding project, my will shall hover boldly and indifferently above the wreckage of the universe. For I have seized my vocation, and it is more permanent than you. It is eternal, and I am eternal like it!"

FOURTH LECTURE
Concerning the Scholar's Vocation

I must speak to you today about the vocation of the scholar.

I find that I am in a peculiar situation in regard to this subject. For all of you, or at least most of you, have chosen the sciences as your life's work, and so have I. Presumably, you devote your entire energies to the goal of being respected members of the scholarly class, and so have and so do I. I am thus supposed to speak as a scholar before prospective scholars on the subject of the scholar's vocation. I am supposed to treat this subject thoroughly and, if possible, exhaustively — omitting nothing true from my presentation. Suppose that I should discover that the vocation of this class is a very honorable and lofty one, more distinguished than that of any other class: how can I say this without being immodest, without depreciating the other classes, and without seeming to be blinded by self-conceit? Yet I am speaking as a philosopher, and as such I am obliged to specify precisely the meaning of every concept; so what can I do if the concept which comes next in the series happens to be the concept of the scholar? It is impermissible for me to suppress anything which I recognize to be true: it remains true in any case. Even modesty is subordinate to truth, and it is a false modesty which stands in the way of the truth. For the time being let us investigate our subject impartially, as if it had no relation to ourselves and were a concept borrowed from a world totally alien to us. Let us demand all the more precision in our proofs. And let us not forget something which I intend to present with no less force in its proper place: that every class is necessary and deserves our respect, that an individual's merit is not determined by the class to which he belongs, but rather by the way he fulfills his role as a member of that class. For every person deserves to be honored only insofar as he approximates to fulfilling his role completely. For this reason, the scholar has reason to be the humblest person of all: since the goal which is set for him must always remain very distant, and since he has to achieve a very lofty ideal—one from which he normally remains very distant.

We have seen that men possess various drives and talents and that the vocation of every individual is to cultivate all of his talents to the best of his ability. One of man's drives is the social drive. This drive offers man a new, special type of education, i.e., education for society, as well as an extraordinary facility for education as such. It is up to man whether he shall cultivate all of his talents immediately within nature or whether he shall cultivate them indirectly through society. The first course is difficult and does nothing to advance society; therefore, within society every individual quite legitimately selects his own special branch of general education, leaving the other branches to his fellow members of society in the expectation that they will share the benefits of *their* education with *him*, just as he will share the benefits of *his* with *them*. This is the origin of and the justification for the difference between the various classes within society.

Such were the results of my previous lectures. A classification of the various classes according to pure concepts of reason (which is entirely possible) would have to be based upon an exhaustive enumeration of all of man's natural talents and needs—not counting those needs which are purely artificial. A specific class can be dedicated to the cultivation of each specific talent or—which amounts to the same thing—to the satisfaction of each of man's natural needs (i.e., each need which has its origin in a basic human drive). We will reserve this investigation for some future time in order to devote this hour to a topic which lies nearer to us.

If someone were to ask about the relative perfection of a society organized according to the above first principles (and as our investigation of the origin of society has made clear, every society, in accordance with man's natural drives, is organized in this way by itself and without any guidance), then in order to answer this question we would first have to investigate the following question: Are all needs cared for in the society in question? Are they all developed and satisfied, and are they developed and satisfied *equally*? If they are, then the society in question is perfect *qua* society. This does not mean that it would attain its goal (which, according to our previous deliberations is impossible), but rather that it would be so organized that it would necessarily have to *approximate* more and more closely to its goal. If all needs are not equally cared for in this manner, then it would of course remain possible for the society in question to make cultural progress through a fortunate accident. This, however, could not be counted on with any certainty; the society might just as well regress through an unfortunate accident.

The first presupposition for seeing to the equal development of all of man's talents is an acquaintance with all of his talents: a scientific knowledge of all of his drives and needs, a completed survey of his entire nature. Yet such complete knowledge of man in his totality is something which is itself based upon a talent, and one which must itself be developed. Man certainly has a drive to *know*, in particular, he has a drive to know his own needs. The development of this drive, however, requires all of one's time and energy. If there is any common need which urgently demands that a special class of persons be dedicated to its satisfaction, it is this one.

But the *acquaintance* with man's talents and needs would be an extremely sad and depressing thing without the scientific knowledge of how to develop and satisfy them. It would also be something empty and quite useless. It is most unfriendly of someone to show me my shortcomings without at the same time showing me the means by which I may overcome them, or to induce within me a sense of my own needs without putting me in a position to satisfy them. It would be far better for him to leave me in my state of animal ignorance. In short, such knowledge could not be the sort which society desires and for the sake of which society requires a special class possessing such knowledge; for such knowledge does not have the aim it is supposed to have, viz., the improvement, and thereby the unification, of the species. Accordingly, this knowledge of man's needs must be joined with a knowledge of the *means for satisfying them*. Both sorts of knowledge are the business of the same class, because neither sort of knowledge can be complete, much less efficacious and vigorous without the other. Knowledge of the first sort [viz., an acquaintance with man's talents and needs] is based upon principles of pure reason; it is *philosophical* knowledge. Knowledge of the second sort [viz., how to satisfy man's needs and develop his talents] is partly based upon experience; to that extent it is *philosophical-historical* knowledge (not merely historical knowledge, since before I can evaluate as means to ends the objects given in experience, I must be acquainted with the ends to which these objects refer, and such ends can only be recognized philosophically). The knowledge in question is supposed to be useful to society. It is, therefore, not enough merely to know what talents man has and the means for developing them. Such knowledge would still always remain entirely fruitless. In order to obtain the desired utility, an additional step is required: one must know the particular cultural level of one's society at a particular time, as well as the particular level it has to reach next and the means it has to employ to do so. Simply on the assumption that there is any experience whatsoever, one can certainly calculate the course of the human species on the basis of reason alone, and in advance of all particular experience. One can specify approximately the various steps it has to climb in order to reach a particular stage of development. One cannot, however, determine the level of a particular society as a particular time solely on the basis of reason. For this one has to examine experience as well. One has to study the events of former ages, albeit with an eye purified by philosophy. One must look around oneself and observe one's contemporaries. The last element in the knowledge which society requires is thus merely *historical*.

Taken together (and if they are not, they are of much less use) the three types of knowledge just indicated constitute what is — or at least should be — called "learning." The person who dedicates his life to the acquisition of this [three-fold] knowledge is called a "scholar."

Every individual scholar does not have to master the entire field of human knowledge in all three of these respects. Such total mastery would be for the most part impossible, and just for this reason the attempt to gain it would be fruitless and would lead to the waste without any gain for society of a person's entire life — a life which could have been useful to society. Individuals may stake out for themselves individual portions of the domain of knowledge, but in his own area each person should cultivate all three: philosophical and philosophical-historical, as well as merely historical knowledge. In saying this I wish to indicate in a merely provisional manner something which I will discuss more fully at a later time. I wish to assert here (on my own testimony at least) that the study of a properly grounded philosophy does not make it superfluous to acquire empirical knowledge — not, at least, if such knowledge is thorough. On the contrary, such a philosophy demonstrates in the most convincing manner that such empirical knowledge is indispensable. We have already shown that the purpose of all human knowledge is to see to the equal, continuous, and progressive development of all human talents. It follows from this that the true vocation of the scholarly class is the *supreme supervision of the actual progress of the human race in general and the unceasing promotion of this progress.* Only with great effort do I here restrain my feelings from being carried away by the lofty idea which is now before us, but the path of cold investigation is not yet at an end. Yet I must at least mention in passing what it is that those who attempt to hinder the advance of science would actually do. (I say "would" do, for how can I know whether there really are any such persons?) The whole progress of the human race depends directly upon the progress of science. Whoever retards the latter also retards the former. And what public image does the person who retards the progress of mankind present to his age and to posterity? With actions louder than a thousand words, he screams into the deafened ears of his own and later ages: "So long as I am alive, at least, my fellow men shall become no wiser and no better. For if mankind were to advance, then, despite all my resistance, I too would be forced to advance at least in some respect, and this I abhor. I do not wish to become more enlightened or ennobled. My element is darkness and perversity, and I will summon up my last ounce of strength in order to keep from being budged from this element." Mankind can dispense with, can be robbed of, everything without risk of losing its true dignity—it can dispense with everything, that is, except for the possibility of improvement. Like that foe of mankind whom the Bible depicts, these misanthropes [who would hinder the progress of science] have deliberated and calculated coldly and cunningly; they have explored the most sacred depths in order to choose where mankind has to be attacked in order to be nipped in the bud. They have found the spot. With indignation mankind turns away from the spectacle presented by such persons, and we return to our inquiry.

Science itself is only one branch of human development—every branch of which must be advanced if all of man's talents are to be further cultivated. Hence, like every person who has chosen a particular class, every scholar strives to advance science, specifically, that area of science which he has chosen. He has to do what everyone has to do in his special area, and he has to do far more than this. He is supposed to supervise and promote the progress of the other classes, but is he himself *not* supposed to make any progress? The progress of all of the other special areas of development depends upon the progress of the scholar. He must always proceed in advance of the other areas in order to clear and explore the path and then to guide them along it, but is he himself supposed to stay behind? From that moment he would cease to be what he is supposed to be, and thus—since he is nothing else but this—he would be nothing at all. I am not saying that every scholar *actually has to advance* his own area; perhaps he cannot do so. But I am saying that every scholar must *strive* to do so, and that he may not rest nor believe himself to have discharged his duty until he has advanced his area of science. And so long as he lives he can continue to advance it further. If he is overtaken by death before he has achieved his purpose then he is of course released from his duty within this world of appearances, and his sincere attempt will be counted as his accomplishment would have been. If the following rule applies to all men, it applies especially to the scholar: he should forget his accomplishments as soon as they are completed and should always think only of what he still has to accomplish. The person whose field is not enlarged with every step that he takes has not yet advanced very far.

The scholar is especially destined for society. More than any other class, his class, insofar as he is a scholar, properly exists only through and for society. Accordingly, it is his particular duty to cultivate to the highest degree within himself the social talents of *receptivity* and the *art of communication*. If he has acquired the appropriate empirical knowledge in the appropriate manner, then his receptivity should already be highly cultivated. He should be familiar with his scientific predecessors. And this is something which cannot have been produced merely by rational reflection, but has to have been learned through oral or written instruction. By constantly learning something new he should preserve his receptivity and try to guard against that total lack of openness to foreign opinions and ways of thinking which one often encounters, occasionally among excellent and independent thinkers. For no one is so well instructed that he could not always learn something new and occasionally something very essential, and seldom is anyone so ignorant that he could not tell even the most knowledgeable man something new. The scholar always needs skills of communication, since he does not possess his knowledge for himself, but rather for society. He has to practice this art from childhood and has to preserve it in all of his activities. At the proper time we will examine *the means by which* he does this.

The scholar should now actually apply for the benefit of society that knowledge which he has acquired for society. He should awaken in men a feeling for their true needs and should acquaint them with the means for satisfying these needs. This does not imply that all men have to be made acquainted with those profound inquiries which the scholar himself has to undertake in order to find something certain and sure. For that would mean he would have to make all men scholars to the same extent that he himself is a scholar, and this is neither possible nor appropriate. Other things also have to be done, and this is why there are other classes of men. If these others were to devote their time to scholarly investigations, then even the scholars would soon have to cease being scholars. But then how can and how should the scholar disseminate his knowledge? Society could not continue to exist without trust in the integrity and the ability of others, and accordingly, this trust is deeply etched in our hearts. Moreover, we are especially favored by nature in that our trust is the greatest precisely in those areas in which we most require the integrity and the ability of others. Once he has acquired it in the manner he is supposed to, the scholar may count on this trust in his integrity and ability. In addition, all men have a sense for what is true. By itself, of course, this sense is not sufficient; it has to be developed, scrutinized, and purified, and this is precisely the scholar's task. Such a sense or feeling for truth is not sufficient to lead the uneducated person to all the truths that he needs, but, unless it has been artifically falsified (something which is often done by persons who think of themselves as scholars), it is always enough to permit him to recognize the truth after another has guided him to it—even if he does not see the deeper reasons why it is true. Likewise, the scholar may rely upon this sense of truth. To the extent that we have developed the concept of the scholar so far, the vocation of the scholar is to be the *teacher* of the human race.

But the scholar does not merely have to make men generally acquainted with their needs and the means for satisfying them. He has to direct their attention to the needs which confront them under the specific circumstances inherent in each particular time and place, as well as the specific means for achieving each purpose as it arises. He does not look only at the present; he looks toward the future as well. He does not see only the present standpoint; he also sees the direction in which the human race must now proceed if it is to continue on the path toward its final goal and is not to stray from this path or go backwards on it. He cannot demand that the human race proceed at once to that point which shines before his eyes. No step along this path can be skipped. The scholar simply has to see to it that we do not remain standing in one place or turn back. In this respect the scholar is the *educator* of mankind. I wish to mention explicitly at this point that when engaged in this activity, as in all of his occupations, the scholar is subject to the ethical law, which commands harmony with oneself. The scholar exercises an influence upon society. Society is based upon the concept of freedom; it and all of its members are free. Thus the scholar may employ none but moral means to influence society. He will not be tempted to use *compulsory means* or physical force to get men to accept his convictions. In our era one should not have to waste any further words on such folly. But neither should the scholar employ *deception*. Quite apart from the fact that in doing so he would wrong himself and that his duty as a person would in any case be higher than his duty as a scholar, he would wrong society at the same time. For every individual in society ought to act on the basis of free choice and on the basis of a conviction which *he himself has judged adequate*. In each of his actions he ought to be able to think of himself as an end and ought to be treated as such by every other member of society. A person who is deceived is being treated as a mere means to an end.

The final aim of every individual person, as well as of society as a whole, and thus the final aim of all of the scholar's work for society, is the ethical improvement of the whole person. It is the scholar's duty always to keep this final aim in view and to have it before his eyes in all that he does within society. But no one who is not himself a good man can work successfully for ethical improvement. We do not teach by words alone; we also teach—far more forcefully—by example. Everyone who lives in society owes it to society to set a good example, because the power of example originates only through our life in society. How much greater is the scholar's obligation to set a good example—the scholar, who is supposed to surpass the other classes in every aspect of culture! How can he think that others will follow his teachings if he contradicts them before everyone's eyes in every action of his life? (The words addressed by the founder of Christianity to his followers apply quite aptly to the scholars: "Ye are the salt of the earth, but if the salt has lost its savour wherewith shall it be salted?" When the elect among men have been corrupted, where should one search to find ethical goodness?) Considered, therefore, in this last respect, the scholar should be the *ethically best* man of his time. He ought to represent the highest level of ethical cultivation which is possible up to the present.

This is the vocation we have in common, the fate we share. It is a happy fate to have a particular calling which requires one to do just that which one has to do for the sake of one's general calling as a human being. It is a happy fate to be required to apply one's time and energy only to something for which one would otherwise have to make time and save up energy with prudent economy. And it is a happy fate to have for one's work, one's business, one's own daily task something which for other persons is a pleasant relaxation from labor. Here is an invigorating thought, one which elevates the soul and which each of you who is worthy of his vocation can have: "Within my special area the culture of my age and of future ages is entrusted to me. My labors will help determine the course of future generations and the history of nations still to come. I am called to testify to the truth. My life and destiny do not matter at all, but infinitely much depends upon the results of my life. I am a priest of truth. I am in its pay, and thus I have committed myself to do, to risk, and to suffer anything for its sake. If I should be pursued and hated for the truth's sake, or if I should die in its service, what more would I have done than what I simply had to do?"

I realize how much I have now said. And realize equally well that an emasculated age which has lost its nerve cannot endure this feeling and cannot bear to have it expressed. And I realize that, with a timorous voice which betrays its inner shame, such an age will call anything to which it cannot rise "muddled enthusiasm." Anxiously, it will avert its gaze from a picture in which it sees only its own enervation and shame, and something strong and elevated will make no more impression upon such an age than a touch makes upon those who are crippled in every limb. I know all this, but I also know where I am speaking. I am speaking before an audience of young men whose very age protects them from such utter enervation. I would like to provide you with a manly ethical theory, and at the same time and by means of this, I would like to place in your soul feelings which will protect you against such enervation in the future. I frankly admit that I would like to use this position in which providence has placed me in order to disseminate a more manly way of thinking, a stronger sense of elevation and dignity, and a more intense desire to fulfill one's vocation despite every danger. I would like to broadcast this in every direction, as far as the German language extends and even farther if I could. This I would like to do, so that after you have left this place and have scattered in all directions I could know that in all those places you are scattered there live men whose chosen friend is truth: men who will cling to truth in life and in death, men who will provide a refuge for truth when all the world thrusts it out, men who will publicly defend the truth when it is slandered and maligned, men who will gladly suffer the cleverly concealed hatred of the great, the insipid smile of the conceited, and the pitying shrugs of the narrow-minded — all for the sake of truth. This is why I said what I have said, and this will remain my ultimate object in saying all that I will ever say to you.

Translated by Daniel Breazeale

A Crystal Clear Report to the General Public Concerning the Actual Essence of the Newest Philosophy

An Attempt to Force the Reader to Understand

Foreword

Certain friends of Transcendental Idealism, or of the system of the Science of Knowledge, have given this system the name of the newest philosophy. Although this appellation looks almost like a mockery and seems to presume a search by its originators for the very newest philosophy; and furthermore, although the originator of this system is himself convinced that there is but one single philosophy, just as there is one single mathematics, and that as soon as this single possible philosophy is found and acknowledged no newer one will arise, but all earlier so-called philosophies will be considered only experiments and preparatory work; still in the title of a popular work he has preferred to risk every danger by following that use of speech rather than using the unpopular appellation of Transcendental Idealism or the Science of Knowledge.

A report concerning these newest efforts to raise philosophy to a science, one which is addressed to the general public for whom the study of philosophy has not become a real enterprise, is, for various reasons, both necessary and appropriate. Of course not all people should dedicate their lives to the sciences and consequently not to the foundation of all other science, a scientific philosophy; penetration into the investigations of such a philosophy also requires a freedom of spirit, a talent, and a diligence encountered in only a few individuals. But each person who lays claim to a general cultivation of mind should know in general *what* philosophy is. Although he does not participate in the investigations of philosophy, he should still know *what* it investigates; although he does not penetrate into the realm of philosophy, he should still recognize *the boundary* separating this realm from the one in which he finds himself, so that no threat from that other world completely strange to him causes him to fear for *this* world in which he stands. Therefore he should at least know it, so that he not act unjustly toward those scientific men with whom, as a person, he certainly must live; and also that he not advise his confidants incorrectly and keep them from that which might revenge itself bitterly on them if neglected. For all of these reasons, every educated person should know at the very least what philosophy is *not*, what it does *not* intend, what it is *not* able to effect.

And to elicit this insight is not only possible, it is not even hard. Scientific philosophy, although it raises itself above the natural view of things and above common human understanding, still stands firmly with its foot in the realm of the latter and proceeds from it, although admittedly it eventually leaves it. Anyone can see philosophy's foot on the ground of the natural way of thinking and can observe its departure from this ground, even those who only possess common human understanding and the usual power of observation presumed of every educated person.

A report like the one promised is, especially for such a system — I take here the Kantian and the newest to be one, since both agree without contradiction, at least in their claim to be science — such a report, I say, is indispensable to a system chronologically following another system which still continues *eclectically* and which formally gave up its claim to science, scientific preparation and study, inviting everyone who could add two and two to participate in its investigations; indispensable at a time when the unscientific public is only too pleased with this invitation, being of the opinion — and not to be dissuaded from it — that philosophizing is as automatic as eating and drinking, and that everyone who simply possesses the faculty of speech has a voice concerning philosophical matters; at a time when this opinion has occasioned such great harm, when philosophical propositions and expressions which can only be understood and judged within a scientific-philosophical system are brought before the court of unscientific understanding and misunderstanding, thus attaching no smaller, meaner reputation to philosophy; at a time when even among genuine philosophical writers one might find perhaps not half a dozen who know what philosophy actually is and others who seem to know raising a miserable little whimper that philosophy — simply is philosophy; it is indispensable at a time when even the most conscientious of contemporary critics believe they have cast no small aspersion on the newest philosophy when they assert that this philosophy is much too abstract ever to become a general way of thought.

Already in several instances and in the most diverse formulations this writer has not failed to deliver such a report to the ostensible friends of the arts. He must not have been completely successful in this, since he still hears the same old story from all quarters. Now he wants to see whether he will be more successful with a public which, at least in the sense of this writer, is non-philosophical. Once again in the most elementary manner in his power, he wants to show what he has already shown several times and, he believes, made quite accessible in some of his essays. Perhaps at least indirectly he will also succeed in this way with his colleagues. Perhaps the fair-minded, unprejudiced man who has no claim to celebrity as a philosophical teacher or writer will become aware that philosophy requires certain abstractions, speculations, and intuitions which he in no way remembers having made, and which he could never succeed in making if he tried. Perhaps he will realize that this philosophy does not think or talk at all about what he thinks and talks about; it never contradicts him because it never speaks with, about, or concerning him. Perhaps he will realize that all of the words which commonly serve both him and philosophy retain completely different meanings which are quite incomprehensible to him as soon as they enter the magic circle of this science. Perhaps from now on this fair-minded and unprejudiced man will just as dispassionately refrain from talking about philosophy as he refrains from talking about trigonometry and algebra if he has not learned these sciences. Whenever he is confronted with something philosophical he will say without prejudice: "Let the philosophers who have learned nothing else settle it amongst themselves; it does not concern me. I tend to *my* affairs." Perhaps after just one example of such reasonable restraint is given by the layman, the scholars will not be so bitterly provoked by the sharply repeated prohibitions against speaking about something they quite clearly *have not even read*.

In short, philosophy is *innate* in man. This is the common opinion, and that is why everyone considers himself justified in judging philosophical matters. However it may be with this innate philosophy, I will leave it in its own place and concern myself only with the *newest*, with *my own* philosophy, which I myself must know best; it is not *innate* but must be *learned* and accordingly only those who have learned it can judge it. I will show the former, and the latter automatically follows from the first.

It is always met with grimaces and, indeed, it seems hard to deny common human understanding the right to pass judgment on matters which one holds to be the final goal of philosophy: God, freedom, immortality. And for this very reason one does not want to accept the given example taken from mathematics or any of the other positive and learned sciences, but rather finds it unsuitable. Those concepts, after all, are grounded in the natural, common way of thinking; therefore, in a certain respect to be sure, innate. Here, then, in regard to the newest philosophy, only this needs to be recalled and kept in mind: that it would deny common human understanding the right to judge in those matters much less and would promise common human understanding more and more forcibly, it seems to me, than any of the previous philosophies, but solely *in its sphere* and in *its own realm*, not at all, however, *philosophically-scientifically*, a ground which for common understanding as such is absolutely not present. Common understanding will *reason* about these matters, perhaps reason quite correctly, only it will not *philosophize*, for no one can do this who has not learned and practiced it.

If one wants to retain at any cost the beloved expression philosophy and the repute of a philosophical head, of a philosophical jurist, historian, newspaper writer, or the like, then one should accept the proposal advanced earlier that scientific philosophy no longer be called philosophy, but rather something like Science of Knowledge. Secured in this name, the latter will do without the other name of philosophy and ceremoniously yield it to *all sorts of miscellaneous reasoning*. The general public and everyone who has not thoroughly studied it recognizes the Science of Knowledge as a newly discovered, unknown science like, say, the Hindenburgian Combination Theory in mathematics, and would believe our assurances that this science nowhere coincides with what they might call philosophy, would not contest it, and in this way could also not be contested. Their philosophy should then remain in all possible honor and dignity; only in consequence of our claim to the natural freedom of all mankind, they should permit us to refrain from their philosophy, just as we ask them not to take notice of our Science of Knowledge in their philosophy.

Accordingly, the following is the actual purpose of this text: it does not intend any conquest for the newest philosophy, but rather only a reasonable peace within its borders. It, this text, is itself not even *philosophy* in the strict sense of the word, but simply *reasoning*. Whoever has read it to the end and fully understood it does not possess one single *philosophical concept*, proposition, or the like because of it; he has rather attained a *concept of philosophy*; he has not taken the first step out of the realm of common human understanding onto the ground of philosophy, but he has arrived at their common border. If he really wants to study this philosophy from now on, he at least knows where he should direct his attention in this enterprise, and where he should turn it away. If he does not want this, he has at least achieved the clear consciousness that he does not want it, and never did want it or ever really have it, and that he consequently must acquiesce in all judgments concerning philosophical matters. He has achieved the conviction that no real philosophy could ever intrude into his private circle and disturb it.

Introduction

Dear Reader,

Before you—please allow me to address you informally—before you come to read this text, let us come to a preliminary understanding with one another.

Of course, I have thought what you will be reading from here on, but it concerns neither you nor me that you should also know what I have thought. As accustomed as you may otherwise be to reading texts only in order to know what the writers of these texts have thought and said, still I hope that you do not treat this one in such a manner. I do not appeal to your memory but to your understanding; my purpose is not that you take heed of what I have said, but rather that you yourself think and, God willing, think just as I have thought. Should what occasionally happens to contemporary readers then happen to you in reading these pages—you continue reading without continuing to think, apprehend the words without grasping their sense—then turn around, double your concentration, and read once again from that point at which you slipped off, or even lay the book aside for the day and read further tomorrow with undisturbed powers of concentration. It is solely on this condition, for your part, that fulfillment of the title's bold promise depends: to force you to understand. You must genuinely come forward with your understanding and place it against mine in battle; and, of course, I cannot force you to do that. If you keep it to yourself then I have lost the bet. You will understand nothing, just as you see nothing when you close your eyes. Should it happen from a certain point on that no contemplation can convince you in any way of the correctness of my contentions, then put the book completely aside and leave it unread for a long time. Go with your understanding along your earlier path in your usual way without thinking about it; perhaps out of nowhere, while you are concerned with something completely different, the condition of understanding will come to you of itself, and, after a short time, you will very well and easily comprehend what you cannot grasp now in spite of your efforts. Such things have happened to others of us, we who credit ourselves presently with a certain capacity for thought. Only do God the honor and keep silent about this matter until the condition of understanding and the real understanding has come to you.

My process throughout is consequential: just one single uninterrupted chain of reasoning. Each and every consequence is true for you only under the condition that in each instance you have found the preceding to be true. You would no longer be able to think as I have thought from that point which you found to be untrue, and to continue reading under these circumstances would have no other positive effect for you than that you *would know* what I had thought. I have always considered this effect to be quite insignificant and have always wondered at the modesty of the majority of people who ascribe such lofty value to the thoughts of others and so little to their own that they spend their lives learning the former rather than producing their own, a modesty which, in regard to my thoughts, I utterly refuse to tolerate.

Let us now get to the matter at hand!

1.

Each person with sound sensory tools maintains a store of knowledge, experiences, and facts through observation of the world outside of him and of his own mind. He is further able to renew, freely and in himself, whatever is given through immediate perception, even without actual perception; he may reflect upon it, holding the manifold of perceptions one against the other to determine the similarities of the singular as well as its differences. And in this way, if he has only the usual sound understanding, his knowledge becomes *clearer, more definite, more useful*, ever more a possession in which he is able to hold sway with complete freedom and dexterity. However, in no way will it be *increased* through this reflection; one can only reflect on the *observed*, only *compare* this with itself as it is observed, but in no way *create* for oneself new objects through mere thinking.

You and I and all of our kind possess this store of knowledge and either a more superficial or a more exact rendering of it through free reflection; and this is without doubt what one means when one speaks of a system or of maxims of common and sound human understanding.

2.

There was once a philosophy which presumed for itself the ability to expand the circle just now described through mere *inference*. According to it, thinking was not only *a dismantling and reconstruction of the thing given* as we have just described it; at the same time it was *a production and creation of something completely new*. In this system the philosopher found himself in exclusive possession of certain cognitions which common understanding had to do without. In this the philosopher could reason himself a god and immortality and could rationalize wisely and well. If such philosophers wanted to be consistent, they would have to declare common under-standing inadequate for the business of life, otherwise their expand-ing system would become superfluous; they would have to look down on common understanding disdainfully; they would have to invite everything that had a human face to become philosophers as great as they themselves in order for them to become just as wise and virtuous as these philosophers.

3.

Does a philosophical system like the one described appear to you, dear reader, to be honorable for common understanding and in keeping with its interests, a system according to which common understanding is healed of its innate blindness in the school of the philosopher, adding an artful light to its natural one?

If against this system another is now posed which undertook to refute this presumption of newly reasoned cognitions hidden from common understanding from the ground up, to clearly demonstrate that we have absolutely nothing true and real outside of experience which is accessible to everyone nothing for life except the system of common understanding described above, that one becomes ac-quainted with life only through life itself but in no way through speculation, and that one does not rationalize wisely and well but lives—would you, as a representative of common understanding, consider this last system your enemy or your friend? Would you believe that it would want to cast you in new bonds, or much more free you from those which have fettered you until now?

If this latter system were now indicted before you as hostile, evil-intending, and threatening your destruction; if, in addition, this indictment originated in people who by all appearances belong themselves to the party of the philosophy first portrayed, what would you think of the honesty, or, looking at the matter most generously, of the relationship of these accusers to the true state of things?

4.

You are amazed, dear reader, and ask whether the case, these indictments against the newest philosophy which are brought before your seat of judgement, actually is as I have just described it.

I am here compelled to transpose myself altogether from the person of the author into my individual personality. Whatever one thinks and says about me, I am certainly not known as a mere blind adherent, and as far as I know, the public has only one voice concerning this point. Several people do me the often declined honor of considering me the originator of a completely new system unheard of before me; and the man who on this point might seem the most competent judge, Kant, has publicly disavowed any connection with this system. Be that as it may, at least I have not *learned* from anyone else what I pronounce. I have not *found* it in any book before I pronounced it, and, at least in its form, it is completely my property. Accordingly, I myself should *know* best what I myself teach. Undoubtedly I will also *want* to say it. For what could it help me to openly affirm something here before the general public, the opposite of which my first, best pupil could explicate from my other texts.

Consequently, I hereby publicly declare what is the innermost spirit and soul of my philosophy: Man has nothing at all other than experience, and all that he arrives at, he arrives at only through experience, through life itself. All of his thinking—whether unrestrained or scientific, common or transcendental—proceeds from experience, and, in return, intends experience. Nothing has unconditioned value and meaning other than life; all remaining thinking, musing, knowing, only have value insofar as they relate in some way to the living, proceed from it, and intend to return to it.

This is the tendency of my philosophy. The same is true of the tendency of the Kantian philosophy, which, at least on this point, will not disavow me; the same for Jacobi, a reformer in philosophy contemporary with Kant, who, if he wanted to understand me, if only on this point, would raise few complaints against my system. This is accordingly the tendency of all *newer* philosophy which understands itself and which definitely knows what it wants.

I do not have to defend any of the others here; I am speaking only about my own, about the so-called *newest*. In the standpoint of this philosophy, in its process, in its entire form, lie the grounds through which one can be misled into believing that it does not at all proceed from the proposed result, but rather much more from the opposed result; that is, if one mistakes its proper standpoint and sees what is only said for itself as valid for the standpoint of life and common understanding. Accordingly, I have only to describe this standpoint precisely and separate it distinctly from that of common understanding, and it will be revealed that my philosophy has no other tendency than that given. You, dear reader, should you want to remain in the standpoint of common understanding, will retain in the same standpoint the most complete security against my philosophy and against every other philosophy; or, should you want to raise yourself to the standpoint of philosophy, you will receive the most intelligible direction possible from that standpoint.

I would like to be understood once and for all concerning the points which I will treat here, since I am tired of always repeating what I have said so often.

I must request of my reader the patience necessary for a continuous process of reasoning where I can only come to the aid of the memory of the reader by repeating the proven propositions out of which conclusions should be drawn.

First Lesson

Do not be taken aback, dear reader, if I seem to wander far afield. It is my concern to make perfectly clear to you several concepts which will be important in the future, not for the sake of these concepts themselves, which are common and trivial in themselves, but rather for the sake of the consequences which I intend to draw from them. Also, I will develop these concepts no more than necessary for my purpose, a fact which you can tell the critic who might expect here an analytical piece of art.

To begin with, you certainly know the genuinely real, that which distinguishes what the true fact of your present experience and life is—what you really *live* and *experience*—from the unreal, the merely imagined and pictured. For example, you are now sitting, holding this book in your hand, seeing its letters, reading its words. This is without doubt the actual event and determination of your present moment in life. While you sit there continuing to hold the book, you can remember yesterday's conversation with a friend, form an image of this friend as if he stood alive before you, hear him speak, let him repeat what he said yesterday, etc. Now is the latter, the appearance of your friend, just as the former, your sitting and holding the book, the real and true event of your present moment in life?

Reader: Not at all.

Author: I should rather have thought that at least something in that latter instance would also be an actual, real event of your life; for, tell me, do you not in the meantime live on; does your life not pass in the meantime; *is it not filled with something*?

R: I think you are right. The true event of my life in the latter instance is precisely that I *place* my friend before me, *let* him *talk*, etc., but not that he *is there*. It is through this placing before me that I fill the time which I am living.

A: In your *sitting there*, your *holding the book*, etc., as well as in your *placing* before yourself your friend whom you saw yesterday, your *representing* his conversation, etc., there must therefore be some *common quality* in consequence of which you judge both to be *genuinely real events of your life*.

Yesterday's actual presence of your friend, his *actually occurring* conversation yesterday as you still judge it today, must not possess that something in consequence of which you would consider it real in the context of the time in which you pose it *today*. Perhaps it even possesses an opposition to this something in consequence of which you do not consider it to be a real event today.

R: It must certainly be so. My judgment must have a ground; a like judgment, the like ground; an opposed judgment, the absence of the first ground, or the presence of a ground for its opposition.

A: What might this ground be?

R: I do not know.

A: But yet you judge every moment concerning reality and non-reality and judge them quite correctly, agreeing with yourself and other rational beings. Yet the ground for those judgments must consequently be continually present to you; only you do not become clearly conscious of this ground in your judgment. Furthermore, your answer is: "I do not know; I know nothing other than: No one has told me that yet." Yet if someone were to tell you, all of this would not help; you must find it yourself.

R: As much as I mull it over, I still cannot arrive at how it might happen.

A: This is not the right way either, mulling it over and making conjectures. In this way empty nonsense systems arise. Just as little can be *concluded* from that. To become truly inwardly conscious of your procedure in that judgment of reality and non-reality, look into yourself and you will become conscious of the ground of your procedure and at the same time inwardly intuit it. All that one can do for you in this regard is lead you so that you hit upon the correct procedure; and this direction is absolutely all that any philosophical instruction can do. But it is always assumed that you yourself actually inwardly possess that to which the other leads you, and that you intuit and contemplate it. Apart from this you receive only the narrative of an unfamiliar observation in no way your own, and in addition to that, an *incomprehensible* narrative; for what it depends on does not allow itself to be fully described in words as composed merely of things already familiar to you. It is rather simply an unknown which only becomes familiar through your own inner intuition and is signified only through analogy with something sensibly familiar. This sign only obtains its perfected meaning through intuition.

Let this be said once and for all and also for similar cases in the future, and try to pass it on to the famous writers who do not know it and who therefore allow themselves to handle the relationship of philosophy to language quite ineptly.

But to the matter at hand! — When you are involved in reading this book, in contemplating this object, in conversing with your friend, do you think about your reading, your contemplation, hearing, seeing, feeling of the object, your speaking, etc.?

R: Not at all. At these times I do not think about myself at all; I forget myself completely in the book, in the object, in the conversation. That is why one also says: "*I am involved in it*"; also, "I am *immersed* in it."

A: And, indeed, this all the more — to recall this in passing — the deeper, fuller, and livelier your consciousness of the object is. That half-consciousness, dreaming and diffuse, that inattentiveness and thoughtlessness which are characteristic traits of our time and the most powerful hindrance to a profound philosophy is precisely the situation, since one does not completely *throw* oneself *into* the object, burying and forgetting oneself in it, but rather vacillates and wavers between it and himself.

But how is it in that case in which you place before yourself an object which you have not judged to be real in this context of time; for example, yesterday's conversation with your friend? Is there then also something into which you throw yourself and in which you forget yourself?

R: Oh yes, it is precisely in this *placing before myself* the absent object that I forget myself.

A: Well, you said above that in the first instance the *presence* of the object, and in the second your *re-presenting* of the object, is the truly real in your life; here you say that you forget yourself in both. Consequently, the search for the ground of your judgments concerning reality and non-reality would be found. Self-forgetting would be the character of reality, and in every instance of life, the focus into which you throw yourself and in which you forget yourself and the focus of reality would be one and precisely the same. The rending of yourself from yourself would be what actually occurs and the fulfillment of your life's moment.

R: I do not yet understand you completely.

A: I had to put forth this concept here and designate it as clearly as possible. Stay with me in attentive discussion, and I hope to clarify myself to you shortly.

Can you again represent the *representing* which you just completed of yesterday's discussion with your friend?

R: Undoubtedly. This is precisely what I have just done during our reflection on that representation. I did not really represent that conversation, but rather a representing of that conversation.

A: What do you now consider to be the genuinely *factual* in this representation of the representing, the *fulfilling* of the flowing moments of your life?

R: Simply the representing of the representing.

A: Now come back with me again, and to the side. In the representation of yesterday's conversation—be truly inwardly conscious of this and look into your consciousness—how did the latter, the conversation, stand in relation to your consciousness and to the genuinely factual, the fulfilling of it?

R: *The conversation* was, as already said, not the actual event, but rather the *picturing of the conversation* was the event. Yet the latter was not a *picturing in itself*, but a picturing of a *conversation* and, in fact, of this *determined* conversation. The picturing, as the main thing, resulted in the conversation; the latter was not the actual, but only the *modification, the thorough determination* of the actual.

A: And in the representing of this representation?

R: If the representing of the representation were the actual event, the *representation* would be the further determination of the former, in that not only would something be represented, but a representation would be represented. Furthermore, *the conversation* was the further determination of the (represented) representation, since not a representation in itself, as might also have been possible, but rather a determined representation of a determined conversation was represented.

A: The prevailing reality, the actual and truly *lived* event, would consequently be that in which you forget yourself, its beginning and the genuine focal point of life, which might carry along with it further subordinate determinations, precisely because it is as it is. I wish and hope I have presently made myself completely clear to you, if you have only been with yourself during this investigation, intuiting yourself inwardly and attending to yourself.

While you represented yesterday's conversation with your friend, or—since I prefer to assume nothing fictional, but to lead you directly into your present, true state of mind—while you reasoned with me as you reasoned above, filling your life and throwing yourself into it, do you believe that during this time something else *outside of you and your mind* has advanced and come about?

R: Certainly. For example, the hand of the clock has advanced in the meantime, the sun has advanced and the like.

A: Have you, then, observed this progression, *experienced* it — have you *lived* it?

R: How could I, since I was reasoning with you and had thrown my entire self into this reasoning and thereby filled it?

A: Then how do you know the hand of your clock advanced, to stick with this example?

R: I actually looked at my clock earlier and I perceived the place where the hand stood. Now I look at it again and find the hand no longer in the same position, but in another. I *conclude* from the arrangement of the hands of my clock which I became aware of earlier in like manner through perception, that the hand gradually advanced during the time I reasoned.

A: Do you assume that if instead of reasoning with me you had looked at the hand of your clock during that time, you would have actually perceived its advance?

R: Certainly I assume that.

A: So both, your reasoning just as much as the movement of the hand of your clock, are, according to you, at the same time true, genuine events; the latter certainly not an event of *your life*, since at this time you lived something else, but yet it could have been an event of your life, and would necessarily have been had you attended to the clock?

R: So it is.

A: And the hand has really and in fact advanced without your cognizance and assistance?

R: So I assume.

A: Do you believe that had you not reasoned, just as you did not look at the clock, your reasoning would have advanced without your cognizance and assistance, just as the hand of the clock has?

R: Not at all. My reasoning does not advance of itself; I must lead it forward if it is to proceed further.

A: How does your representing of yesterday's conversation stand in this regard? Does this also come without your assistance, like the movement of the hand, or must you bring it forward yourself as you do with reasoning?

R: When I really think about it, I do not know. In this instance, I am certainly well aware that I actively produced that representation in myself at your request. But since images go through my head otherwise without my knowing assistance, diverging from and supplanting one another just as the hand advances, so I cannot know whether that representation would not also have come of itself without your request and without my assistance.

A: With all of the respect an author owes his reader and which I actually bring to you, still I must confess that your admission does not bode well for the success of my discussion with you. In my view one should only dream when sleeping, but with waking eyes let no images coming of themselves pass through one's head. This absolute freedom to willfully give the mind a particular direction and to keep it in the same direction is the distinguishing condition not only of philosophical, but even of common, sound, and correct thought. Nevertheless, in the hope that at least during this discussion you will resist that blind inclination toward association of ideas and restrain those foreign images and thoughts, I want to drop the equivocal point concerning sensible representation and simply hold to your above admission concerning the freedom of reasoning.

Would there then be, in consequence of this, two kinds of reality, each of which is equally real; of which, however, one makes itself, while the second must be made by him for whom it should exist, and without whose making it would not exist at all?

R: So it seems.

A: Let us consider the matter a bit more closely. — The hand of your clock has really advanced while you reasoned, you say. Would you be able to say this, would you know it, if you had not attended to the hand at some time since your reasoning and made your conclusion in consequence of the *actual perception* that it is in another position than before?

R: I would undoubtedly not know it then.

A: Do not forget this. It is important to me. All reality of the first kind — whether it makes its way for itself without any of your assistance and cognizance, and whether it exists *in itself*, that is, without reference to any possible consciousness, are points which we want to leave completely undecided here — it exists, I say *for you* and as an event of *your* life, only insofar as you at some time attend to it, place yourself in it, and frame that reality in your consciousness. With this in mind, your contention that the hand has advanced from one of your perceptions of it to another, without which latter one it would never again enter your consciousness, since, in the meantime, you did not perceive it, can mean nothing other than: *You would have perceived it advancing in this interval had you attended to it.* Accordingly, through a contention concerning an event outside of your life you assert what is still only a *possible* event of your life, a possible moving forward and fulfillment of this life from the first perception of the hand to the second; you supply and insert a series of possible observations between the end-points of two actual ones. Were I only to give you my word that here, in all respects, I only speak of a reality *for you* and never do I posit a reality in place of it *without reference to you* — neither do I want to maintain and assert anything about it — then, under this condition, you will permit me to consider the movement of an outer reality without your assistance simply as a movement of your own *possible* consciousness and life, since you have realized that only in this way does it become reality for you.

A Reader (who, in addition, might be a famous philosopher in his area): I do not want to hear anything about it. Have I not made it sufficiently clear to you that this is pure craziness? I always proceed from a reality in and for itself, from an *absolute Being*. I cannot and will not go higher. The distinction which you make there between a reality in itself and one for us, and the abstraction in the former which occupies you and which, as I note, is the cornerstone of your building, you must first—demonstrate to me.

A: So! You are able to *speak* of a reality without *knowing* about it, without at least framing it vaguely in your consciousness and relating it to it? You are capable of more than I. Put the book away; it is not written for you.

A second, reasonable Reader: I will accept your qualification only to speak of a reality for us only on the condition that you remain faithful to it and not refer to reality in itself, whether in a good or bad way. As soon as you go beyond your limits and draw a conclusion to the detriment of the latter, then we will part company.

A: —That is reasonable enough!—

Therefore, given this perspective that the discussion will only concern itself with our relationship to reality and actuality, the following will be the case concerning our consciousness: *All reality,* whatever name it might have, would originate for us through the eclipse and forgetting of our self in certain determinations of our life; and this forgetting of our self would be precisely that which gives to the determinations in which we forget ourselves the character of reality, and would give to us *life itself.*

In the first place, it would give certain *fundamental* and *primary* determinations—the opposition immediately following will clarify these expressions about which I request your thorough reflection— certain fundamental and primary determinations of our life, the true roots of our life which make themselves and drive themselves on, to which one need only *surrender*, allowing oneself to be seized by them in order to claim them as one's own and to make them one's own actual life; the continuing chain of which, even if one lets it fall somewhere, can be taken up again at will and can supply the missing links from any point, moving forward and backward.

One need only *surrender* oneself to them, I say; for even these fundamental determinations do not have the irresistible power to *seize* us.

For furthermore, we have the capacity to again tear ourselves loose from those determinations in which we forgot ourselves, to lift ourselves above them and freely, out of our own selves, to prepare for ourselves a higher order of life and reality. We can, for example, think and conceive of ourselves as the *knowing* in that fundamental consciousness, the *living* in that fundamental life — the *second power* of life, if I call that resting in the fundamental determinations the *first power*. One can further conceive of oneself as the *thinker* in that thinking of the original knowledge, as the *intuiter* of one's own life in the positing of the same, which would give us the *third power*, and so on into infinity.

The entire difference between the first and the higher powers, between the life which is, as it were, pre-given and presented to us, which we need only accept in order to make it into our actual life, and the life not given, which only allows itself to be brought forth through one's own activity, may simply be that difference that from each of the higher powers one can look down on and descend into a lower one. But from the lowest, one sees nothing but itself and one cannot go deeper except into the realm of non-being; consequently, in regard to the *descent*, one is limited and constrained in it, although not at all in regard to *ascent* through reflection; so that for this reason, it is the real foot and root of all other life. That is why I called it above the primary and fundamental determination of all life.

It is enough for us here, in consequence of our agreement, to consider this sphere of the first power as the sphere of these fundamental determinations of our life; in no way, however, as the sphere of things in and for themselves, a view we disregard here. Though they may always be the latter in and for themselves, only for us do they exist, and only to us do they come as determinations of our life, in order that we live and experience them. And we are satisfied here to talk about these things in relation to us. One also calls that which lies in this sphere preferably *reality*, *fact of consciousness*. One also calls it *the experience*.

Know, dear reader, that from now on we will reflect purely and simply on this system of the first power. Do not forget this for a moment, but separate everything which lies in higher powers from it and disregard it.

I include in this system of the first power everything which we perceive in part through our external senses in space and discover in part through the internal sense in our mind. In regard to the latter, what I have called higher powers fall within this sphere; certainly not according to its *content*, but rather in view of its *form*; that is, the laws according to which it acts and comes to be exactly as it comes to be. For these laws belong to the facts of the internal sense and are perceived when one carefully observes oneself during those functions of the mind.

The main purpose of the present discussion with you, dear reader, has been this: that you—by the way quite arbitrarily and only designed for my future ends—divide everything that goes on in your consciousness into two classes, and clearly understand the differences between them by what is included in one or the other; that you distinguish what is a product of freedom and belongs to the higher powers and put it aside in the following investigation, and, on the other hand, think about and look exclusively at what I have called the first power. Only insofar as you have recognized this difference, hold fast to it and not mix it up with what has already been separated, will you correctly grasp what we will discuss further.

Second Lesson

A: Do not forget, dear reader, the distinction we have made between the two fundamental determinations of any possible consciousness, and bear in mind that in this treatment only the first, what we have called the fundamental and primary determinations of all life, will be discussed. Proceed with me once again in our conversation, dispassionately and unconcerned as to how we will return to our path.

Let us consider the inner workings of a mechanical artifice, for example, a clock. In it you see interconnected gears of various sorts, springs, chains, etc. You pass over the manifold of the mechanism observantly and look at one gear after another. Is it a matter of importance to you in this observation, whether you apprehend the separate parts of the machine from above, or whether you move from the bottom up; from right to left, or from left to right?

R: Not at all. I can apprehend the parts entirely in any of these directions.

A: Or do you perhaps orient yourself in your apprehension not at all according to the sequence in which the parts are juxtaposed, but rather, say, according to other viewpoints; for example, according to the external uniformity and similarity of the parts?

R: It is all the same for my ends.

A: Now, however, as certainly as you have apprehended each single part, you have accomplished this apprehension according to some kind of order. I want to posit that you have followed the juxtaposition from top to bottom. Why have you chosen precisely this one and no other, since several sequences of apprehension were certainly possible?

R: I cannot say that I have chosen it at all. I did not at all think that several sequences of apprehension could be possible. I came to this one immediately. Chance — that is what I call it when I can give no reason for it — ordained it to be so.

A: Yet, the manifold of the fundamental determinations of consciousness itself, as described above, proceeds according to a certain sequence in your consciousness?

R: Undoubtedly. I notice in the world before me now this, now that, now something else, etc.

A: Do you find at first glance that exactly this order of your observations is necessary, or might others have been possible, in your judgment?

R: In my judgment others might also have been possible. I judge further that I did not freely choose that one among the several possibilities which actually arose here, but that it came to me by chance just as the sequence of my apprehension of the manifold in the clock.

A: Now back to our machine and your apprehension of its individual parts! —

In that you consider each individual part alone and for itself — this gear, this spring — and find each entirely determined in a certain manner by this determinate form, this determinate size, etc., does it seem to you impossible that it could be otherwise, or can you possibly think that, in the most diverse manner, it could be otherwise formed, either larger or smaller?

R: In my judgment the individual part, considered in and for itself and as an individual part, certainly has the unlimited possibility of being otherwise. But all parts should work together and in their union bring forth one single result, and when I look at it, all parts must, in my judgment, fit together, mesh with one another; all parts must affect each individual part, and each individual part, in turn, must affect all others. When I look at it, it would certainly have been possible, in my judgment, to make another whole, for example, a larger clock or one which had other functions apart from the designs of what is actually at hand; and in this other whole, the individual gear which I am considering could not only be otherwise, but in fact it would have to be. But should *this* whole already have existed, this large clock with these functions, this individual part, this gear which I am considering, would necessarily have to have been precisely as it is with not a hairsbreadth of difference, because the whole is as it is; which means here, because all remaining parts apart from this gear are as they are. Or, if I begin my consideration of this individual part, this part posited as a part of such an artifice, then it is necessary that all remaining parts be as they are if they are supposed to fit with such a part in such an artifice.

A: Consequently, if you only properly understand the mechanism of this artifice, it would not have been necessary at all, as we posited above, for you to apprehend one part of the machine after the other through actual perception; but rather after you have seen and correctly understood only one part, and from it complete the perception without further perception and represent its place through mere inferences; then through mere inferences you could figure out which parts, assuming the machine fulfills its purpose, belong with the given part.

R: Undoubtedly.

A: Is it all the same to you for this purpose which of the single parts of the machine I give you?

R: It is all the same to me, because to each possible part all the remaining must fit. From each possible part it can consequently be inferred how all remaining parts, insofar as they are determined through the mere mechanism of the work, must be constituted.

A: Now posit the possible case—according to a certain scope and in a certain respect, the more exact determination of which does not belong here—that in the manifold of the above described fundamental system of all consciousness there is a connection similar to the mechanical such that each individual part must fit with the whole and the whole with each, and each is determined by the whole. Would it not then be possible to learn through mere inference from each individual part of actual consciousness how all of remaining consciousness will fall in place — and must fall in place — without the actual appearance of this remaining consciousness, just as you believe that from the observation of a single gear you can learn how all remaining gears must be constituted through mere inference?

Furthermore, posit the case that philosophy, or, if you rather, the Science of Knowledge, precisely in the search for this manifold of consciousness, exists in the way of an inference from the given to the not-given; then you would already have a very clear concept of this science. It would be the demonstration, the deduction of the whole of consciousness, which is always to be understood according to its primary and fundamental determinations, from any given determination in actual consciousness, just as you can picture to yourself a demonstration of the entire clock quite well from one single given gear; a demonstration of this consciousness independent of the actual perception in consciousness, just as you do not at all need to see the remaining parts of the clock in order to know how they are — most assuredly how they are in reality — if only the clock fulfills its determination.

R: Oh yes; if I only think about what you say superficially and hold to the similarity in what you are comparing. But if I reflect on it a bit more deeply, then your concept appears self-contradictory to me. The Science of Knowledge should provide for me a consciousness of the fundamental determinations of my consciousness without these determinations really presenting themselves in my consciousness. How can it do that? Will I not become conscious of what the Science of Knowledge teaches?

A: Undoubtedly. Just as you become conscious of the gears whose presence in the machine you only infer, but not as conscious as when you see and feel them. It should have already become clear to you from our first investigation that there might be a difference in the manner of becoming conscious. We will confront this quite extensively for our purposes more clearly below. Therefore, because of this difficulty, do not refrain from concerning yourself with our premise.

R: I seriously have no desire to concern myself with what would follow, if the merely possible were real, or the impossible possible.

But your premise of a systematic connection of fundamental determinations of our consciousness certainly seems to me to belong among the impossibilities.

A: I hope I can overcome your objections to the possibility of my premise. For the time being, draw with me just one single conclusion from that premise, which cannot be done too quickly in order to destroy misunderstandings of another kind and to suspend their hidden sequence of effects in your mind.

If you now apprehend one single part of that clock, observe it and continue to infer which parts are still required in order to give to the one part perceived by you the entire determination and efficacy you detect in it according to the laws of mechanics well-known to you, do you now really see these parts in this function of inference, do you touch them, do they pass before any one of your external senses?

R: Not at all. Relating to the examples you used in the first discussion, they do not stand in relation to my consciousness in the same way as this book which I have in my hand, but rather like the representation of yesterday's conversation with my friend; disregarding, of course, what should be disregarded. What is really factual in this operation, that in which I immerse and lose myself, is not the presence of such gears, but my representing—not really *re*-constructing, but *pre*-constructing such gears.

A: Do you or any other rational person propose that such a representation, the inner design and sketch of such a machine, is the actual, moving machine executing its functions in life? And does someone tell you after he has described and demonstrated a pocket-watch, for example: "Now put this watch in your pocket, it works fine; you can take it out whenever you want and look at it to see what time it is"?

R: Not that I know of—unless he is a complete fool.

A: Be careful talking that way. Because the philosophical system which I mentioned in the introduction, and against which the newer system is really directed, proceeded in this manner and no other. It proposed that the demonstration of a clock, and, moreover, an incorrect demonstration, was a real clock, a superb clock.

But if someone to whom you had demonstrated a pocket-watch says to you in the end: "How can all of this help me? I do not see that I will get a pocket-watch this way, nor can I see by your demonstration what watch it is"; or, if that same person accused you of ruining his real watch with your demonstration, or demonstrated it out of his pocket, what would you say of such a person?

R: That he is just as much a fool as the first one.

A: Be careful talking that way. Because precisely this—the demand for a real clock when, however, one has only promised a demonstration of it—is the most thorough reproach which has been lodged against the newer philosophy to the present time—lodged by the most respectable scholars and the most profound thinkers of our time. In the end, all misunderstandings to which this philosophy has been exposed are based on this confusion of the actual thing with the demonstration of the thing.

All of these objections and misunderstandings are based on this alone—I say this unequivocally. Because what is to prevent my immediately asserting what this science to be described actually is historically, which its originators undoubtedly will know, instead of asserting all of its presuppositions?

(1) Philosophy, or, since this term could give rise to controversy, the Science of Knowledge, first of all completely disregards that which we characterized *above as higher powers of consciousness*, just as has been required of you until now, dear reader, and absolutely limits itself with the contention we will immediately advance, to *the first and fundamental determinations of consciousness*, entirely in the sense we have explained it and you have grasped it.

(2) In these fundamental determinations, the Science of Knowledge makes yet a further distinction between that which each rational being contends is the same for every other rational being and therefore must be valid for all reason, and that which each presumes is there only for our species, for us as *people*, or even for us as *particular individuals*. It likewise disregards the latter and therefore the content of the former remains to be investigated.

Should the reader remain in doubt concerning the grounds and limits of this last distinction, or should he be unable to make this entire distinction as clear as the first distinction became for him, which was indicated above according to our presupposition, then this is without meaning for all of the conclusions we propose to draw in this text, and without detriment for the construction of the concept of the Science of Knowledge as we here intend it. The latter, which is merely determined by species and individuality, already automatically excludes itself from the actual system — but our intention here is not to lead the reader into this system.

We set forth the following in passing for those readers acquainted with philosophical terminology: the fundamental determinations of consciousness, which is the sole concern of philosophy and the first point valid for all reason, is the Kantian *a priori*, or the original and primary; the second, determined only by species and individuality, is the *a posteriori* of the same author. The Science of Knowledge does not require that this distinction be presupposed for its system, since the distinction is made and grounded in the system itself, and through this distinction the expressions *a priori* and *a posteriori* have completely different meanings.

(3) Initially, in order to gain entry into itself and to set itself a particular task, the Science of Knowledge presupposes that in the manifold of those fundamental determinations, according to the given scope, there might be a systematic coherence in consequence of which, given one thing, all the remaining are, and must be, exactly as they are; so that that which lies in the presupposition, those fundamental determinations, according to the given scope, comprise a system completed and closed within itself.

The Science of Knowledge *itself*, I say, presupposes this. In part, the Science of Knowledge is not yet this system itself, only becoming possible through it; in part, this system is also only presupposed, not yet proven. Those fundamental determinations are, so to speak, familiar to the Scientist of Knowledge; where they come from is beside the point. He hits upon the thought — how he does it is likewise beside the point here — that between them there might possibly be a systematic coherence. He does not yet assert this coherence, neither does he claim to prove it directly, and still much less to prove something different from its presupposition. His thought might be a conjecture, a vague notion that should mean nothing more than any other vague notion.

(4) In consequence of this presupposition, the Scientist of Knowledge proceeds to the attempt to deduce from one single fundamental determination of consciousness familiar to him — which one is not relevant here — all of the remaining ones as necessarily connected with the first and determined by it. Should the attempt fail, then it is still not proven that it will not succeed at some other time; consequently it is not proven that the presupposition of a systematic

coherence is false. It retains its validity as a problem just as before. Should the attempt succeed, if all fundamental determinations of consciousness can really be deduced — apart from the familiar — completely deduced and exhausted, then the presupposition is proven by this act. But even this presupposition, which has been raised to a settled proposition by this time, is foreign to us in the description of the Science of Knowledge itself. The enterprise of that deduction alone is the Science of Knowledge itself. Where this deduction begins, the Science of Knowledge begins; where this deduction is completed, the Science of Knowledge is completed.

Therefore, dear reader, let this be settled and established between us, and keep it in mind always: the Science of Knowledge is the systematic deduction of a reality, the first power in consciousness; and it relates to this real consciousness like the demonstration of a clock to a real clock, as described above. As mere Science of Knowledge, it does not want to be more than this in any possible way, not tangentially nor anything like it, and it does not want to be at all, if it cannot be this. Anyone who presents it as something else or something more does not know it at all.

In the first place, its object is the fundamental determinations of a consciousness as such, as determinations of a consciousness; not at all as, for instance, things at hand which actually exist outside of consciousness. We will learn in greater depth below that both might well be one and the same thing in and for the Science of Knowledge; but that the science can only contain the first view, and why this is so, we will also see. It is sufficient here simply to assert that it is so.

Just as the perception conveys these fundamental determinations of consciousness in itself, so does the Science of Knowledge pose them as its object; or more, those fundamental determinations of consciousness are themselves the perception. Only both pose the same thing as object in different ways. The actual clock relates to the demonstration of the clock as the consciousness of the actual presence of your friend to your representing of this presence; actual consciousness relates to the Science of Knowledge in just this manner. The self becomes immersed in philosophizing not in those fundamental determinations of consciousness themselves, but rather in the picturing and diagramming of these determinations.

Accordingly, the Science of Knowledge deduces *a priori*, without regard to perception, what shall come forth in perception in consequence of it; that is, *a posteriori*. These expressions consequently do not mean different objects for it, but only one differentiated view of one and the same object, similar to the way the same clock is used by it in the demonstration *a priori*, in actual perception *a posteriori*.

The Science of Knowledge has given itself this determination since its inception and has clearly displayed it in its name. It is hard to comprehend why people do not want to believe what it is.

Limiting itself to this determination, it can let any other philosophy be whatever it will: fondness for knowledge, wisdom, wordly wisdom, wisdom of life, and whatever kinds of wisdom there might be. It makes only this demand, without doubt fair, neither to be held the equal of these others, nor to be judged and refuted by them; just as the practitioners of the Science of Knowledge insist that they not be required to participate in, or even know of, these other philosophies. The Science of Knowledge will not enter into the controversy concerning what philosophy might seem to be to this person or that, or what philosophy was considered to be all along. It invokes its right to set its own task; and if philosophy is something else apart from the resolution of this task, then it does not desire to be philosophy.

I hope, dear reader, that this description of the Science of Knowledge, as a mere historical description, is completely clear and comprehensible, and does not allow for ambiguity at all. I must simply request that you at least note it and not forget it again at the first opportunity; and that you believe I am completely serious in this description, that it should remain fixed, and that everything which contradicts it will be repudiated by me.

Third Lesson

R: I now believe I have grasped your opinion of the Science of Knowledge and know quite well what you mean. As long as I remain with the simple likeness of it to the demonstration of a mechanical artifice, I can also conceive of the possibility of it roughly and in general. But as I look at the necessary difference between them, and at the characteristic distinctions of their mutual objects, a science such as you describe appears to me to be completely impossible.

The concept of the systematic linking of the manifold in the artifice to the manifestation of the intended result was present in the mind of the artist before the artifice existed; and this was brought about in reality only through this concept and according to it. We others do nothing more than reconstruct that concept of the artist, *re-invent* the artifice for the artist. And so there is a significant meaning here when it is said that there is a systematic coherence in the manifold. This systematic coherence is *in the artist's concept* and in all of those who think of themselves as artists.

Is your contention that in the manifold of consciousness there is a systematic coherence supposed to mean that this consciousness is brought about in the same way, according to the concept of such a coherence, by some artist, and the Scientist of Knowledge re-invents this concept? Where is this artist; how and out of what has he brought about this consciousness?

A: What if it did not mean this, and the likeness between the things compared should not be stretched so far? What if the proposition which appears ambiguous is only supposed to say this much: that one *can* view the manifold of consciousness, *also among other things*, as standing in a systematic coherence? Or that there are two ways to view and apprehend the determinations of a consciousness; partly an unmediated way in which one just gives in to the determinations, and so finds them to be however they present themselves; partly a mediated way in which one systematically deduces how they present themselves as a consequence of this systematic coherence: — That this view could only be grasped after the actual consciousness was there, yet without regard to its content, but not before the presence of the consciousness, and that it would have been nowhere except in him who grasped it with wilful freedom. Consequently, the Scientist of Knowledge, and he alone, would be the artist of consciousness, if indeed there should be an artist here; really the *re-inventor* of consciousness, yet without there being presupposed and seriously assumed an original, primary master craftsman and a concept according to which he had brought about his work.

R: So, if I have understood you correctly, I should conceive of it in the following manner: There is a consciousness which, as fundamental determination of my life, is as certain as I am of myself. Granted. This consciousness appears as an unconnected manifold. Granted. What kind of consciousness it is I know precisely because I have it and I need not ask after anything further from this standpoint.

Moreover, it is now still possible to deduce this manifold systematically as having to be as it is if consciousness is to be at all. This view, this deduction, this systematic coherence, which manifests itself in the deduction, are only for the individual who grasps this view and for absolutely no one else. And nothing further will be asked of this second point of view.

A: This is how I understand it.

R: So it is; although I again only apprehend your meaning here historically rather than grasp it, and although very many questions still remain for me.

But to proceed. — The artist who outlines the concept of a mechanical artifice traces the manifold in this concept back to the unity of a single result. The artifice should fulfill this or that determined purpose. The manifold and the harmony of the manifold comprise, according to the concept of the artist, the sole conditions under which the work can fulfill its purpose, and this unity is prior to the artifice, even prior to the concept of the manifold. The latter only arises through the concept of the unity for its own sake and is determined by it. Precisely such a manifold is required, because this purpose is to be achieved.

Such a concept of unity appears to me to be completely inseparable from that of a systematic coherence. Thus your Scientist of Knowledge certainly had to have a concept of such a unity, of such a purpose and result of all consciousness, to which he traces the manifold back as its condition.

A: Undoubtedly.

R: And indeed, he cannot find this unity first in the system, but he must already have it before he begins his systematic deduction; just as the artist must know what purpose is to be achieved in his work before he can look for the means to these ends.

A: The Scientist of Knowledge must undoubtedly have the concept of unity prior to the system.

R: The artist conceives this purpose out of freedom; he creates it through his thinking, since the existence of the artifice, as well as its constitution, depends purely on the artist. Since the Scientist of Knowledge need not first bring consciousness forth, being there independent of him and so there as it is, according to your own statement, he cannot *freely think up* this unity, because the actual manifold, present without the assistance of the philosopher, must likewise relate to consciousness without the assistance of the philosopher. As was already stated, neither can he find it in his systematic deduction, because for the possibility of this deduction, the unity is presupposed. Nor can he find it through perception in actual consciousness, since here, according to the presupposition, only the manifold, and in no way the unity, presents itself. Consequently, how, and in what manner, is he supposed to arrive at this unity?

A: For you it is enough to accept that this happens purely through a fortunate flash of insight. He surmises this unity. This, of course, only results in an assumption, and he must begin building up his system relying on luck. If it is now found in this investigation that the complete manifold of consciousness actually allows itself to be traced back to what was assumed, as if to its unity, then it is thereby, and only thereby, proven that his presupposition was correct. It is proven by the act, by the establishment of the system.

R: I grant you this, too; but once again let us proceed. — Prior to his concept of the artifice, the artist knows the necessary and immutable laws of the mechanism on which he relies in the connection of the manifold to the production of the proposed result; he knows the materials and their characteristics, from which he wishes to construct the manifold, and on whose constancy he likewise relies in his concept. In the same way, the philosopher had to know, prior to his deduction, the immutable laws according to which the manifold of consciousness would have produced its presupposed main result, and, if I am not deceived in all of this, the material that would already have been determined according to these laws; *would have been*, I say, without the assistance of the philosopher.

To stay with the first for now, how does the philosopher gain knowledge of these laws? Does he perhaps hit upon them, also through a fortunate flash of insight, until it becomes clear that they are the right ones when the presupposed main result can be deduced according to them out of the manifold of consciousness; just as, in its turn, the fact that these laws yield precisely this result reveals that the presupposed result was the right one?

A: You are making fun of the Science of Knowledge, and with more perspicacity than is customary. No, the Science of Knowledge does not behave in the way you assume. This would be a vicious circle.

Always keep to our chosen comparison. The Scientist of Knowledge is the artist who constructs the artifice of consciousness, which, nevertheless, is already there, as he himself maintains; and thus he only *re*-invents it, yet genuinely invents, since he does not look at the artifice already present during his work.

But the major difference is this: The producer of a mechanical work deals with dead matter which he sets in motion; the philosopher with living matter which moves itself. He does not so much produce consciousness as allow it to produce itself before his eyes. Were consciousness subordinate to laws, then it would undoubtedly direct itself according to them in its self-production; he would look on and at this moment simultaneously discover those laws, although he is not even concerned with this, but rather simply with its result, with consciousness as a whole.

R: Consciousness which produces itself, and yet is not the actual, familiar consciousness granted to us all?

A: Not at all; because this does not produce itself systematically, but its manifold is connected by mere chance. The consciousness that produces itself before the eyes of the philosopher is simply a representation of actual consciousness.

R: A representation produces itself? I no longer understand you, and I will not understand you until you give me a short sketch of your method.

A: Very well. We begin with this presupposition: That to which the complete manifold relates like a condition to the conditioned, like the gears, springs, and links of the clock to the hour hand, that is the last and highest result of consciousness, nothing other than *clear and complete self-consciousness*; just as you, I, and all of us are conscious of ourselves.

I say just like you, I, and all of us, and, in conformity with a remark made above, thus neatly separate out everything individual, which, according to our presupposition, can no longer fit into our system. Whatever you ascribe to yourself, but not to me, just as I do in my turn, is excluded; except the fact that you do ascribe something to yourself at all, befitting no one else, just as I do and we all do.

Now this, that complete self-consciousness is the highest and the last result of all consciousness, is, as was said, merely a presupposition which awaits confirmation from the system.

The deduction now proceeds from this self-consciousness in its fundamental determination.

R: In its fundamental determination? What does that mean?

A: In regard to self-consciousness, whatever is in it which is completely unconditioned by any other consciousness; hence, that which cannot be found in the deduction, but which must proceed from it. It is assumed that the manifold of consciousness includes the conditions of complete self-consciousness. Now, however, there may be something in this self-consciousness which would be conditioned by nothing else. This is to be asserted, and here the deduction begins.

R: But how do you find this?

A: Again, only by a fortunate flash of insight, which, however, when found, neither requires nor is capable of further proof, but makes itself immediately clear.

R: What is it in the asserted which is immediately clear—even if, for the time being, I wanted to excuse you from accounting for this clarity itself, this direct evidence?

A: That the asserted is the absolutely unconditioned and the characteristic of self-consciousness.

R: I will not understand you until you specify for me this direct evidence from which you proceed, the absolutely unconditioned and characteristic of self-consciousness.

A: It is the *I-ness*, the subject-objectivity and nothing else whatsoever, the positing of the subjective and its objective, of consciousness and what it is conscious of as one, and absolutely nothing else except this identity.

R: I have heard from various sources that people have found you to be quite incomprehensible—and ridiculous on top of it—concerning this first point, which you, nevertheless, must consider to be completely clear and generally comprehensible, since you begin all of your understanding with it. In case others ask, will you not give me something to help me make it a bit more comprehensible for them, without, however, allowing yourself to stray from your path; if, of course, this point does not also belong only in the actual Science of Knowledge, and not at all in a provisional commentary to it.

A: It certainly does belong in this commentary, because it is the common point already mentioned above which is shared by the Science of Knowledge and actual consciousness, and from which the former raises itself above the latter. Whoever shall attain a completely clear concept of this science must recognize this point from which the science proceeds, and such a concept should certainly be produced through our commentary.

The complaint has been voiced that people have not understood us concerning this point, which is absolutely unfathomable, since every child who has simply stopped speaking of himself in the third person and calls himself I has already achieved what we have set out for and can understand us.

I must simply repeat what I have already frequently said: Think of anything at all, for example, this book which you hold here in your hand. Now you can undoubtedly become conscious of the book as that which you have thought, and of your self as that which thinks the book. Do you see yourself as one with the book, or as separate from it?

R: Obviously as separate from it. I will never confuse myself with a book.

A: And, in order not to confuse yourself, the thinking one, with what you are thinking about, is it necessary that it be a book, and precisely this book?

R: Not at all; I distinguish myself from *every* object.

A: Accordingly, in thinking of this book, you can disregard everything which makes you think of it as a book and as this book, and simply reflect on the fact that in your thinking you distinguish yourself, the thinker, from what you are thinking about?

R: Undoubtedly. And as I answered the above question, whether I distinguish myself from the book, I have actually and in fact reflected on nothing more than the latter.

A: Consequently, you distinguish every object from yourself, the thinker, and for you there is no object except through and by means of this investigation?

R: So it is.

A: Now think yourself. Here you can undoubtedly also become conscious of a thinker and a thing thought. Does it seem to you that here the thinker diverges from the thing thought also? Are both supposed to be of two kinds?

R: No. Precisely in that I think *my self*, I am, of course, the thinker, for otherwise *I* would not have thought. At the same time, I am that which is becoming in thought, otherwise I would not have thought *me*, but rather something like an object, like the book.

A: Well, initially you have certainly thought *yourself*; that is, this determined individual, this Cajus or Sempronius, or whatever you may be called. However, you can undoubtedly disregard these particular determinations of your individuality, just as you could disregard the particular determinations of this book above, and simply reflect on the *convergence* of the thinker and the thing thought, as you reflected on their *divergence*. And you have actually done it the moment you explained your thinking yourself to me. In this, thinker and thing thought converge for you.

And so in this convergence you find the I — in opposition to the object — in whose thinking the thinker and thing thought diverge for you. Thus you find the essential character of the I, that notorious *pure* I about which contemporary philosophers have racked their brains for years, still explaining it psychologically — read, as psychological deception — and finding it infinitely amusing.

R: They might well have believed that such a pure I should first be found originally in the mind, something which converges and returns into itself — roughly like a pocket knife — just like the Kantians' waffle-iron of forms. They have eagerly searched for this pocket knife and, having found none, now conclude that those who wanted to see it deceived themselves.

A: It could well be. Then how did you find this convergence?

R: In that I thought myself.

A: Do you suppose other people think themselves?

R: Undoubtedly; if they do not talk without thinking, because they all talk about themselves.

A: Do you suppose they proceed in this thinking of themselves as you proceed?

R: I think so, yes.

A: Do you suppose they are also able to observe their procedure as you observed your own just now?

R: I do not doubt that.

A: Then if they do this, they will likewise find that convergence in their thinking themselves; however, if they do not do it, they will not find it: this is our meaning. We are not talking here of finding something already completed, but rather of finding something that is only to be produced by thinking freely. The Science of Knowledge is not psychology, which itself is nothing.

Now I would like a definite answer from you as to whether you seriously assume other rational beings and I proceed in the same way as you do in thinking of ourselves; that is, consider the thinker and thing thought as one in this thinking.

R: I do not merely assume it, I maintain it is absolutely certain and consider any exception to it to be simply impossible. The thought *I* does not come into being except by this procedure, and this procedure is itself the thought I. Consequently, anyone who merely thinks himself proceeds in the same way.

A: I bid you, dear reader, think into my soul and into the soul of all rational beings, and if you have been able to do this, have you then surveyed and traversed all rational beings in order to maintain something about all of their souls?

R: Not at all; and yet I cannot take back what I maintained. Indeed, by being inwardly conscious of myself, I find that I maintain even more than what was said. Beyond this I maintain that each person, from within himself, must maintain the same in regard to all others.

A: And how do you arrive at these contentions?

R: If I am inwardly conscious of myself, I find that the irresistible and undeniable conviction that neither I nor any other rational being will ever be able to proceed otherwise is directly linked with my procedure.

A: Hence you prescribe a law for yourself and all rational beings through this procedure; and here you have, at the same time, an example of the direct evidence mentioned above.

Now back to our project!

The philosopher finds this fundamental and characteristic determination of self-consciousness outside of his science and independent of it. It cannot be proven in the science and is, as a proposition, absolutely incapable of being proven. It is immediately evident. Also, as a fundamental proposition of the Science of Knowledge it cannot be proven except by the act itself; that is, by the fact that beginning with it, the required deduction is actually possible.

The deduction proceeds as follows: The Scientist of Knowledge says to himself, "In thinking myself, I proceed as we have just seen."

Now, does another one attach itself to this process so that we obtain a new characteristic of consciousness, and to this last perhaps another, etc., until we arrive at completely determined self-consciousness and so obtain a systematic deduction of the whole?

R: Once again I do not understand you. You ask whether something other, which is undoubtedly a determination of consciousness, can attach itself. How then should it attach itself; on what and in what? At least in the process of thought just completed I have become aware of nothing other than the identity of the thinker and the thing thought.

A: And yet, in keeping with my request and your own observation, have you disregarded many other things that you thought simultaneously with your thinking of yourself? You certainly should; and once again to take up what had been separated, which now lies in confusion, would lead science nowhere.

But even in that abstraction in which you are to apprehend your thinking, something attaches itself and you will find it if you only look closely. Does, for example, your thinking of yourself not seem to you to be a transition from some other circumstance to this determined one?

R: Indeed it is.

A: Do you also believe here that it will seem so to everyone else, and that if they will only look closely, they will find it so?

R: Certainly. I believe this if I become inwardly conscious of myself and expect it of them. Here there is the same direct evidence as above.

A: In the same way, if one keeps it properly in view, another attaches itself to this appearance, and to this second, under the same conditions, a third; and so the Science of Knowledge advances step by step until it has exhausted the complete manifold of consciousness and comes to an end in completely deduced, determined self-consciousness.

And so, in a certain respect, it is the Scientist of Knowledge himself who produces his system of consciousness; yet, in another respect, it produces itself in its turn. That is to say, the former provides the impetus for and condition of self-production. However, insofar as he thinks and construes what he intended, something else arises for him which he did not at all intend, which is simply necessary and accompanied by the apparent conviction that it must arise in just this way for all rational beings.

The Scientist of Knowledge only produces the source and first link of his chain with absolute freedom. From this source he is led, but not driven. He must construe each new link that arises for him in the construction of the preceding separately and in its turn with freedom, and as each new one attaches itself to the previous one, he will proceed as he did before; and in this way, his system gradually comes into being. Hence, in this linking of one manifold to another the laws of consciousness, about which you raised questions, manifest themselves. Ultimately he is not even concerned with their *apprehension*, but simply with their result.

R: I remember having heard people reproach you, saying that your system would probably be correct and consistent if one were to grant you your fundamental proposition. What kind of case can possibly be made with this reproach?

A: If the place and the meaning of the whole system as well as of the fundamental proposition is not completely misunderstood and not taken in a sense in which it is incorrect and therefore can never be proven; in short, if it is not taken psychologically, then the demand to prove the fundamental proposition can only have the following meanings: On the one hand, they might demand a proof of our right to philosophize as we do and not as they do. In making such a demand, they would be dismissed without further ado for the perfectly natural reason that every person has the indisputable right to pursue whatever science he wants. Let them only accept our Science of Knowledge as a special science still unknown to them; in return we will allow their philosophies to count for as much as they would claim for them. Only then, if we were to say their philosophies are nothing at all—as we certainly think and also say in the appropriate place—only then could they demand proof from us. But this proof is completely and decisively conveyed only in our entire Science of Knowledge; hence, provisionally, and before a proof of the validity of this procedure can be delivered to them, they must begin to study this science. On the other hand, they might require that the proposition as the fundamental proposition of the system be proven prior to the system, an absurd demand. Or they might want to have the truth of the substance of that proposition demonstrated by a dissection of the concepts lying in it. This would prove that they have absolutely no concept of, or sense for, the nature of science, which is never founded on concepts, but rather always on the intuition of immediate evidence. One would then have to let them be, without wasting more time on them.

R: But I am very much afraid that precisely this last point is their stumbling block. If each person is allowed to call only on his intuition and to presume it for all others without deriving his proof in an orderly manner from concepts, then he can maintain anything he wants; every stupidity must remain unchastised and all doors are left open for all kinds of foolish enthusiasm: that, I am afraid, is what they will say.

A: No one can prevent their doing this, and those who are like them might also believe them. Science has lost its hold on them. But to you, my dispassionate reader, to whom a concept of philosophy should be imparted, although you yourself want neither to begin the study of philosophy, nor to raise yourself to the intuition proper to this science; to you the nature and possibility of the intuition can be described with other, simpler examples.

You certainly assume that a right triangle is completely defined by two sides and the enclosed angle, or by one side and the two adjacent angles; that is, that on the basis of the given parts, precisely such other parts must be added, as they are added, if it is to be a triangle?

R: I assume that.

A: Are you not afraid that a case might yet present itself in which it is not so?

R: I do not fear that at all.

A: Or are you afraid that any rational being who could only understand your words will deny your contention?

R: I am not afraid of this either.

A: Have you tested your proposition on all possible triangles; or have you asked all possible rational beings whether they agree?

R: But how could I do this?

A: How, then, do you arrive at that conclusion, which for you is initially supposed to be valid in all cases absolutely and without any exception, and then for all other rational beings, likewise without exception?

R: I want to keep to the first case, where two sides and the enclosed angle are presupposed. If I become inwardly conscious of myself, I proceed as follows: In my fantasy I sketch some kind of an angle with finite sides, since I cannot do otherwise, and I close the opening between the sides of this angle with a straight line. I find that there is only one straight line which could possibly close this opening; this line lies at a certain incline against both legs on both sides (making certain angles), and it could plainly only lie at these inclines.

A: Now, however, your arbitrarily drawn angle was a determined one of so and so many degrees. Or is it otherwise; did you perhaps describe an angle in general?

R: How could I? I cannot describe anything but a determined angle, even if its dimensions are neither known nor intended by me. By virtue of its mere description, it becomes a determined one for me.

A: And so, the presupposed sides were determined to be of a certain length in the same way. Hence you could rightly say (I will spare you a great many other difficulties) that in this determined case, presupposing *this* determined angle and *these* determined sides, the triangle can be closed by only one possible side — the determined one which arises for you — and only by one possible pair of angles, the determined ones which arise for you; because nothing lies beyond this in your inner *perception*, which obviously begins with determined presuppositions. You would like to try it with other angles and other sides, and you could say the same of them, if it turned out to be so in the perception; and so forth. However, you could never extend this to cover all cases in which you have not tried it, least of all so boldly and brazenly extend it to cover the infinity of all cases which you could not possibly exhaust in your experiments.

Do you not therefore want to revise your terms, perhaps, and restrict your contention to the cases you used in your experiments?

R: Not at all, if I observe myself correctly and look to my inner self. I certainly cannot fail to ascribe general validity to my contention absolutely without exception.

A: You may well arbitrarily raise the many cases in which it has turned out to be true without exception to a generality and only expect similar cases by analogy, habit, association of ideas, or whatever else you want to call it.

R: I do not believe this. One single example is sufficient for me, and compels me, as much as would a thousand examples, to a general judgment.

A: Seriously, I believe it as little as you. And that proposition concerning the arbitrary raising of the many accomplished cases to a generality seems to me to be the fundamental proposition of absolute unreason.

But now, dear reader, allow me the small importunity of keeping you here until you have given me an account of how the generality of your contention, which you certainly do not want to give up, might be grounded through the procedure you described above in the construction of the triangle.

R: In the generality of my contention, I obviously disregard the determinateness of the angle and the sides, which I presupposed and which were closed by the third side. This is factual and proceeds from the mere analysis of my contention itself.

Accordingly, I must also have disregarded that determinateness in the same way in the construction of the triangle itself and in my observation of it as that upon which my contention is grounded, only without becoming completely conscious of it; because, over and above this, that which necessarily lies in the conclusion must have been in the premises. But if one disregards the determinateness of the angle or the sides, then there remains neither angle nor sides as present and given objects; there would remain nothing at all for my observation, or, of course, if you call the observation of something present and given exclusively *perception*, as I believe I have noticed, then absolutely no perception would remain. Since, however, an observation now must certainly remain, and something to be observed, in that apart from this I would be contending nothing at all, what remains can be nothing other than my simple *drawing* of the lines and angles. Consequently, this has to have been what I actually observed. This presupposition also agrees quite well with what I am actually and clearly conscious of concerning this process. As I described my angle I did not proceed from an angle of such and such a degree, but rather from an angle as such; neither did I move from the sides of some particular length, but from sides as such. They were determined for me not by my design, but rather by necessity. When it came to the actual description, they just occurred to me as determined, and only God might know why they were determined *precisely* as they were.

Now this consciousness of my drawing of lines, which lies beyond all perception, is undoubtedly what you call *intuition*.

A: So it is.

R: Now in order to ground my general contention, this intuition of my construal of a triangle must be directly linked with the absolute conviction that never and in no case could I construe it otherwise. In the intuition, I consequently grasped and encompassed my entire capacity for construction at one instant and with one glance through an immediate consciousness not of this determined construal, but simply of all of my construals as such; and indeed, *as* such a construal. Hence the proposition that through the three parts of the triangle the other three are determined is actually to say: Through my construal of the three parts, my construal of the remaining three parts is determined. And the generality which I posit would not in any way have arisen through the apprehension of the manifold in the unity, but much more through the derivation of the infinite manifold out of the unity of the same apprehended in a single glance.

A: Do you now expect further for your proposition in its generality that it is likewise general and without exception for all rational beings?

R: I do. And I can no more renounce this claim of general validity *for* all, than renounce the claim of the general validity *of* all. In order to ground it, I would have to assume that in that unmediated intuition of my procedure I intuited this *my* procedure not as the procedure of this or that determined person, which I certainly am, but rather as the procedure of a rational being as such, with the unmediated conviction that it simply is so. The intuition would thus be the apprehension of the manner of activity of reason in itself, constituting itself directly as such, all at once and with one glance. And this general validity for all individuals would not have arisen through the accumulation of the many in the unity, but much more through the deduction of the infinitely differentiated individuals from the unity of the same reason. Thus it is comprehensible how in this intuition, and in it alone, direct evidence, necessity and the general validity of all and for all, hence all scientificality, grounds itself.

A: You have understood yourself quite well and I hope you might be able to make the matter just as comprehensible for all readers, whose representative you are.

You can now judge for yourself what merit that objection to the grounding of our science through intuition might have, and to what degree one can count on those raising this objection in scientific deliberations.

If the Science of Knowledge now grounds itself in the intuition like that just demonstrated and described by you as the condition of geometry, but intuition in its highest abstraction, and if the Science of Knowledge sets forth the entire series of this intuition; indeed, if it proceeds from this in its highest abstraction; if this intuition for itself, therefore general reason itself, apprehending itself in its single mid-point and determining for all time; if this intuition is the first link in its chain, this reason which grasps *itself* as reason and consequently the pure I in the highest sense of this word already described above; — then it will be quite comprehensible to you, if you are otherwise acquainted with the literature of our age, why the scholars of the last half of the eighteenth century were completely unable to find this pure I in themselves. It will be immediately clear to you what kind of people these are who want to go still farther beyond the principle of the Science of Knowledge, i.e., beyond the absolute intuition of reason through itself, and who believe that one has actually gone beyond it.

R: Then from this pure I, or from the intuition in its highest abstraction, the Science of Knowledge begins; but with every step it takes, a new link attaches itself to the chain, a necessary connection which is ascertained in that very intuition?

A: So it is, as it also is in geometry, where in every new proposition something new is added to the previous one, the necessity of which is likewise demonstrated only in intuition. It must be this way in every real and truly progressive science which does not spin in circles.

R: I have been told that you have spun your entire science out of the presupposed concept of the I, as out of an onion; that you have done nothing but analyze this concept and shown that all other concepts which you advance are already contained in it, however obscurely; and that one calls just such a concept fundamental concept, and the proposition in which it comes forth, fundamental proposition.

A: You were quite good-natured to let yourself be caught up in such a thing.

R: I believe I now clearly recognize how you might establish your science. I also see what its claim to general validity as science is grounded on; namely, on the intuition, which, of course, is the intuition of the procedure of all reason, hence valid for all who will proceed as you do; that is, those who will *produce this science in themselves*. In short, the product of your science, starting from the accepted presupposition, can only be established simply as you have done it; just as the triangle, after the three parts had been presupposed, could only be closed by this side and these angles. Assuming that you could actually ascertain in intuition what you maintain, I have nothing against your claim as long as you do not represent the product of your science as anything more than a mere product of your imagination, just as this often mentioned triangle is also nothing more than such a product.

However, as I conclude from what you have said above, in doing this you are not at all satisfied to let the matter rest. You are not content to represent your product as existing in itself and agreeing with itself, but you go beyond this. It is supposed to be a picture of true and actual consciousness, which we all possess, present without the assistance of philosophy. The manifold is said to lie in this consciousness, and to stand in precisely that relation to it in which the manifold stands in the product of your system. Nevertheless, I confess that I myself do not quite comprehend what you are actually maintaining in this regard, and even less, how you will ground any further claim apart from that just now granted you.

A: You also give geometry an application to actual consciousness in life, and you consider it to be a picture of a part of actual consciousness, just as we consider the Science of Knowledge. Now just explain and ground your claim. Perhaps in doing this, our claim will also be grounded.

In scientific geometry you draw the line with which you close your arbitrarily designed angle with its arbitrarily drawn sides. You find in the field a triangle with an angle determined by itself, and two sides determined by themselves, which you measure. Now do you also need to measure the third side?

R: Not at all. I can find the actual length by simple computation using the immutable relation, known to me from geometry, of this third side to the other two and to the opposite angle.

A: Its *actual* length. What does this mean?

R: If I were to actually measure it with instruments, as I measured the first two, this measurement would yield precisely the same length I arrived at by computation.

A: And you are unshakably convinced of this?

R: I am.

A: And you are prepared to apply the same procedure with all possible triangles you might encounter in the field? You are not afraid that one could present itself to you which would prove an exception to the rule?

R: I am not afraid of this, and it is simply impossible for me to have such a fear.

A: What, then, might be the ground for your firm conviction that your determination of the actual size of this third side is correct, independent of all actual measuring of it and preceding all actual measuring?

R: If I become conscious of myself, I must conceive of it in this way, and I can express it in approximately the following manner:

If two lines and the enclosed angle are presupposed as determined, this angle can only be closed by one possible side, determined as standing in a definite relation to the presupposed parts. This is valid for the construction of the triangle in the free imagination and becomes immediately clear and certain through intuition.

Now I treat the actual triangle according to the laws of that which was only constructed without going any further and with the same certainty, *just as if this was also contained in the intuition*. Hence, I presuppose as a *fact* that the right to this application is really contained within the intuition. I consider the actual line as if, I say as if, it has arisen through my free construction, and I treat it as such. How it may be that it has arisen in fact, is a question I do not pose. The *measuring* is at least a re-construal, a construal after the fact of the present line, and from this I am compelled to assume that it is completely the same as an original construal of this line only presupposed analogically, the reality or unreality of which, however, is of no concern to me.

A: And in this way you have also very clearly described how it is in regard to the claim of the Science of Knowledge to validity in actual consciousness. Just as the third side finds itself determined by the other two sides and the enclosed angle in the original construction of the triangle, so, in consequence of the Science of Knowledge, does something certain in consciousness find itself determined in the original construction by something other in consciousness. These are only formed, however, by the free imagination and in no way are they actual determinations of consciousness, just as the lines of the geometrician are not the lines in the field.

Now a determination of consciousness, formed there, actually enters; just as an angle and two sides, whose free construction was possible, are found in the field. You can believe just as firmly that along with the present, actual determination, those which entered into reality in the picture as inseparable from what was first found have, at the same time, entered as determined and as there described, and you will actually find it to be so if you undertake the observation. Anyone who rises to this speculation is as certainly convinced of this as the geometrician is that the measurement of the actual line will confirm his computation. The determinations of actual consciousness, to which he is compelled to apply the laws of freely construed consciousness, just as the geometrician is compelled to apply the laws of the freely construed triangle to that found in the field, are now also, *as it were*, results to him of an original construction and are treated as such in that judgment. Whether such an original construction of consciousness actually preceded all consciousness is of no concern to him; indeed, this question is completely senseless for him.

At least the *judging* is a construal after the fact, as is the measuring for the geometrician. This must agree with the analogically presupposed, original construal of the thing judged, and very definitely does agree with it if the judgment is made correctly, just as the measurement of the line certainly agrees with the computation, if the measuring is done correctly. This and nothing else should signify the claim of the Science of Knowledge to a validity which is yet outside of it, for actual consciousness in life; and so this claim is grounded, as is the entire Science of Knowledge, on this same immediate intuition.

And so I believe I have given you a sufficiently clear concept not only of the purpose of the Science of Knowledge itself, but also of its procedure and the grounds of this procedure. It construes the entire common consciousness of all rational beings absolutely *a priori*, according to its primary characteristics, just as geometry construes the general modes of limitation in space for all rational beings absolutely *a priori*. It begins with the simplest and most thoroughly characteristic determination of self-consciousness, intuition or I-ness, and proceeds in the presupposition that completely determined self-consciousness is the last result of all other determinations of consciousness until this is deduced, since to the Science of Knowledge on every link of its chain a new link always attaches itself. Accordingly, it is clear to it in immediate intuition that for every rational being it must attach itself in just this way.

Posit I = A and it will be found that in the intuition of the construal of this A, a B inseparably latches onto it; in the intuition of the construal of this B, in its turn, a C latches on; and so forth until one arrives at the last link of A, complete self-consciousness which is closed by itself and appears complete.

Fourth Lesson

A: It is said that a particular system of consciousness for a rational being exists just as this being itself exists. Can we presuppose what is contained in this consciousness for every person?

R: Undoubtedly. It is already contained directly in your description of that system that it is common to all people.

A: Can we also presuppose that everyone will correctly judge objects from this point and that each will draw conclusions from one step to the other without error?

R: If he has practiced to some degree the faculty of judgment innate in all and in the same way belonging to that system, certainly. It is even reasonable that one readily presuppose this moderate practice of judgment until the contrary is proven.

A: But something which is not contained in that general system which is, as it were, part of each person's equipment, but which can only be brought forth by a wilfull and free abstraction and reflection, might this also be readily presupposed by all as known?

R: Obviously not. Each person attains it only in undertaking the requisite abstraction with freedom and, apart from this, he does not have it.

A: Hence, if someone, say, wanted to pass judgment on the I which was sufficiently described above, and from which the Science of Knowledge proceeds, and if he looked for this I in common consciousness as a given, could the talk of such a person then be to the point?

R: Obviously not, since what is being talked about will absolutely not be found in common consciousness but must first be produced by a free abstraction.

A: Furthermore, as has become familiar from his procedure, the Scientist of Knowledge describes a continuous series of determinations of consciousness from this first link on; a consciousness in which on each preceding link in the series a second, and on this a third link is hung, etc. Now it is about these links on his chain that he speaks and asserts his propositions and contentions. In what way, then, can one pass from the first to the second, from this to the third, etc.?

R: According to your description, simply by actually construing the first inwardly in himself and by looking into himself at the same time to see whether in this construction a second link arises and what it might be. He then construes this second link in its turn and looks to see whether a third arises and which one, etc. Only in this intuition of his construal does he attain the object about which something is asserted, and without this construal there is nothing for him there to talk about. So the matter stands, according to the above description, and so you undoubtedly wanted me to answer you.

Here, however, the following doubt still occurs to me. This series which the Scientist of Knowledge describes consists of discrete, particular determinations of consciousness. But also in actual common consciousness, which belongs to every individual without any Science of Knowledge, there are differentiated manifolds of consciousness. Now if the first of *these* are separated out and sorted precisely as the latter are, then the elements in the series of the Science of Knowledge are also known from actual consciousness and the intuition is not at all required in order to make this discernible.

A: Here it is completely sufficient to say to you briefly and historically that the distinctions of the Science of Knowledge and those of actual consciousness are not the same at all, but are entirely different. Indeed, those of consciousness present themselves likewise in the Science of Knowledge, but only as the last deduced. However, on the way to their deduction there lie in the philosophical construction and intuition still quite different elements through whose union alone a differentiated whole of actual consciousness itself arises.

If I might cite an example of this: Certainly the I of actual consciousness is also particular and separate; it is one person among several people, each of whom, for himself and in the same way, calls himself I; and it is precisely to the consciousness of this personality that the Science of Knowledge pursues its deduction. The I from which the Science of Knowledge proceeds is something entirely different; it is absolutely nothing more than the identity of the conscious-being and the conscious; and for this distinction one must raise oneself by abstraction above all that remains in the personality. Those who aver that they cannot disregard the concept of individuality in the concept of the I are completely correct if they are speaking of their state in common consciousness, because there in the perception, indivisibly united, is that identity which they usually completely overlook; and it is individuality with which, and almost exclusively to which, they attend. Should they, however, be completely incapable of abstracting from actual consciousness and its facts, then the Science of Knowledge has lost all claims on them.

In previous philosophical systems, all of which proceeded to a description of the same series which the Science of Knowledge describes only without their knowing it quite clearly, and which also, in part, hit the mark quite well; in these systems some of these distinctions and their names appeared: for example, substance, accidence, and the like. But, in part, no one understands this without intuition. He has only empty words instead of the matter at hand, which were then considered to be actual, existing things by uninspired philosophers. And, in part, since it raises itself to a higher abstraction than all of those systems, the Science of Knowledge puts these particulars together out of much simpler elements, therefore quite differently than the others. Finally, those artificial concepts present in previous systems are, in part, false.

Accordingly, for those who actually construe the series, everything about which this science speaks is only there in and for intuition, and, apart from this condition, they are nothing at all. Without this construction, all propositions of the Science of Knowledge are entirely without significance and meaning.

R: Are you completely serious? Should I take this in its strictest sense without allowing for exaggeration?

A: Certainly, you should take this most seriously. I only want people to believe us once and for all on this point.

R: But then in relation to the Science of Knowledge there would be only one of two possibilities: either understanding, or absolute lack of understanding; to see correctly, or to see nothing at all. But by far the fewest declare that they have not understood you at all; they believe they understand you quite well and think you are simply incorrect. And you declare that they *mis*understand you. Therefore they must certainly garner some kind of understanding from your remarks, only not the same one intended by you. How is this possible, according to what you have just said?

A: It is possible because the Science of Knowledge had to begin its discourse using the existing words in the language. Had it been able to begin immediately as it certainly will end, having created for itself a completely unique system of signs in which the signs signify *only the intuitions of the Science of Knowledge and the relations of them to one another*, and absolutely nothing apart from these, then they could not have been misunderstood, but they also never would have been understood and transposed from the mind of its first originator into other minds. Now, however, the Science of Knowledge has the difficult task of enduring, out of the confusion of words, whatever thoughts in the belly have recently been raised even to be judges over reason, in order to lead others to intuition. Until now each person has thought something on hearing a word, and in hearing it, he calls to mind what he had thought until then; and this he should admittedly do, also for our purpose. If, however, he is unable to rise above these words, which are mere guidelines, and he cannot get beyond their previous meaning to the matter itself, to intuition, then he necessarily misunderstands, even when he understands the best; because what matters here *has neither been said earlier, nor has it been signified by the word, nor can it be said; it can only be intuited*. The most which can be accomplished by word clarification is a determined *concept*, and, precisely for this reason, in the Science of Knowledge, something completely false.

This science describes a progressive series of intuition. Each following link attaches itself to the preceding and is *determined* by it; that is, precisely this coherence clarifies it and belongs to its characteristic. Only intuited in this coherence is it correctly intuited. The third is determined in its turn by the second, and, since the latter is determined by the first, the third is also indirectly determined by the first, and so forth to the end. So everything passing earlier clarifies what follows, and in return (and it can be no other way in an organic system whose parts are connected not simply consequently, but also by a reciprocal determination) each thing that follows further determines all that preceded it.

Can one therefore correctly grasp any link in the Science of Knowledge if one has not correctly grasped all of the preceding, and if one does not have it present in the apprehension of the latter?

R: No.

A: Does one understand any link completely and entirely before one has completed the whole system?

R: According to what you have just said, not at all.

One can judge each point only in its coherence but, since each is connected with the whole, one cannot judge any point completely without having grasped the whole.

A: It is understood that this only concerns points taken from *the actual science*. Because one can make judgments concerning the mere *concept* of this science, its essence, goal, procedure, without having the science itself, since the concept is taken and deduced from the realm of common consciousness. I have invited you, the layman, to become acquainted with this concept and to judge it. I would be on my guard against doing this concerning any inner point of the system.

In this way, the end of the system, its last result, falls within the sphere of common consciousness, and also, in its design, everyone can judge not whether it is correctly deduced, being something about which he understands nothing, but rather whether it presents itself this way in common consciousness.

The constitutive elements and propositions of this system do not fall within common consciousness and the limits of each reasonably trustworthy judgment. They are only created through freedom and abstraction and are determined through their coherence; and no one has the least judgment concerning objects of this kind who has not undertaken this abstraction and construction and developed them to their end while also holding fast to the whole, always present and unwavering?

R: So it admittedly is, as I realize quite well. Accordingly, anyone who wanted to speak on the subject must have invented the system itself.

A: Exactly. — Yet, since it has been shown that mankind has philosophized for millennia and, as can be clearly shown, has repeatedly come within a hairsbreadth of the real point without actually finding the Science of Knowledge, this leads us to expect that if it were to be lost now, it would not soon be found again. So it would be good to put to use the invention which has finally been accidentally made, to let it be provisionally pre-invented, and to re-invent it for the originator and the people possessing it. Just as it is, for example, with geometry, the invention of which might well have cost time, so must one have studied the system to the point that he has made it his own invention.

Is it therefore so, that absolutely no one could have a judgment concerning any proposition of this science, and, in case it should be the only possible philosophy, which it certainly maintains, concerning any philosophical proposition; — no one who has either not proven in fact that he himself has invented the Science of Knowledge, or, if this is not the case, who is not conscious of having studied it long enough to make it his own invention, or — *because this is the only possible alternative — who can ascertain another system of intellectual intuition opposed to that of the Science of Knowledge?*

R: Try as I might, I cannot deny that it is so.

On the other hand, I cannot blame other philosophers when they react in an unfriendly manner to your demands that they return to school. They are themselves aware of having studied their science as well as you, and some had been considered masters of their science at a time when you yourself were learning the first rudimentary principles. They assume, and you yourself admit, that it was through them that you were first drawn from your mind's dream. And now they, many with grey beards, are supposed to return to their studies with you or else be forbidden from speaking.

A: If they love anything in the world more than truth and science, then their fate is admittedly hard. But it cannot be changed. Since they are very well aware that they never even believed they possessed what we assert we have, evident science, and have denied such a thing, then they must examine how it really is with these unheard of assertions of ours, as bitter as they might seem to them. Apart from the study of the Science of Knowledge, do you know another way out for them other than their keeping silent and leaving the stage in good faith, without a convenient memory?

R: Then—I have already heard such a little bird sing—they will say: "You have such a fine worm, you expect others to despise themselves in comparison with you."

A: This is just an invidious turn of speech which does not help their cause. We do not expect them to think little of their talents as such and of the cognitions which they actually have claimed they possess until now; much more, we offer the first deference by bringing our science to them for clarification and judgment. That it is we who made the invention and not they we ascribe to fortunate coincidence and to the point in time, and we presume for our part no reward at all from this. That they should deem we are in possession of this invention and not they, as they never before asserted; that they should examine our report about this invention, is no more a demand that they despise themselves, than that we should despise ourselves when we read their books in the assumption that they could have thought something which we have not.

Anyone who seeks to study anything scientific assumes that the teacher knows more about it than he does, otherwise he would not undertake such study; and the teacher assumes the same, or else he would not take the task upon himself. But the former truly does not despise himself because of this, since he hopes to comprehend the science just as well as his teacher, and this is precisely his goal.

R: Moreover, they can never know beforehand whether there is also something behind your subject matter, whether the effort of this difficult and continuous study you expect of them will be rewarded by it. They have already been disappointed by the promises of great wisdom so often.

A: Of course they cannot know this before they make the attempt; the expectation that they believe our assurance would be ridiculous. However, neither we nor they knew the benefit and significance of any science we have learned beforehand, and yet we have always had to risk the danger of wasting our time. Or was this encountered only as long as they stood under the scourge of their teachers, and have they never again done it since they have become their own masters?

They would have to take a chance in this matter also as they have in other matters. Or, if they are frightened away from this risk for their entire lives, then the safest way out remains open to them: to remain silent and to throw themselves into some discipline in which it is to be hoped the claims of the scholars of science will not soon extend.

R: If they only had the prospect that you and your Science of Knowledge could become fashionable. But you yourself have obstinately blocked this path against all warnings from those well-disposed to you. You have kindled too little confidence and love for yourself in your colleagues to make yourself fashionable. You are not old enough. You have neglected the old, honorable customs of the guild; not letting yourself be first introduced as an industrious student in a preface from one of your teachers, then looking for alliances along the proper and respectable paths, through dedications, requests for advice and instruction, citations and praise of others, to gain praise and applause, associating yourself with a reviewing society and raising yourself in this way quite slowly and unnoticed. No, you have sprung up all at once, as if from the soil, with all of your claims, just as arrogant as you now are. You have cited and praised hardly anyone but yourself. But how you have criticized and waged your war. Against all literary conventions and tradition, you have never offered accord and conciliation; you have immediately refuted your opponents, allowing them to be right in no instance in which they were not actually so; not mentioning one syllable about their perspicacity, you are bent on destruction. You are capable of denying the best known truth held valid from time immemorial, and turning it to dust at the feet of your poor opponent, and there is no honest man who knows on what basis he is to take up the dispute with you. For this reason, many have made up their minds and affirm it loudly, that they certainly do not want to learn anything from you, since you are not worthy; and others even doubt the possibility of honorably speaking your name.[1]

A: Well, we will have to be content that these people will learn nothing.

Does every person possess this fundamental intution we described above?

1. A reviewer in the *Erlanger Literatur-Zeitung* before the appearance of the second editor doubts that one can honorably speak my name.

R: According to your description, he necessarily does if only once in his life he asserts one single, generally valid proposition as such, not simply repeating it, but asserting it with conviction, or if he simply expects of some other person that he consider a matter precisely as he finds it to be; for we have seen that this necessity and generality only proceed from that intuition and are grounded in it.

A: But does everyone also raise himself in turn to a clear consciousness of this intuition?

R: This at least does not immediately follow from the fact of an absolute contention as does the intuition itself, for this is grounded absolutely and in itself without further questioning after a higher reason and without the consciousness of such a thing being enunciated. In order to raise oneself to this consciousness, it seems one must first reflect on that absolute contending itself and give an account of it. And this does not appear to be nearly so generally and necessarily grounded in the nature of rational beings as the absolute contending itself, without which almost all communication and understanding between people would cease.

Yet anyone *could* undertake the deliberation which we undertook in the preceding lesson, for example, and in this way raise oneself to consciousness of that intuition.

A: Undoubtedly anyone could, just as anyone could raise oneself to pure morality through freedom or, through another intuition very closely related to the philosophical-scientific, to poetry.

In this regard, it is sufficient to express our opinion to you historically. One cannot deny any person's ability to raise himself to consciousness of scientific intuition, just as little as one can deny the capacity to be morally reborn or to become a poet. But one can just as little clarify — precisely because these abilities and capacities are absolutely *primary* and do not lie in any elapsed sequence of grounds — why they present themselves here, yet are absent there. Experience, which is not to be clarified through reasons, however, teaches this much: that some people, no matter what one tries and how one may lead them, do not raise themselves to this point. In youth, when a person is still educable, he raises himself quite easily to science as to poetry. If he has let his youth slip by and ruined half of his life through memory work, dilletantism, and reviewing, then one can probably dispute his capacity for science and poetry without any great danger of being contradicted by his success, although one cannot demonstrate his incapacity.

No one should take it amiss if his gift of intuition is denied by intuition; no more than he who is denied poetic talent. In regard to the latter, people have long consoled themselves with the maxim that poets are born and not made. Why, then, is there no rush to extend this consolation to philosophy? Reasonable people will deny him as little in the latter regard as they have denied him in the first. Unfortunately, we have become accustomed to considering philosophy to be merely a matter of common judgment and we believe we have denied this in denying philosophical talent. This would admittedly be an insult, but, from the lips of the Science of Knowledge, that proposition truly has a completely different sense.

However, it is not enough just to have that ability in general. At the same time, one must possess the capacity to hold fast to intuition, to be able to call it forth at whatever moment it is required, to place oneself at will in the altogether unique world which it opens up for us, and to remain in that world, wherever one is, with a good consciousness. It is not unusual, especially among young people, for a light to be suddenly turned on, penetrating the old darkness like lightning; but before one knows it, the eye is again closed, the previous night is there, and one must await the moment of a new illumination. This situation does not lend itself to continuous and systematic study. The intuition must become altogether free and it must come under our complete control. This freedom, however, is obtained only through continuous exercise.

Furthermore, to systematic thinking as such belongs the intellectual freedom to give direction to thought absolutely at will; to fix it on this object, and to keep it there until the object is adequately treated for our purpose, withdrawing it from everything else and restraining its progress against itself. This freedom is not innate in people, but must rather be obtained through diligence and exercise of a nature which is inclined toward unchecked rambling. Transcendental thinking in particular is altogether distinct from the usual, in that the latter is held and, as it were, carried by something underlying which is already differentiated and determined by its nature; the former, however, has absolutely nothing as its object apart from itself, therefore it is borne only by itself and only distinguished, divided, and determined by itself. Even the geometrician has the lines and figures on the board by which he fixes his intuition. The Scientist of Knowledge has absolutely nothing other than himself and his free reflection. This he is to carry through a long series and, with every new link, he must keep present everything which came previously as entirely determined; and yet in this constancy the entire series is to remain, at the same time, suspended; he is not to conclude any determination finally, since with each link to follow, he will have to further redetermine all that went before. It is clear that not merely the usual capacity for concentrated attention and self-activity of the mind is assumed in him, but also an ability, which has become habitual, to place and fix his entire mind before him; in the finest or coarsest manner to break it down, put it together, and to break down the synthesis again with firm and steady hand and with the certainty that all will always remain for him as he has ordered it. It is clear that this is not merely a higher level, but an entirely new *kind* of intellectual labor the likes of which has never before existed. It is also clear that the exercise for such labor can only be obtained in the single object present to it, and that even the thinkers who are sufficiently practiced and accomplished in other regards will need time and diligence to establish themselves in this science. There is, however, no way that they will be able to judge it on the first or second reading. Should it then be supposed that unrefined, unscientific people, who have cultivated nothing other than their memory and who are not even capable of conducting a coherent, objective-scientific line of reasoning, are capable from the outset of passing judgment on every point torn from its context which they may have noticed in their newspaper; as if they had only to assert whether they had already heard the same thing somewhere else?

In another respect, however, there is nothing easier than the study of this science as soon as the first flicker of light concerning it has come to the student. It presupposes absolutely no previous knowledge of any kind, but only the usual intellectual exercise. It does not exhaust the mind, but rather strengthens and animates it. Its development is uninterrupted and its method is extremely simple and quickly comprehended. Each single understood point in it opens the eye to the understanding of all of the rest.

Therefore, the Science of Knowledge is not innate in man like his five senses; it can only be attained by applying oneself at some time in life to a systematic study of it. I want to convince you of this, dear reader, so that, in case you have not studied it and you also have no desire to study it, you refrain from speaking out on matters of this kind as you would from any other absurdity; and also so that you know how to take it when others, even highly educated people, speak out on such matters, even though they have studied the Science of Knowledge as little as you.

Fifth Lesson

A: That which is deduced by the Science of Knowledge should be, by design, a fitting and complete picturing of fundamental consciousness. Can that deduced contain more or less, or something determined other than what occurs in actual consciousness?

R: Not at all, as long as the Science of Knowledge fulfills its purpose. Every deviation of it from actual consciousness would be the surest proof of the fallacy of its deduction.

A: Therefore, in consequence of everything said previously, in the total consciousness of a finite, rational being, only the following would be possible:

In the first place, the primary and fundamental determinations of life as such, the common consciousness, that which occurs in immediate experience or whatever one wants to call it, would be possible. This is a completely closed, perfected system, entirely the same for everyone with the sole exception of purely individual determinations. The first power characterized above would be possible; then reflection on it and representation of it, the free division, synthesis and judgment to infinity, which depends on freedom and which varies according to its various uses. The above so-called higher powers would be possible; the middle region of our mind, as it were. In this regard, it should be kept in mind that nothing can occur in these higher powers which has not, at least according to its elements, been situated in the former. Freedom of the mind can separate and unite to infinity what is given in fundamental consciousness, but it cannot create.—Finally, a complete deduction of that of the first power without regard to actual experience, but rather from the purely necessary procedure of intelligence itself, immediately, as if fundamental consciousness were the result of this procedure, would be possible: the Science of Knowledge as the absolute highest power above which no consciousness can raise itself. Also, absolutely nothing can occur here which is not situated in actual consciousness or in experience in the highest sense of the word.

Hence in consequence of our fundamental propositions, in absolutely no respect can anything enter into the consciousness of any rational being and find access there which is not situated in experience according to its elements and in the experience of all without exception. Everyone has retained the same equipment and the same freedom to develop and refine that common equipment; but no one can create something for himself. Our philosophy is thus certainly well-disposed and inclined toward common human understanding, and it assures the rights of that understanding, as we promised above. Any other philosophy which is opposed to this design is an opponent of common understanding.

We have said that the Science of Knowledge should give a fitting picture of fundamental consciousness. Can this picture now be the thing itself, and does it present itself as such?

R: As I have understood it from you and now see quite well myself, not at all. That which penetrates and grips us in the determinations of life established in and through the thing itself, which tears us away from our self and immerses our self in it, that must necessarily be lacking. We throw ourselves into *the construal* of the determination here, not at all into *the determination* itself, as determination; just as I had thrown what was mine and forgotten myself in the process of representing my friend's presence yesterday; not at all, however, in this presence itself.

A: So it is. The Science of Knowledge represents itself merely as a picturing of life, not at all as actual life itself. Whoever takes it to be the latter misunderstands it entirely.

Not a single one of its thoughts, propositions, or statements is one of actual life, nor does it fit actual life. They are really only thoughts of thoughts, which one has or should have; propositions of propositions, which one makes one's own; statements of statements, which one should express oneself. That it is so difficult to be broken of the habit of considering it to be more than this comes from the fact that the preceding philosophies claimed to be more, and it is not easy to refrain from seeing the new philosophy as being like the others. Those wanted to represent not only science but at the same time wisdom itself, world-wisdom, wisdom of life, or whatever else they might have been called; and they became neither

wisdom nor science. Our philosophy is satisfied to be science and
has solemnly dispensed with any other claim from the outset, as its
name suggests. It cannot make man wise, good, or religious by
demonstration, as little as any of the preceding philosophies could;
but it knows that it cannot and it will not do what it knows it
cannot. It only wants to make those who are able to dedicate themselves to it *scientific*. What it says about wisdom, virtue, and religion must first be actually *experienced* and *lived* in order to cross
over into actual wisdom, virtue, and religiosity.

R: For this reason it probably does not make the study and understanding of it a condition of wisdom and a good way of life?

A: So little, that it is much more a sworn opponent of whatever
poses all cultivation and education of man in the enlightenment of
his understanding, and whatever believes it has won everything
when it has made man into an accomplished reasoner. The Science
of Knowledge knows well that life is only formed through life, and it
never forgets this.

R: And it probably does not expect such study of everyone?

A: So little, that it rather deplores the fact that there have now
already been many half-true philosophical propositions brought to
the masses from other systems. This, however—because nothing is
stopping the Science of Knowledge from revealing all of its claims
now, although it may well be a century before they are filled—this it
demands: that everyone who practices science possess it, and also
everyone who has anything to do with the education of man in
general and whose business is government or the education of the
people.

R: But in spite of the agreement of your teachings with common
human understanding, of which you assure us, you certainly cannot
deny saying that everything which is there for us is brought forth by
ourselves. This is undoubtedly a contention which flies in the face
of common consciousness. We are not conscious that we bring forth
what exists there, but rather that it just *is there*, simply is there; that
we find it and are met with it.

A: I do not quite correctly understand the contention which you
ascribe to us, so I do not know if I should recognize it as our own or
disavow it. However, let us think it over.

In the Science of Knowledge, everyone produces this science for
himself, bringing forth the picture of actual consciousness and

hence the sequence of pictures of everything which is found existing there in consciousness. One also observes how they are brought forth. This lies in the description of our science and everyone who studies and understands it will find it in himself as an immediate fact. That this sequence is now produced in this way in common consciousness would contradict not only this immediate consciousness itself, but also the very contention of the Science of Knowledge, and suspend its entire system. Consciousness is a complete system, according to this doctrine, and no single part of it can exist without all of the remaining parts; neither can all of the remaining parts exist without each individual one. Thus, according to the same doctrine, it cannot at all be produced in common consciousness in a gradual sequence—first a single A, then B, etc.—since, of course, any one is impossible without the other; but if one will talk about a production, then the whole with all of its individual parts would have to be produced simply in one stroke.

But why would we even want to talk about production here? Actual consciousness exists; it is complete and entirely finished, just as only we ourselves are finished and possess self-consciousness, with which the Science of Knowledge concludes, as with its last link. Our existing world is finished, indisputably, by all accounts, as only we are. Our actual life can do nothing further than become conscious of this world, piece by piece, however inexplicable coincidence causes it to be; walk through it, analyze, and judge it. It makes absolutely no sense to assert this production in actual life.) Life is not a producing, but a finding. Our philosophy even contradicts the supposed productions of other philosophies and rejects them.

In consequence of our philosophy, this absolute presence allows itself to be *examined and judged* in actual life, *just as if* it had arisen through an original construction like the one carried out by the Science of Knowledge; actual life can be completed and supplemented according to the laws of such a construction, and one can be certain that actual observation will confirm such a completion. One does not need absolutely everything, all intermediate links, to live and to experience, just as one supported by scientific geometry does not actually need to measure all lines but can find many through mere computation.

To consider this *just as if* to be a categorical *that*, this fiction to be a narrative of some true event which occurred at some particular time, this is a gross misunderstanding. Do they then believe that in the construction of fundamental consciousness in the Science of Knowledge we want to deliver a history of the acts of consciousness before that consciousness existed, the life history of a man before his birth? But how can we, since we ourselves declare that consciousness only exists simultaneously with all of its determinations, and since we covet no consciousness before all consciousness, and without all consciousness? These are misunderstandings against which one cannot take precautions, because they do not occur to someone until they actually happen.

Therefore, all cosmogonies are attempts at an original construction of the universe from its fundamental elements. Does the originator of such a construction now want to say that it has actually happened as he pronounces it in his cosmogony? Certainly not, as certain as he himself knows and understands what he says. For the universe is undoubtedly an organic whole for him, of which no part can exist if the remaining do not exist. Thus the whole can certainly not arise gradually, but at each moment it is there; it is there in its entirety. The unscientific understanding, which one holds within the scope of the given and to which research of this kind should not be allowed to come, admittedly believes it is hearing a narrative, because it can think nothing other than narratives. Does the present assumption of so many, that we believe because of our gnosogony that we are offering a narrative, lead to the conclusion that they themselves would not be disinclined from taking it to be a narrative, if only the seal of authority and antiquity rested on it?

R: Yet I still continually hear only about determinations of a consciousness which are there, and of a system of consciousness which is there, and the like. Even the others are not satisfied with this. A system of things should be there in consequence of their requirements, and only from these is consciousness produced.

A: You are now reading into the soul of the professional philosopher, whom I thought I had already dismissed above, and not into that of common human understanding and actual consciousness, which I have just confronted.

Tell me, and before you answer, collect your thoughts: Does a thing enter into you, does it occur in and for you, except at the same time through and with your consciousness of it? Consequently, can the thing, in and for you, ever be separated from your consciousness of it, and, if it is just one of the described first power, a thoroughly determined one, can that consciousness be separated from the thing? Can you conceive of a thing without its consciousness or a completely determined consciousness without its thing? Does reality arise for you in any other way than through your immersing your consciousness in its lowest power; and does your thinking not cease entirely when you want to conceive of it otherwise?

R: If I reflect well on myself, I must grant you this.

A: Then it is certainly you yourself who speaks, out of your soul and into your soul. So you must not desire to leap beyond yourself and grasp something in any way other than you are able: as consciousness *and* thing, as thing *and* consciousness; or, more correctly, as neither one of the two, but as that which only later is distinguished in the two, the absolute subjective-objective and objective-subjective.

Common human understanding does not find it in any other way; it always holds consciousness and thing together and always speaks of the union of both. Only a philosophical system of dualism finds it otherwise, in that it divides the absolutely indivisible and believes it thinks quite sharply and profoundly after all thinking has ceased for it.

Now the contemplation you have just undertaken and one's reflection on oneself seem to us so easy and natural that it requires no study; each and every person must find it by himself, and it can be expected of him at once. Everyone who only awakens to self-possession and steps forth from the intermediate position between plant and man finds it to be this way; and whoever simply cannot be brought to the point of finding it so cannot be helped in any way. Occasionally this reflection on oneself has been taken for the Science of Knowledge itself. If this were true, nothing would be more quickly and easily accomplished than this science. But it is more, and that reflection is not the science itself, but merely the first and simplest, but necessary, condition for understanding it.

What should be thought of the minds of those who still search here for the outlet of critical and transcendental scepticism; that is, those who believe it can be doubted whether one must also really know what they are talking about, and who place in this doubt true, philosophical enlightenment?

I beg you, dear reader, shake these dreamers up and say to them: "Do you ever know without having a consciousness? Can you ever get beyond the determinations of consciousness with all of your knowledge, and with your entire essence, since knowledge, as long as you are not changed into sticks and stones, is inseparable from your essence? If you have recognized this just once, then root yourself in this conviction, mark it forever, and do not allow yourself to be swayed from it, or misled into forgetting it for a moment."

We are admittedly well aware that when you again judge those determinations of consciousness and so produce a consciousness of *the second power*, this now appears to you in this context quite particularly as consciousness, and as a pure consciousness removed from the thing; and now that first determination, in regard to this pure consciousness, appears as a pure thing, just as the *measuring* of your line should still be something other than *the line itself*. But you will not allow yourself to be deceived by this appearance after you have once recognized that for you there can be nothing there at all apart from determinations of consciousness. Then you will also grasp very well that that thing is also nothing but such a determination, which is called a thing only in relation to a higher consciousness; just as you are able to be inwardly aware every moment that the measuring of your line is nothing other than the line itself, only in a different relation and more clearly conceived.

We are equally aware that if you should conceive an immobile system of fundamental determinations of consciousness, as you certainly should, if only to grasp the concept of the Science of Knowledge, then it is probably impossible for you to fix the living, that conceived in constant agitation and becoming, as your consciousness appears to you; impossible to place it before yourself as something permanent and solid, which no one expects of you anyway. But this system rather unfolds over against your consciousness as a system of the world, just like your entire world, itself conceived from the standpoint of common consciousness, is nothing other than precisely that tacitly presupposed system of fundamental determinations of consciousness in itself. However, you should recognize from the earlier self-reflection and recall that as certainly as you conceive it, know and talk about it, and not—not think, not know and talk about it—it can actually only be a system of determinations of your consciousness.

Sixth Lesson

I see, dear reader, that you stand there perplexed. You seem to be thinking: "Is there nothing more than this? A mere picture of actual life is handed to me which spares me nothing in life; a depiction in reduced scale with pale colors of what I have before me all the time without effort or work in nature. And for this purpose I should subject myself to a tiring study and interminable exercise? Your art seems to me to be no more important than that of the well-known man who threw millet seeds through the eye of a needle, which certainly must also have cost him effort enough. I do not need your science and want to hold to life."

Only follow this resolution dispassionately and hold firmly to life. Stand fast and unflinching in this decision and do not be led astray by any philosophy or become leary of that decision. In this I will have achieved the greatest part of my purpose with you.

However, so that you do not fall into the danger of advising against a study which we do not advise for you and to which nothing urges you, disparaging it in your own circle, slandering it with our statements, suppressing it, insofar as you have the power to do so, then listen to what influence and use this study could have.

One has always recommended mathematics as a means of intellectual exercise, especially geometry, its most immediate, stimulating part for intuition; and one has studied it a great deal simply for the sake of this exercise without, however, wanting to put its material content to any use. It is by all means worthy of this recommendation, although it has become possible—through elevated formal training in it, through its authority based on antiquity, and through its special standpoint lying intermediately between intuition and perception—to learn it historically rather than to re-discover it as one should, to accept it on faith rather than be convinced by its evidence; so that scientific education, which alone was intended, is not achieved, and the claim of a great, i.e., erudite mathematician to a scientific head nowadays has become entirely uncertain. Whether one has actually comprehended the earlier propositions or only accepted them on good faith does not matter for life's customs nor for induction in science. In this respect alone, the Science of Knowledge is to be recommended to a far greater degree. Without an actual elevation to intuition and, thereby, to scientificality, one cannot at all grasp it, at least not as it is now being pronounced; and it may well take centuries before it takes a form in which it could be learned from memory. However, if we are not very mistaken, it will probably never come to the point where one can apply it and, with it, bring forth another knowledge without having grasped it scientifically. Moreover, for the reason already mentioned above—that it has absolutely no means of assistance, no carrier of its intuition except intuition itself—it raises the human mind higher than any geometry can. It gives the mind not only powers of concentration, agility, and constancy, but at the same time absolute independence, in that the Science of Knowledge compels the mind to be alone with itself and to live and rule in itself. Every other intellectual enterprise is infinitely easy in comparison; and for him who has exercised himself in it, nothing else is difficult. In addition, the Science of Knowledge, in that it pursues all objects of human knowledge to the mid-point, accustoms the eye in all that comes before it to come upon the actual point at first glance and pursue it steadily; for this reason there can no longer be anything obscure, complicated and confused for a practiced Scientist of Knowledge, if only he recognizes the object of concern. It is always easiest for him to erect everything new and from the beginning since he carries the plans for every scientific building within him; therefore, he orients himself very easily in every confused structure. To this belongs the security and the trust in his glance which he has acquired in the Science of Knowledge as guide of all reasoning; the imperturbability with which he confronts every deviation from the usual path and every paradox. In all human affairs, things would be completely different if people could only decide to believe their eyes. Now they inquire of their neighbors and forebears about what they actually see, and because of this mistrust in themselves errors become immortalized. The possessor of the Science of Knowledge is forever guarded against this mistrust. In a word, through the Science of Knowledge the spirit of humanity comes to itself and rests in itself from now on without foreign help, and it gains mastery over itself like the dancer over his feet and the fencer over his hands.

If the first friends of this science, which could only have been attempted with so few until now, are not completely mistaken, then independence of mind leads also to independence of character, a predisposition which, in turn, is itself a necessary condition of an understanding of the Science of Knowledge. True, the Science of Knowledge is just as little able as any other knowledge to make someone an upright virtuous man; but, if we are not very mistaken, it sweeps the mightiest hindrance to uprightness out of the way. He who in his thinking has completely torn himself away from all foreign influence and, in this respect, has built himself up from himself anew, will undoubtedly not take maxims of behavior from where he disdained to take maxims of knowledge. Undoubtedly, he will no longer form his feelings for happiness and unhappiness, honor and shame, from the invisible influence of the whole of the world, nor allow himself to be drawn by its secret pull; rather he will move himself and search for and produce the main springs of this movement on its own ground.

This would be the influence of this study, if only seen simply in its scientific form, even if its content meant nothing and was of absolutely no use.

But let us look at this content! That system exhausts all possible knowledge of the finite mind according to its fundamental elements and poses these fundamental elements for all eternity. These elements can be infinitely divided and put together in other ways, and here finite life has room for free play; however, absolutely nothing new can be added to them. What is not already present in its depiction according to its elements is certainly contrary to reason. Through this science it is crystal clear to all whose eyes are open to it. Therefore, absolutely no overarching of reason, no foolish enthusiasm, no superstition can take root from the moment the Science of Knowledge becomes dominant; that is, after all those possess it who lead the great mass of people who can never possess it. All this is attacked to the depths of its foundation and annihilated. Everyone who has undertaken that general measurement of finite reason with us knows at each moment to indicate the point where the unreasonable oversteps the bounds of reason and contradicts it. He knows how to bring to light the contradiction to everyone who only has a sound understanding and the good will to be reasonable. So it is with judgment in common life. It is no different in that type of philosophy which prowled among us, made claims, provoked attention, and brought forth numberless confusions. All of these confusions are forever suspended from the moment the Science of Knowledge becomes dominant. Until now philosophy wanted to be and to be something, but *what* it did not quite know itself; this was even one of the main points of contention. By measuring the entire realm of finite thinking and knowledge, it is ascertained which part of this realm devolves to it, after which all that remains is either nothing or taken up by other sciences. In like manner, there occurs no further dispute over particular points or propositions after all that is thinkable is identified and determined in a scientific sequence of intuition. No longer is any error possible, because intuition never errs. Science, which is to help everything else out of a dream, finds itself no longer in a dream from this time on.

The Science of Knowledge exhausts all human knowledge according to its fundamental characteristics, I said; it divides knowledge and distinguishes these fundamental characteristics. The object of every possible science therefore lies in the Science of Knowledge. The manner in which the object must be handled proceeds in the Science of Knowledge from its coherence within the entire system of the human spirit and from the laws valid in this region. The Science of Knowledge tells the practitioner of the science what he can and cannot know, what he can and should ask; it gives him the sequence of the investigations to be undertaken, teaches him how to undertake them and how to direct his proof. Accordingly, that blind groping and fumbling about of the sciences is likewise suspended by the Science of Knowledge. Every investigation which is undertaken there comes to a final decision, in that one can certainly know whether it has been correctly undertaken. The Science of Knowledge, through all this, guarantees culture, since it tears it away from blind chance and brings it under the dominion of circumspection and principle.

This is its success for the scientific, which is determined to penetrate into life and, if it is pursued correctly, penetrates into it necessarily; consequently indirectly also for life.

But the Science of Knowledge also affects life directly. If it is not immediately in and for itself the correct, practical way of thinking itself, philosophy of life—since, in addition, it lacks the lived urgency of experience—it still gives a complete picture of it. He who actually possesses the Science of Knowledge, but who, in life, does not have and does not act according to that way of thinking which is advanced there as the only reasonable one; if he only compares his actual thinking with his philosophical thinking, he, at least, does not labor under any misapprehension about himself. He knows that he is a fool and cannot spare himself this name. Furthermore, he does not lack the capacity to find the true principle of his folly and the true means of his improvement in every instance. He can know, with the most minimal, if serious, reflection on himself, which habits he must cast off, which practices he must undertake in their place. If he does not advance from being a philosopher to being a sage at the same time, then the fault lies simply with his will and his indolence; for no philosophy can improve the will and give a person strength.

So the Science of Knowledge presents itself to those who, in and for themselves, are able to possess it. Those who are not capable of this are steeped in the Science of Knowledge by those who are led by it, by the regents and school teachers.

As soon as the Science of Knowledge is understood and accepted, public administration will blindly grope about and make experiments no more than other arts and sciences; it will rather come under firm principles and fundamental propositions, because that science establishes such fundamental propositions. Of course, it is not able to teach public administrators good will or give them the courage to put through what they know is right; but at least from that moment on they will no longer be able to say that it is not their fault if human relations do not change for the better. Everyone who possesses the science himself will be able to tell them what they had better do; and if they still do not do it, then they will stand exposed before the whole world as deficient in good will. Accordingly, from that moment on, human relations will be able to be brought to such a state that it will not only be easily possible, but rather almost necessary for people to be order-loving and honorable citizens.

Only after this task has been accomplished will educators and school teachers be able to hope to work successfully. The external condition of their purpose, which is not dependent on them, is given to them. They have, in themselves, the aptitude to reach it because their enterprise has also been freed from its superstitious heritage and work habits and brought under firm principles by the Science of Knowledge. From now on, they definitely know from what point they must proceed and how they must continue.

In a word: Through the acceptance and general dissemination of the Science of Knowledge among those to whom it belongs, the entire human race will be freed from blind chance and fate will be destroyed. All of humanity takes itself in its own hand under the dominion of its own concept from now on, it makes everything out of itself that it can possibly want with absolute freedom.

This everything I have maintained here is incontrovertibly demonstrable and proceeds from the mere concept of the Science of Knowledge as it has been advanced in this text. Consequently, only whether this concept is itself feasible can still be questioned; concerning this, those and only those will answer who actually put it into effect, and who, for themselves, will bring about and re-invent the Science of Knowledge, which, it is maintained, is already present. However, the success of the given promises depends on the Science of Knowledge coming into control of all who as practitioners of any science or as educators of the people raise themselves above the people; and future ages will come to a decision concerning this. In the present age, the Science of Knowledge wants and hopes for nothing more than that it not be rejected without a hearing and sink into oblivion; it only wants to win over a few who will be able to hand it down to a better age. Were the Science of Knowledge only to achieve this, then the purpose of this text and the past and future texts of the author would be fulfilled.

Afterword:
To philosophers by profession who, until now, have been opponents of the Science of Knowledge

This text, to be sure, has not been written for you. Still it will fall into your hands and, of course, if you follow your earlier practice, you will not understand it and will not actually read it but, most likely, review it.

Before you begin your review at least read this afterword expressly intended for you, if the pressing urgency of your business allows. It would indeed be written in vain were you not to read it.

"The difference between the conflicting opinions is not really so great. May the conflicting parties each give up something and settle their differences with one another!" This is one of the wise sayings of our humane age which was also expressed in relation to my conflict with you when one still retained one's composure. Even if you have only leafed through the above text, which is all that is needed for a review, still this much must have struck you: that the difference between you and me is certainly very large, and that what I have already often said and what you have never wanted to accept as my true sincerity—that between you and me there is absolutely no common point about which and from which we could come to an understanding about something else—might well be true. Also, the reason this is so, the actual dividing line between your minds and my own, could have dawned on you.

But since it is just as likely that it could not have occurred to you or dawned on you, I will once again specify this point—historically that is, as one must specify something for you.

I look to apprehend science in its original source; not just the external systematic form, but the interior of a *knowledge* on which alone the fact is founded that a knowledge, a conviction, an imperturbability of consciousness exists. You, on the other hand, good reasoners as you might be—according to logical form at any rate—whose repute I will here grant each of you to whatever degree you are able to maintain, you have not the least idea of such an interior of knowledge. The entire depth of your being does not go that far but only to historical belief, and your business is to further reason about and analyse the transmission of this belief. You have not *known* in your life, and therefore do not at all know the state of mind of someone who does know. Remember how you laughed when *intellectual intuition* was mentioned? Had you ever known, and known about knowledge, you truly would not have found this intuition laughable.

But it is not enough that you have no inkling of it; a shadow of that unknown has even reached you in a dark tradition, according to which you consider it to be the worst detour and the most monstrous aberration which the human mind can fall into. These are foolish enthusiasms, splitting of hairs, scholastic fog, miserable sophistries; these you pass over wherever you find them in order to quickly arrive at—the results (that is, the historically learnable and memorizable propositions) and, as some of your representatives say, to stick with things that interest the head and heart. The lofty enlightenment, education and humanity of this philosophical centu-

ry consists precisely in this: You have rid yourself of this old Frank-
ish pedantry.

I, on the other hand, respect and strive with all of my powers for
precisely that which you despise and from which you flee with all of
your powers. We have completely opposed views of what is worthy
as a goal, what is decent and praiseworthy; and if this opposition
has not violently broken out sooner, it is simply because of your
good-natured belief that that scholasticism is only a temporary aberration; that, in the end, I too would aim at the same thing you aim
at: a popular, edifying philosophy of life. You probably have said of
the signs of the times, that one seems to aim at reintroducing the old
barbarism—which I, of course, call something else, the old thor-
oughness—and that the enlightenment and *belles lettres* of the Germans—which I call the shallowness and frivolity of the Germans—
threaten to fall into decay just now when they have rightly begun;
you have presumably done this in order to prevent the decay. It will
become increasingly clear how bad it is with the Science of Knowledge concerning this point, and, if things went according to it, that
barbarism would certainly return and this pretty enlightenment
would totally perish.

So your being arrives at historical belief and goes no further. In
the first place, you have your own life in whose presence you believe
because others also believe it; for if you only *knew* that you live, it
would already be totally different for you because of that. Secondly,
shattered shards of former science swim in the stream of time. You
have let yourselves be told that these had worth and you look to fish
out as much as you can to show it to the curious. You take great care
with these shards so that you do not break them, mishandle them,
or change their form in any way; so that you can hand them down
undamaged to your heirs and successors, and they, in turn, can
show them to the curious of future generations. At the most, you
polish them occassionally.

I have come among you and you have done me the honor of
considering me one of your colleagues. You have tried to offer me
collegial assistance, to consult with me, warn and advise me. So you
have fared and always will fare if you do not give up the business
entirely.

In the first place, you considered what I pronounced to be a
history; first as fragments from the Kantian stream. You then want-

ed to compare them with your collections, and when this did not work, then at least as fragments from the stream of empirical life. Whatever I might say, assure, and assert, however I might protect myself, you absolutely could not refrain from transforming my scientific propositions into propositions of experience, my intuitions into perceptions, my philosophy into psychology. Just a short while ago in the *Erlanger Literatur-Zeitung*, I encountered such a thing from one of you in regard to the second book of my *Vocation of Man*, in which I truly believe I was clear. This person reproaches the spirit of speculation, there introduced as the speaker, for merely questioning the *consciousness* of hearing, seeing, etc., and already in this questioning happily discovers the deception. For his own person, he knows *through* hearing, seeing, etc., without knowing *of* hearing, seeing, etc.; and, in his own way, the man is completely right. I know very well that this must happen to you in this way and I also know the reason for it. You do not have the intuition and you cannot manage it; therefore, you are left with only perception, and should you not have this, then you have absolutely nothing palpable. But I could want you to have precisely nothing, as I will explain to you more thoroughly below.

Furthermore, you considered every single bit to be a complete bit existing for itself, just as is the case with your collections; you believed that each could be carried away individually and established in the memory, and you attempted the task. However, the individual pieces would not fit together in the way you grasped them and you screamed: "Contradiction!" This happened to you because you have absolutely no concept of a synthetic-systematic discourse, but only recognize collections of utterances of the wise. For you, every discourse is a flood of quicksand in which every little grain exists whole and for itself and is absolutely understandable as a grain of quicksand. You know nothing of a discourse which resembles an organic and self-organizing body. You tear a piece from the organic body, show the edges hanging all around and scream: "This is supposed to be smooth and rounded!" The above mentioned reviewer treated the above mentioned book in this way. You know—or rather you need not know, but the popular reader who may also read this page knows that, as all scientific discourse should, my discourse proceeds from the completely undetermined and determines this further before the reader's eyes; therefore, of course, in pursuit of the objects, completely different predicates are added than were added in the beginning. You also know, or should know, that this discourse very often establishes and develops propositions that it later refutes, in that it advances through antithesis to synthesis. The thoroughly determined, true result with which it remains is only found here at the end. You, of course, only look for this result, and the way in which it is found does not exist for you. In order to write appropriately for you, one would have to say what one actually means in the shortest way possible, so that you could quickly check whether you mean it that way too. Were Euclid a writer of our day, how you would uncover his contradictions, which are legion. "Every triangle has three angles." Good, we want to remember that. "The sum of the three angles in every triangle equals two right angles." What a contradiction you would cry. On the *one* hand: any three angles at all, the sum of which can be various totals; on *the other hand*: only three angles of the type whose sum is equal to two right angles!

You have improved my expressions and taught me to speak, since, because you are my judges, it is understandable that you can speak better than I. Only you have not taken into consideration that one cannot appropriately advise anyone on *how* he is to say something until one knows *what* he wants to say. You have shown yourself to be anxious for my reader and complained that I write incomprehensibly, and you have often asserted that the public, for whom I determine my work, cannot understand it. If you follow your accustomed practice, you will assert the same of the present work. This, however, you have believed only because you yourselves have not understood it and assumed that the general public has a great deal less understanding than you, since you, of course, are scholars and philosophers. But in this assumption you are very much mistaken. I have spoken about philosophy for many years, not only with beginning students but also with adults from the educated classes of all walks of life, and I have never in my life heard in conversation the same kind of misunderstanding as you write every day for publication.

The peculiar phenomena which show themselves arise from that radical difference of our respective minds. When I say something that seems to me very easy, natural, and self-evident, you find it to be a monstrous paradox that you cannot clear up; whereas what you assume to be uncommonly plain and well-known and could simply never cause you to dream that someone might have anything against it often appears to me to be so confused I would have to talk for days in order to disentangle the confusion. Your plain propositions have come down to you through tradition, and you believe you understand and know them because you have heard and said them yourself so often without experiencing contradiction.

For you, the present text is certainly filled again with such monstrous paradoxes which you will knock down with one of your simple propositions. To cite only one of these paradoxes as an example, the first one that comes to mind: "What one solves by a mere definition of a word is, in the Science of Knowledge, never correct, but rather most surely incorrect," I said above. If you follow your accustomed practice, you will cite this sentence as a clear proof of how far I have gone in my nonsense: "For how in all the world can one come to an understanding anywhere except by the correct definition of the words used," you will mock in your manner; you will wish the Illuminati luck, those who desire, by way of Fichtean intuition, to raise themselves to the sense which yet lies above and beyond the words, and assert of yourselves that you have no such desire; and whatever else your wit is capable of. You will now find, if you would just pay attention to yourselves when reading a political newspaper, that you do not even understand this if you only apprehend and analyse the words; that you, on the contrary, even here draw up a picture of the narrated event in your imagination and allow the event to proceed, *construe* it for yourselves in order to really understand it; and that you also have actually done this always and without exception, and still do it, as sure as you have ever understood a newspaper and still understand one. Only you have never noticed this and I greatly fear that even now you will not find it so, even though I draw your attention to it, because it is precisely this blindness of the inner eye of imagination which is the defect for which we have always reproached you. But had you even noticed it or could you notice it now, it would still not fit into science for you at all. You have always believed of this that it is only learned and it has not occurred to you that it must actually be construed just like the narrated event in the newspaper.

For this reason, which is now sufficiently analysed for you, you have understood the Science of Knowledge so little until now, that none of you has even caught sight of the ground on which it rests. Yet, when one tells you this, you become angry. But why would you want to get angry over this? Are we not obliged to say it? Were one to believe that you have grasped it and that it must be grasped as you have grasped it, then it would be just as if the Science of Knowledge never existed, and it would, in this easiest of ways, be cast out of the world in complete silence. You cannot reasonably expect us to allow this to happen so very quietly, simply to prevent your capacity for understanding from falling into disrepute.

But neither will you understand the Science of Knowledge in the future. Now, disregarding the fact that several of you have put yourselves under the suspicion of being inspired by passions other than enthusiasm for philosophy through the extraordinary means which have served you in order to bring the Science of Knowledge into ill repute—disregarding that and giving the suspicion up as unfounded, one would still like, perhaps, to harbor some hope concerning you had you not declared your heartfelt opinion, not declared it so loudly, not laid it out so openly in the light of day. But, unfortunately, you have done this; are you now supposed to suddenly transform your nature and step into a light in which the things you have asserted until now as well as your entire intellectual condition—I cannot describe how poorly they would have to appear? It has probably happened to all who have quietly furthered their development, provided they have ever come to understand, that they now rest securely in their mind and, after the passage of some time, look back on their former confusion with a melancholy smile. But that he who has made the entire public a witness to his mistakes must continue to rise to the podium, he who continues to write and review day after day, that he would acknowledge and take them back is an extremely rare case.

Since everything is in fact so, as you yourselves would admit to me—of course never out loud and publicly, but yet quite certainly in some quiet hour in a secret corner of your soul—no other way out is left for you than to be completely silent concerning everything regarding the Science of Knowledge, indeed, philosophy, from this hour on.

You *can* take this way out, because you will never convince me that your speech-organs form those words which you bring forth without your assistance, and that your pens set themselves in motion and set those things down on paper which later get printed with or without your name. I will always believe that you first set both in motion with your wills before what happens happens.

Since you can do it, why should you not want to? I have considered and thought about it all and have simply found no rational ground why you should not follow this advice, or even resent me for it.

You cannot allege your enthusiasm for truth and against error; for, since you do not at all know what the Science of Knowledge actually wants, as your own conscience tells you whenever you question it, and since, after all, the entire region in which it resides is not at all present for you, you cannot even know whether what it reports from that unknown region is truth or error. Therefore, relinquish this business quietly to those others whom it concerns on their own responsibility; just as we all allow kings to rule their states and make war and peace completely on their own responsibility without talking it over with them. Until now, you have only stood in the way of the dispassionate investigation, complicated the simple, clouded what was clear and set everything on its head. Why do you positively want to stand in the way?

Or do you believe that it would damage your honor if you, who until now have been vociferous, fall silent? You are not concerned with the opinion of the irrational, are you? Because by falling silent, you would gain in the opinion of the rational.

It is rumored that Professor Jacob in Halle has given up higher speculation entirely and devotes himself to political economy, in which discipline much of excellence is to be expected from his renowned exactitude and his diligence. In this case he has shown himself to be a wise man by giving up philosophy. I hereby publicly pay him my high respects and hope that every rational person who knows what speculation is will share this respect. Would that the Abichts, the Buhls, the Bouterwecks, the Heusingers, the Heydenreichs, the Snells, the Ehrhard-Schmids likewise give up a discipline with which they have now sufficiently tortured themselves and found that they are not made for it. Let them take up another useful business: lensgrinding, forestry and provincial law, poetizing and novelizing; let them serve in the secret police, study the healing arts, herd livestock; let them write edifying memorials to the dead every day of the year, and no one would deny them his respect.

But since I still cannot rely on them and their like all the way on through the alphabet to follow good advice, I add the following so that they cannot say they were not told beforehand what would happen:

This is now the third time that I report on the Science of Knowledge. I would not like to be obligated to do it a fourth time and I am tired of seeing my words negligently passed from mouth to mouth so that soon I do not recognize them anymore. Therefore, I will assume that even modern literati and philosophers can understand this third report. Furthermore, I have assumed for a long time, because I *know* this, that absolutely every human can know whether he understands something or not and that no one's mouth will be forced open to talk of a thing before he is aware that he understands it. Therefore, I will no more leave this text to its fate than my future scientific texts, but rather watch over the remarks they stir up and observe them in a periodical. If these babblers are not improved by this, then I still hope to make it evident to the general public what manner of people have undertaken to guide their opinions until now, and continue to do so.

Translated by John Botterman and William Rasch

FRIEDRICH HEINRICH JACOBI

Open Letter to Fichte

Nous sommes trop élevés à l'égard de nous mêmes, et nous ne sensions nous comprendre.

—*Fenelon according to Augustus*

"How does genius manifest itself?" Through that whereby the Creator manifests himself in nature, in the infinite universe! The ether is clear and yet of unfathomable depth; visible to the eye, it still remains eternally hidden from reason.

—*Schiller*

PREFACE

I now promulgate the following letter just as I have written it directly and solely for the man to whom it is addressed, with his permission, without having had even the remotest thought that it should ever appear publicly, in order to come to terms with him philosophically, and satisfied if he only comprehended and did not misunderstand me, for this reason among others, that I consider it better that it circulate in a reliable edition rather than in unreliable rumors or in excerpts taken from memory.

Since no one will feel compelled to read this letter by virtue of its public appearance, I therefore expect from the fairness of spontaneous readers that they be satisfied with it just as it is and will not demand that I should have either deliberately drafted it especially for the public right away or at least now, prior to publication, revised it to something better. A new entirely different work would have resulted from such a revision, and that was not supposed to occur.

What disturb me most by the publication of this text are the incidental, although not unconsidered opinions, hastily jotted down about our great Königsberger—his moral philosophy and theology. The closer determination of these opinions, their detailed justification, will be found in another text, which I hereby pledge and now myself feel pressed to have appear as soon as possible. It would distress me if in the meantime one chose to understand and interpret that which is to be found here (e.g., the passage where I call Kant, with regard to transcendental philosophy, merely the forerunner of Fichte) differently than its setting, tone and context involve. In the present case, the forerunner is obviously the more distinguished. Fichte himself, as a noble man, has declared himself beautifully and emphatically about this and shown rather too much than too little modesty.[1] This matter presents itself to me, however, in another light. Since I, after all, consider the consciousness of not knowing as the highest in the human being and the site of this consciousness as the site of the true, inaccessible to science, so I must be pleased with Kant that he preferred to sin against the system than against the majesty of this site. Fichte sins against it, according to my judgment, when he wants to include this site in the area of science, and from the standpoint of speculation as the osten-

---

1. In the Preface to the essay "On the Concept of the Science of Knowledge." See V where he says: "The author is fervently convinced up to now that no human reason could advance farther than up to the boundary on which Kant stood, especially in his Critique of Judgement, which he, however, has never ascertained for us, and declared as the last boundary of finite knowledge. He knows that he will never be able to say something which Kant had not already indicated, directly or indirectly, more clearly or obscurely. He leaves it to future ages to fathom the genius of the man, who from that standpoint upon which he found the philosophizing power of judgment, often as if led by higher inspiration, carried it so powerfully along towards its last goal. He is just as fervently convinced that following the genial mind of Kant, no loftier gift could be bestowed than through the systematic mind of Reinhold. . . . He certainly does not consider it personal merit to be summoned to work on the heels of splendid workers through a happy coincidence, and he knows that any merit which could perhaps reside in this rests not upon the luck of finding, but upon the honesty of seeking, for which each one can guide and reward only himself."

sibly highest, as the standpoint of truth itself, wants to have it looked down upon. But Kant, if he doesn't do the same thing, Fichte will say, is inconsistent and stops midway. That I admit, and had already made this remark twelve years ago.[2] But isn't Fichte also inconsistent? One has unjustly accused his philosophy of atheism because transcendental philosophy as such can be atheistic just as little as geometry and arithmetic can be. But for the same reason, however, it can by no means be theistic. If it wanted to be theistic, and indeed exclusively, it would then be atheistic, or at least gain such an appearance, by showing how even God is caught in the very fact of non-existence in itself, becomes philosophically valid, yes, even a reality through this alone. Why then did Fichte give it the reputation that it wanted to and could? Why wasn't he more carefully on guard against the appearance that through transcendental philosophy a new unique theism were to be introduced, and through it, that old one of natural reason were to be banished as absurd? He thereby brought himself and his philosophy completely unnecessarily into ill report. That it knew nothing of God did not bring about any reproach against transcendental philosophy, since it is generally acknowledged: God cannot be known, but only believed. A God who could be known would be no God at all. But a merely artifical belief in him is also an impossible belief; for insofar as it wants only to be artificial or only scientific or purely speculative, it negates natural belief, and with that, itself as belief; hence all of theism. I refer to Reinhold's open letter to Lavater and Fichte about the belief in God (Hamburg at Perthes 1799).

To him, the pure and charming, the one courageously disavowing himself and everything for the sake of truth, I also refer here and in advance, should be I attacked in one way or another because of the following text. Then, dear friend and brother, you will have to step into the breach, to carry the older companion out of the tumultuous quarrel on your shoulders, as Socrates did with the younger one. Would I have dared to venture forth this time without your encouragement, your repeated entreaties? — "I should, I would have to — at your peril and risk!" Now see to it how you endure it. From this moment on this text is no longer my affair and property, but yours.

F. H. Jacobi

2. See the appendix to the "Conversation about Idealism and Realism."

Eutin, March 3, 1799

Today, my worthy friend, the sixth week is approaching that I wait impatiently and in vain for a serene day within my inner self to write to you; and today, since I am less capable of that than on any of the preceding ones, I take pen in hand with the best intention of not putting it down until I have written it out in full. What I propose to do with this resolve, which I form out of desperation, I myself don't know; it is, however, for this reason even more in keeping with my non-philosophy which has its essence in not knowing, just as your philosophy has its solely in knowing; for which reason too, the latter alone, according to my innermost conviction, deserves being called philosophy in the strictest sense.

I say it at every opportunity, and am prepared to acknowledge it publicly, that I consider you the true Messiah of speculative reason, the genuine son of the promise of a completely pure philosophy, existing in and of itself.

Undeniably the spirit of speculative philosophy is, and it therefore had to be its unceasing endeavor from the beginning, to make that for the natural human being equal certitude of these two sentences—I am, and there are things outside of me—unequal. Speculative philosophy had to seek to subjugate one of these sentences to the other, to derive the former from the latter or the latter from the former,—ultimately completely; so that only One Essence and only One Truth would come into existence beneath its eye, the All-seeing one! If speculation succeeded in producing this unity, in that it continued this making unequal for so long that out of the destruction of that natural equality another artificial equality arose out of the same, in a certain knowledge evidently previously existing Ego and Non-ego—a completely new creature which completely belonged to it—if it succeeded in this, then it could also thereupon succeed in producing a complete science of truth solely through its own activity.

In this manner the two main approaches: materialism and idealism, the attempt to explain everything out of self-determining material alone, or solely out of a self-determining intelligence, have the same goal; their direction against each other is by no means divergent but rather gradually approximating the final contiguity and permeation. Speculative materialism, which elaborates its metaphysics, must ultimately transfigure itself into idealism of its own accord because aside from dualism there is only egoism, as beginning or end, for the power of thought which thinks through.

Little was lacking for such a total transfiguration of materialism to have already occurred through Spinoza. His unifying substance similarly underlying both extended as well as thinking essence, both inseparable, is nothing but the invisible absolute identity itself of object and subject, verifiable only through inferences, upon which the system of the new philosophy, the independent philosophy of intelligence, is founded. Strange, that the thought never occurred to him to invert his philosphical cube once; to make the uppermost side, the side of thinking, which he called the objective, the lowermost, which he called the subjective, formal one, and then examine whether his cube still remained the same, the only true philosophical form of the matter for him. Inevitably, with this experiment everything would have transformed itself under his hands; the cubical, which had hitherto been substance for him, the single matter of two completely different essences, would have disappeared before his eyes; and instead a pure flame, burning solely out of itself, requiring neither abode nor nourishing stuff, would have flared up: transcendental idealism!

I chose this image because I first found entry into the science of knowledge through the mental image of an inverted Spinozism. And even now its representation is in me, the representation of a materialism without matter, or of a *mathesis pura*, in which pure and empty consciousness imagines mathematical space. How pure mathematics, presupposing the drawing of a straight line (thus movement, with everything this concept presupposes and carries with it) and the construction of a circle (measurement, surface, figure, quality, quantity, etc.), is able to produce in thought mathematical bodies, then an entire world out of nothing, I do not first have to explain. Thus only anyone ignorant and tasteless enough to despise geometry and arithemetic—the former because it produces no substances; the latter no numerical meanings, no existing value—only such a one might also be inclined to despise transcendental philosophy.

I demand and expect of Fichte that he understand me through hints; that which is not casually thought through causal words, characteristics, and jotted down images. Were I not able to do that, what kind of a book would I have to write? and never in my life would I write such a book!

And so I continue and first proclaim you, more ardently and audibly, once again among the Jews of speculative reason their king;

threaten the obstinate with recognizing you as such and accepting the Baptist of Königsberg merely as your forerunner. The sign which you have given is the union of materialism and idealism into *One* inseparable essence — a sign not completely unlike that of the Prophet Jonah.

Just as 1800 years ago the Jews in Palestine repudiated the Messiah, for whom they had yearned for so long, at his true appearance because he didn't bring with him that by which they wanted to recognize him, because he taught: neither circumcision nor foreskin mattered, but rather a new creature, so you too have had to become a stumbling block and rock of anger for those whom I call the Jews of speculative reason. Only one acknowledged you openly and honestly, an Israelite open and above board, Nathanael Reinhold. If I had not already been his friend, I would have then become it. And since then a completely different friendship than had previously existed has arisen between us.

I am a Nathanael only among the heathens. Just like I didn't belong to the old league but remained in the foreskin, so I also refrain from the new, out of the same incapability or stubbornness. According to the opinion of an eminent one among your disciples, this incapability or stubbornness is supposed to derive from the fact that I lack purely logical enthusiasm, the Sole-mind of the Sole-philosophy. Perceptive enough! It has eluded the perceptive one, however, in which form the Sole-philosophy and my Non-philosophy come into contact with each other through the highest degree of antipathy, and in the moment of contact, permeate each other to a certain degree. You, my friend, have felt this, as I have felt it; you have recognized me as the one who stood at the door of your lecture hall long before it was opened, stood expecting you and speaking prophecies. Now, as a privileged heretic and exempt in advance from any papal edict which could strike me in categories, I occupy an excellent seat in this lecture hall. I am even permitted to give a few lectures outside of class because my really true opinion obviously promotes rather than impairs the *coge intrare* of science.

Both living in the mind and honest scholars at any risk, we are, I think, sufficiently in agreement about the concept of science; that it, namely, science as such, consists in the autonomous production of its object and is nothing other than this production in thought itself; that therefore the content of every science as such is only an internal action and the necessary mode of this in itself free action constitutes its entire essence. Like you, I say every science is an Object-Subject, according to the archetype of the Ego; which Ego alone is science in itself, and thereby principle and solvent of all objects of knowledge, the power of its destruction and construction in merely scientific intention. In everything and from everything the human mind, forming concepts, seeks out only itself again, striving and counterstriving, incessantly tearing itself loose from momentarily limited existence which seeks to entangle it, as it were, in order to save its existence in and of itself, to continue it autonomously and with freedom. This activity of intelligence is a necessary activity within it; it does not exist where this activity does not exist. It would therefore be the greatest folly, according to this insight, to seek to inhibit the lust for science in oneself or others, the greatest folly to believe that one could indeed exaggerate philosophizing. To exaggerate philosophizing would mean to exaggerate reflection.

We therefore both want, with similar seriousness and zeal, that the science of knowledge—which in all sciences is one and the same, the World-soul in the world of knowledge—become perfected; with only one difference: that you want it so that the basis of all truth, as lodging in the science of knowledge, reveal itself; I, so that this basis be revealed: the true itself is necessarily present outside of it. My intention, however, does not in any way thwart yours, just as yours doesn't mine, because I distinguish between truth and the true. You take no cognizance of what I mean by the true, and as a teacher of science, should not take any cognizance of it.

On March 6

If I am to keep my word and carry out the resolve not to use pen, hand and eyes intentionally for anything else until I have brought this writing to a conclusion, then I have to form a second bold resolution, namely this: to continue my course even more rhapsodically, even more at a grasshopper's pace; the resolution not to present you anything but patchy pieces of trains of thought out of which you may read my understanding and lack of understanding as well as it is possible. Let it be so!

The secret of the identity and difference between Fichte and me, our philosophical sympathy and antipathy, would have to be, it seems to me, obvious to every one who wanted to take pains to read correctly and understand completely merely the single epistle to Erhard O. in the back of Allwill's letter collection.

I can shift myself to Fichte's point of view and isolate myself intellectually to it to such a degree that I am almost ashamed of having another opinion and hardly like to express my objectives against his system. But I can also feel from my opposite point of view such a force of gravity, soundness, and support, that I am annoyed by him and almost irate about his artificial departure from sanity, through which I, following his example, should liberate myself from my natural insanity and out of impatience heartily fling at him not too many subjects, but instead, too few. I shall not complain if Fichte in return flings too many subjects at me.

A pure, that is, completely immanent philosophy, a philosophy all of a piece, a genuine system of reason, is only possible in the Fichtean manner. Obviously everything must be given and already included in and through reason, the Ego as Ego, in the Ego-ness alone, if pure reason alone is supposed to be able to derive everything out of itself alone.

From understanding comes the root, to understand. Pure understanding is an understanding which understands only itself. Or: pure understanding understands only itself.

The philosophizing of pure understanding must therefore be a chemical process through which everything outside of it is transformed into Nothing and leaves only it behind, a spirit so pure that it cannot itself exist in this its purity but can only generate everything; this again, however, in such a purity that it likewise cannot itself exist but can only be present, contemplated, as in the production of the spirit: the whole thing a mere deed = deed.

All human beings, insofar as they strive at all for knowledge, establish, without being aware of it, pure philosophy as the ultimate goal because the human being knows only by comprehending, and he comprehends only by transforming a thing into mere form—form into a thing, something into nothing.

More distinctly!

We comprehend a thing only insofar as we can construct it, make it originate, come into existence before us in thought. Insofar as we cannot construct it, cannot ourselves produce it in thought, we do not comprehend it.

If, accordingly, an essence is to become an object completely comprehended by us, then we must negate, destroy it in thought objectively—as existing of itself—in order to allow it to become completely our own creation subjectively, a mere scheme. Nothing may remain in it and constitute an essential part of its concept that were not our action, now a mere representation of our productive imagination.

Thus the human spirit, since its philosophical comprehension simply cannot reach beyond its own production, must, in order to penetrate within the realm of essences, in order to conquer it mentally, become a world-creator and—its own creator. Only to the degree to which it succeeds in the latter, will it perceive progress in the first. But it can even be its own creator only under the stated general condition: it must destroy itself in essence in order to arise, to have itself solely in concept; in the concept of a pure absolute emerging from and entering into, originally—from nothing, to nothing, for nothing, into nothing; or the concept of a pendulum movement, which as such, because it is pendulum movement, necessarily sets barriers for itself in the general but has specific barriers only as a particular, through an incomprehensible restriction, in analogy to the expanding and contracting power of matter.

A science which has only itself as science alone for its subject and has no content aside from this is a science in itself. The Ego is a science in itself, and the only one: It knows itself, and it contradicts its concept that it know or become aware of anything outside of itself, etc., etc. . . . The Ego is therefore the necessary principle of all other sciences and an inevitable measurement (*menstruum*) with which they can all be dissolved and evaporated in *Ego* without leaving anything of a *caput mortuum—Non-Ego—*behind. It cannot be mistaken: If *Ego* gives all sciences its foundations, then all sciences must be able to be deduced from the *Ego*: if they can all be deduced from *Ego* alone, then all must also be able to be constructed in and through *Ego* alone, insofar as they are construable, i.e., insofar as they are sciences.

Abstraction forms the basis of all reflection to such a degree that reflection is possible only through abstraction. Conversely, the facts of the matter are thus: Both are inseparable and basically one, an action of dissolving all of essence into knowledge; progressive destruction (in the manner of science) through ever more general concepts. What now has been involvingly destroyed can also be evolvingly restored: in destroying I learned to create. Thereby, namely, that in dissolving, dissecting, I reached the Nothing-Outside of-Ego, it proved to me that everything was nothing outside of my, only in a certain way limited, free power of imagination. Out of this imagination I can then again allow all essences to emerge autonomously, all creatures as they were before I perceived them, as existing in themselves, as Nothing.

In a mischievous moment last winter in Hamburg, I conveyed the result of Fichtean idealism into an image. I chose a knitted stocking.

In order to form an idea other than the usual empirical one of the origin and composition of a knitted stocking, one need only untie the end of the fabric and allow it to unravel on this thread of the identity of this object-subject. One then clearly sees how this individual thing reached actuality by means of a mere weaving back and forth of the thread, that is, through a constant limitation of its movement and prevention that it follow its striving out into the infinite — without an empirical touch or any other admixture or garnishing.

Let me give this, my stocking, stripes, flowers, sun, moon, and stars, all possible figures, and perceive how all of this is nothing but a product of this productive power of the imagination of the fingers suspended between the Ego of the thread and the Non-Ego of the strands. All these figures, together with the stocking essence, viewed from the standpoint of truth, are the single naked thread. Nothing has flowed into it, neither out of the strands nor out of the fingers. It is solely and purely that Everything, and there is in that Everything Nothing outside of it. It is it completely, solely — with its movements of reflection on the strands which he has continously held on to and thereby become this specific individual.

I should like to hear how one would deny this stocking that with all its infinite multiplicies it is still certainly and truly only one thread; and deny the thread that it Alone is this infinite multiplicity. The latter, as I have already said, need only return to its original identity by displaying the series of its reflections in order to make it evident that the former infinite multiplicity and manifold infinity was nothing but an empty weaving of its weaving, and the only reality was merely itself with its action out of, in and upon itself. It also wants this return, namely, liberation from the bonds of the

Non-Ego adhering to it; and there is no one who wouldn't know
and had experienced it just as: All stockings have the tendency to
abolish their boundaries in order to fill up infinity—highly inpru-
dent! since they can probably know that it is impossible to be
Everything and, at the same time, One and Something.

Should this image be so inappropriate that it obviously betray a
gross misunderstanding on the part of its inventor, then I would
therefore not know how the new philosophy could truly be a new
and not merely an altered enunciation of the old philosophy based
on one or the other dualism; it would not then be a truly and
honestly immanent philosophy, a philosophy all of a piece. What in
the old had been called perception would in the new necessarily be
called imagining, but mean basically exactly the same. Should it in
any way mean only the same, then empiricism ultimately still remains at the top, relating to science as the living limbs to their
artificial organs. Therefore, in the human intellect a higher site than
the site of scientific knowledge must be assumed, and it is looked
down from the former upon the latter: "the highest standpoint of
speculation is" not then "the standpoint of truth."

I therefore don't fear that reproach. I can much sooner imagine
that the new philosophy might like my image and use it to its
advantage.

"Just think, it might say to me. Repent! What are all stockings,
and what is all wearing of stockings in heaven and on earth compared with the insight into its origin, compared with the observation of the mechanism through which they are produced at all,
compared with the reinvention in general and ever more general of
its art: a reinvention, through which art itself is first created as
essential art. Scoff as much as you want at this pure joy at the pure
knowledge of pure knowledge alone, which has not improperly
been called a merely logical enthusiasm. We do not deny that we are
blissful in it, don't care anything more about heaven and earth; and
even if body and soul languish away from us, do not esteem it on
account of that sublime love of knowledge merely for the sake of
knowing; of perception merely for the sake of perceiving; of doing
merely for the sake of doing. Scoff at it childishly unaware, pitiable,
as we meanwhile demonstrate and prove irrefutably: There necessarily lies at the basis of all originating and being, from the lowest
animals on up to the highest Holy and Sub- or Full-God, a merely

logical enthusiasm, that is: *An action intending and considering only itself, merely for the sake of acting and considering, without another subject or object; without in, out, for, or to.*"

I answer to this by simply presenting my stocking again and asking: What would it be without the relationship to and purpose for a human leg, by which means alone reason enters its essence? How would it be, from the animal below up to the sacred, with a mere weaving of a weaving? I assert that my reason, my whole interior flares up, shudders, is horrified by this mental image, so that I turn away from it as from the most monstrous of all monstrosities, implore annihilation, like a deity, against such a Danaid- and Ixion-bliss.

Our sciences, merely as such, are games which the human spirit devises to pass the time. Devising these games, it merely organizes its ignorance without getting even a hair's breadth closer to a knowledge of the true. In a certain way it thereby rather distances itself from it, in that with this business it simply distracts itself from its ignorance, no longer feels its pressure, even grows fond of it, because it is infinite; because the game that ignorance plays with the human spirit becomes ever more varied, delightful, larger, intoxicating. Were the game with our ignorance not infinite, and not so constituted that out of each of its changes a new game arose, then it would occur to us with science just as with the so-called Nürnberger cricket game, which disgusts us as soon as all of its movements and possible turns of expression are known and familiar to us. The game is spoiled for us because we understand it completely, because we know it.[3]

All sciences have first originated as a means to other ends, and philosophy in its proper understanding, metaphysics, is not exempted from this. All philosophers aimed at getting behind the form of the thing, that is to the thing itself, behind the truth, that is to the true: they wanted to know the true—ignorant of the fact that if the true could be humanly known, it would have to cease being the true in order to be a mere creation of human invention, of an imagining and forming of incorporeal imaginations.

3. Because of this passage I have been scolded repeatedly and quite harshly by young and old. I am supposed to have equated science with the Nürnberger cricket game, notwithstanding that in fact the clearly opposite had occurred through me, as anyone who knows how to read even a little bit must discover. My true and real opinion can be found more fully worked out in the essay on divine things.

From this ignorance and presumption the two great men, Kant and Fichte, have freed us; only the latter completely. They have discovered the higher mechanics of the human spirit, expounded completely in the intellectual system the theory of movements in resisting properties, and achieved in another sphere what Huygens and Newton had previously done in theirs. Through these most recent discoveries a useless and ruinous waste of human power has been stopped forever, a path to err completely broken off. From now on, no one can excusably rapture with the intellect, no one any longer hope to find the true cabbala after all and produce essences and living powers with letters and numbers. Truly a great blessing for our race if it now, smitten with the science of its ignorance, doesn't seek salvation merely by eagerly squinting with both eyes merely at the tip of its nose.

By the true I understand something which is prior to and outside of knowing; which first gives knowing and the capacity for knowing, for reason, a value.

Understanding presupposes something capable of being understood; reason, the true: it is the capacity for the presupposition of the true. A reason which does not presuppose the true is an absurdity.

With his reason, the human being is not given the capacity for a science of the true, but merely the feeling and consciousness of his ignorance thereof: *presentiment* of the true.

Where this direction towards the true is lacking, there is no reason.[4] This direction — the compulsion to consider the true, hovering only in presentiment, as its object, as the ultimate intention of all lust for knowledge — constitutes the essence of reason. It is directed exclusively to the concealed beneath appearances, to its meaning, to the existence which emits only an appearance and which must indeed shine through in the appearances, if these are not to be abstract ghosts, appearances of Nothing.

Reason places the essence of the imagination in contradictory opposition to the true essence, towards which reason is directed exclusively as towards its ultimate purpose. It distinguishes not merely between imaginations and imaginations (such as necessary and free ones) but absolutely. It contrasts true essence with the

4. Animals lack it. The direction towards the true is simultaneously the direction towards the good.

essence of the imagination as it contrasts waking with dreaming. With this direct, apodictic distinction between waking and dreaming, between imagination and true essence, reason stands or falls.

If the human being is cut off from the reason expressed in the physical world which surrounds him, which orders his imagination by force; if he loses his senses in dream, in fever, becomes in-sane; his own inherent pure reason does not thereby prevent him from thinking, accepting, and considering the absurd a certainty. He loses his wits and his human reason, just as he loses his senses, just as perception becomes impossible for him, because his limited human reason is pure perception, inner or outer, direct or indirect; but as reasonable perception (a definition already given by the literal meaning of the word perception)—with reflection and intention; ordering, continuing, active, spontaneous—full of presentiment.

A not merely perceiving reason, but a reason producing all truth out of itself alone, a reason which is itself the essence of truth and has within itself the perfection of life—such an autonomous reason, the fullness of the good and the true, must certainly be present, or everywhere there would be nothing good or true; the root of nature and all essences would be a pure Nothing, and to discover this great secret the ultimate intention of reason.

As surely as I possess reason, so surely do I possess with this, my human reason, not the perfection of life, not the fullness of the good and the true; and as surely as I do not possess the latter with it and know it, so surely do I know it is a higher essence and I have my origin in it. For this reason then, my watchword and that of my reason is not: I, but rather more than I! better than I!—a completely different one.

I am not, and I do not wish to be, if He is not!—Indeed, I myself cannot be the highest essence for me. Thus my reason teaches me instinctively: God. With irresistible force the highest in me points to a highest being above and outside of me: it forces me to believe the incomprehensible—yes, that conceptually impossible, in me and outside of me, out of love, through love.[5]

Because reason keeps the godhead in mind, necessarily has God

---

5. God, i.e., to be God, is obviously impossible for me, i.e., it presents itself to me as something impossible.

on its mind, for that reason alone we consider it higher than the self in popular understanding; and to that extent it may make sense and be considered as truth "that reason is the end; individuality only the means."[6]

"God is," says Timaeus loftily, "that which everywhere produces the better."—The origin and power of the good.

But the good—What is it? I have no answer if there is no God.

Just like this world of appearances, if it has its entire truth and no inherently deeper meaning in all these appearances, if it has nothing outside of itself to reveal, becomes a repugnant apparition to me before which I curse the consciousness in which this abomination originates for me and like a deity call for its destruction; so too does everything which I called good, beautiful, and sacred become an absurdity merely destroying my mind and tearing my heart from my breast as soon as I accept that it is without any relationship to a higher true essence within me, not merely a symbol and image of it in me: if I am to have everywhere within me merely an empty consciousness and *poem*.

I therefore confess that I do not know goodness, just like the true, in itself, that I also have only a distant presentiment of it; declare that it infuriates me if instead of it, one wants to impose on me the will which wants Nothing, this hollow nut of autonomy and freedom in the absolute indefinite and when I resist accepting it in return, accuses me of atheism, of true and essential ungodliness.

Yes, I am the atheist and ungodly one who, contrary to the will which wants Nothing, wants to lie as Desdemona lied while dying, who wants to lie and deceive like Pylades who impersonated Orestes, wants to murder like Timoleon, break the law and oath like Epaminondas, like Johann de Wit; decide for suicide like Otho, attempt temple robbery like David—yes, pull out sheaves on the Sabbath if only for this reason that I am hungry and the law is made for the sake of the human being, not the human being for the sake of the law. I am this godless one and defy the philosophy which therefore calls me godless, defy it and its highest essence because with the most sacred certainty I have within me, I know that because of such crimes against the pure letter of the absolutely general

6. Fichte's words.

law of reason, the privilegium aggratiandi is the proper sovereign prerogative of the human being, the seal of his dignity, his divine nature.[7]

Don't teach me what I know and understand how to prove better than you might like, namely, that that will which wants Nothing, that impersonal individuality, that mere egoism of the Ego without Self; that, in a word, nothing but pure and bare immaterial things *must* necessarily be taken as a basis if a generally valid, strictly scientific system of morality is to be accomplished. For the sake of the secure course of science you would have to (oh, you could not do otherwise!) subject the conscience to a living death of rationality, make it blindly legal, deaf, dumb, and insensitive; you would have to tear from it its living root, which is the heart of the human being, up to the last fibre. Yes, by all your heavens and as truly as Apollo and the muses are merely categories for you, you have to! For only thus are unconditional general laws, rules without exception, and rigid obedience possible. Thus alone does conscience know itself certain, even externally, everywhere, and unerringly sets the course for all highways, a wooden hand from the professorial chair.

But do I want that no general, strictly proven doctrine of duty be set up which can only take place in and above a pure system of reason? Do I misjudge the value, do I deny the advantage of such a discipline? Or do I dispute the truth and sublimity of the principle from which the moral doctrine of pure reason proceeds? Not at all! The moral-principle of reason: Unanimity of the human being with

7. "Force may influence life, in that it holds certain misfortunes before man to frighten him off from wrongdoing, but the morally evil itself is a greater misfortune than those which force is capable of inflicting; and therefore the obligation of honesty and humaneness is as complete as it can be through the fear of a misfortune or the consideration of happiness. Whoever reflects upon the behavior which is appropriate to him in a certain situation will often find himself less strongly impelled to grant one person that which one calls his right than another help and support. A boy lay almost naked upon the grave of his father, whom he had recently lost; a man who was just going to his creditors to pay his debt which had come due according to his promise saw him; the man raised the boy up and bestowed upon this dear fellow the money for which the creditor was already waiting; the latter was therefore disappointed. Who would want to disapprove of this deed as though a stricter obligation had clashed with it? Even before the courts, the extreme need of one person sometimes forms the basis for not discharging the right of another. Thus it will be permitted the one who is in danger of starving to infringe on other people's property for his own preservation and the demand for humaneness regarded more sacred than that of an unconditional and exclusive right." Ferguson, *Principles of Moral and Political Science*, P. II, ch. 5, sect. 1.

himself, constant unity, is the highest in the concept because this unity is the absolute, immutable condition of reasonable existence altogether; consequently, also of all reasonable and free action. In it and with it alone does the human being have truth and higher life. But this unity itself is not the essence, is not the true. It itself, in itself alone, is bleak, desolate, and empty. Thus its law can also never become the heart of the human being and truly elevate him above himself; and then indeed only his heart, which is the proper faculty of ideas, not of empty ones, truly elevates the human being above himself. Transcendental philosophy shall not tear this heart from its breast and place a pure drive solely out of egoism in its stead. I do not permit myself to be freed from the dependence of love in order to attain salvation solely through pride. If the highest upon which I can reflect, what I can contemplate, is my empty and pure, naked and mere ego, with its autonomy and freedom: then rational self-contemplation, then rationality is for me a curse—I deplore my existence.

Here I had to break off or seek to make a book out of this letter. I would not have ventured the few words I have jotted down about morality if in my earlier writings there had not been scanty explanation given about it. I remind you especially of the aphorisms on non-freedom and freedom inserted in the preface to the new edition of the Letters on the Doctrine of Spinoza. I have never comprehended how one could find something mysterious and incomprehensible in Kant's categorical imperative, which is so easy to deduce from the drive of correspondence with itself (I refer to the aphorisms cited above), and could, with this incomprehensible thing, subsequently attempt to make the stopgaps of theoretical reason conditions for the reality of the laws of practical reason. In no philosophy have I come across a greater annoyance for me than this. Just imagine my jubilation at the appearance of your text on the Vocation of the Scholar, in which I found the most complete agreement with my opinions about these matters right on the first pages.

But precisely for this reason, just as not before, I have not even subsequently been able to make the identity-drive my highest essence and love and worship it alone.

And thus I am altogether and throughout still the same person who in the letters on Spinoza proceeded from the miracle of perception and the inscrutable mystery of freedom and ventured in this manner with a *salto mortale* not so much to prove his philosophy, but rather daringly present his unphilosophical obstinacy to the world.

Since outside of the mechanism of nature, I come across nothing but miracles, mysteries, and signs and have a terrible aversion to Nothingness, the absolutely indefinite, the utterly empty (these three are one, the Platonic infinite!), particularly as the object of philosophy or goal of wisdom; but in the investigation of the mechanism of the nature of the Ego as well as that of the non-Ego, reach nothing but Nothing-in-itself and am so tainted, struck, and exhausted by it in my transcendental essence (personally, so to speak), that in order to empty out the infinite, I even must want to fill it up, as an infinite Nothingness, a purely totally In-and-of-Itself, were it only not impossible! Since, I say, that is the way it is with me and the science of the true, or more accurately, the true science; I therefore do not see why I, for reasons of good taste, should not be allowed to prefer my Philosophy of Not-Knowing to the Philosophical Knowing of Nothing, even it were only in *fugam vacui*. I have nothing against me but Nothingness; and with that, even chimeras can probably compete.

Truly, my dear Fichte, it should not vex me if you, or whoever it might be, want to call what I contrast to idealism, what I chide as nihilism, chimerism. I have made a display of my Not-Knowing in all of my writings; I have so boasted of being unknowledgeable with knowledge, completely and extensively to such a high degree, that I should be allowed to despise the mere doubter.[8] With earnestness and fervor I have strived from childhood on for truth as have few, have experienced my incapacity as have few, and my heart has thereby become tender—oh, very tender, my dear Fichte, and my voice so gentle! Just as I, as a human being, have a deep sympathy with myself, so I have it with others. I am patient without effort; but that I am truthful without effort costs me a lot. The earth will be light above me—before long.

My heart becomes soft as I am writing this. I would like to get up and hurry to you, to reveal to you, eye to eye, breast to breast, my entire soul. This was my feeling, my fervent longing while reading the lines written by your hand among the published letters; they moved me deeply. The address in your text moved me even more

8. S. Th. 1, p. 244.

deeply. The hand which you grasp full of confidence answers you with a friendly squeeze. And it would be the same even if I had to call your doctrine, just like Spinoza's doctrine, Atheistic; I would still not, for that reason, consider you personally an Atheist, an ungodly one. Whoever really knows how to elevate himself above nature with the mind, above every degrading lust with the heart, he sees God face to face, and it is too little to say of him that he believes only in him. Were even the philosophy of such a one, were his opinions according to the (I believe correct) judgment of natural reason atheistic which call a non-personal God, a God who is not, an absurdity; were he to give his system this name himself, then his sin would still be only a thing of thought, a clumsiness of the artist in concepts and words, a transgression of a melancholy brooder, not the human being. Not the essence of God, but only a name would be denied by him. That is what I thought of Spinoza when I wrote the following passage located in my justification against Mendelssohn (p. 84): "Eh proh dolor . . . And God bless you, great, yes, holy Benedictus! however you have philosophized about the value of the highest being and gone astray in words, his truth was in your soul and his love was your life."

The great correspondence between the religion of Spinoza (His philosophy presents itself throughout as religion, as doctrine of the highest essence and the relationship of the human being to the same) and the religion of Fenelon has already been cited several times, but not once carried out in a manner encompassing all philosophies. To undertake such an exposition myself has been my favorite thought for a long time. Here I just want to note that the reproach of either Atheism, or of Mysticism, but especially of Enthusiasm and of Nonsense, will be made in all times until the end of days by the great mass of those who call themselves philosophers and teachers of religion against every philosophy, whichever form it may take, which invites the human being to elevate himself above nature and above himself, insofar as he is nature, with his mind. This reproach cannot be prevented because the human being cannot elevate himself above nature outside of and within himself without simultaneously elevating himself with the mind above his reason, the temporal, up to the concept of freedom.

In view of this concept of freedom surpassing reason, we can hardly come to a complete agreement as to how it is to be defined, what it comprises, presupposes, and implies.

Thus some diversity of opinion would probably become evident among us even in the distinction which we both make, by the way, in exactly the same manner, between religion and idolatry.

I maintain: the human being finds God because he can only find himself simultaneously with God; and he is unfathomable to himself because the essence of God is necessarily unfathomable. Necessarily! because otherwise a super-godly capacity would have to reside in the human being, and God would have to be able to be invented by the human being. God would then only be a thought of the finite, an imagined, and certainly not the highest being, existing solely in itself, the free creator of all other beings, the beginning and the end. That is not the way it is, and for that reason the human being loses himself as soon as he resists finding himself in God as his creator in a manner inconceivable to his reason; as soon as he wants to base himself in himself alone. Everything then gradually dissolves before him into his own Nothingness. But the human being has such a choice, this single one: Nothingness or a God. Choosing Nothingness, he makes himself into God; that is, he makes an apparition into God because if there is no God, it is impossible that man and everything which surrounds him is not merely an apparition.

I repeat: God is, and is outside of me, a living being, existing in itself, or I am God. There is no third.

If I do not find God, so that I must postulate him: A self-existence outside of me, before me, above me; so I am myself, by virtue of my egoism, completely that which is thus called, and my first and highest prayer is that I shall have no other gods aside from me or that egoism. I then know and completely comprehend how that foolish, tasteless, basically godless idolatry originates for the human being with a being outside of him; investigating, deducing and constructing this delusion, I destroy it forever.

In that I destroy and disgrace that idolatry, however, while coming to an understanding of it, I must also eradicate everything which is connected to it. I must eradicate from my soul the religion of love, of example, must ridicule every impulse and inspiration of a higher being, banish from my heart every devotion, every worship.

Far be such a salvation from me! Determined, candidly, without hesitation and doubt, I give preference to the merely external idolatry above that, for me, too pure religion which presents itself to me as self-divination. If one wants to call my weakness irreligion, if one wants to call the effect of this weakness or my superstition atheism, one should then not be angry if against those who reproach me with such a harsh *You* or *I* of atheism, I affirm the *You*. With you, my friend, I am not in this situation, since you expressly explain in your Appellation (pp. 61 and 62) that superstition does not necessarily exclude morality, hence also not true devotion to God. And thus I have likewise already admitted for my part that that spiritual idolatry which postulates a concept, a thing of thought, a generality in place of a living God (I should like to call it idolatry with an adjective), does not exclude morality and the true inner religion inseparably connected to it. The living God is then denied only with the lips.

On the whole, in relation to superstition and idolatry, it is my opinion that it is all the same whether I practice idolatry with images of wood and stone; with ceremonies, stories of miracles, gestures, and names; or with utterly philosophical concepts, cold literal essences, empty forms of the imagination; whether I make the form into a thing this way or that, but adhere superstitiously to the means and delude myself about any true purpose. I frequently said to certain pious ones: You just don't want to practice magic with Satan's help, but indeed with the help of God, because your religion is composed of nothing but sheer magic charms, visible and invisible, compounded, and basically only a practicing of sorcery against and in rivalry with the devil. But even among these I found several infuriating me by their disgusting superstition, by their irrational opinions, people causing me the most severe annoyance, for whom this superstition, this defiance of irrationality and an idol-fearing fervor connected to it, nevertheless dwelled only on their lips. Inwardly, in heart and mind, with their inverted figures of speech and strange imaginations, they nevertheless meant the true. But it was impossible for them, honestly impossible, and it seemed to them therefore absurd, also ungodly, to separate this true essence from those words and images of irrationality. One could just as easily have expected them to think without words and images at all and to isolate everything individual and what is called form from their representations and feelings. Since even the best or purest philosopher is not capable of the latter, if everything is not to be thought to death, everything is not to be exalted to utterly impossible concepts of a pure void, and void purity, and true eternal bliss is to consist in this exaltation alone; so I would think the accusation of idolatry and supersitition should not fall so easily from our lips. One could easily reproach us from the other side that we were shamelessly exalting ourselves with a greater sin above the lesser one of our neighbor, since our thoughts and endeavors and capacity were only to lay waste to the site of the true—that one which every people of the world had in its own way marked with altars—and to strew salt on that spot. It would be infinitely wiser, in my judgment, if we were to persuade ourselves and then also make attempts to persuade others: "Not the idol makes the idolator, not the true God the true worshipper. Because if the true God were to make the true worshipper, then we would all be it, and all to the same extent, since the presence of the true God is only A Universal."[9]

Hail to the human being who constantly feels this presence, for whom that old assertion: By the living God! is in every moment the highest archetype of truth. Whoever touches the sacred and noble simplicity of this belief with a corrupting hand, he is an adversary of the human race; because neither science nor art, nor any other talent, whatever name it might have, would compensate for what had been taken from it. A benefactor of the human race is, on the contrary, whoever is permeated by the nobility, sanctity, and truth of that belief, whoever does not tolerate that one destroy it. His hand will be strong by re-erecting the sunken altars of the only Living and True even higher. The moment he extended it, the hand of the assailant already fell and withered. So it was until now, so will it henceforth be: He never becomes obsolete.

You do not expect me to apologize for the length of my letter. I am at least of the opinion of having rather to excuse myself because of fatigue for already concluding it here, after I have merely rather told than described, incompletely and rhapsodically, my Science of Ignorance to you. Yet I didn't promise any more and basically consider only my egoism offended, which tells me this doctrine would still have probably been capable of a more philosophical exposition and indeed not unworthy of it. All at once, with one miracle, all philosophies, without exception, are affected. Each has a special site, its holy place, where its own miracle appears as the exclusively true,

9. From the text on godly things.

making every other superfluous. Taste and character determine, for the most part, the direction of the view towards the one or the other of these sites. You have yourself admirably noted this on page 25 of your new presentation where you say: "Which philosophy one chooses depends upon what kind of person one is: Because a philosophical system is not inanimate household furniture which one could reject or accept as we pleased, but it is animated by the soul of the human being who has it." You are probably amazed that I cite this passage and am inclined to call it excellent, since what precedes and follows (pp. 23–26) declares to me with biting wit your disdain, at least your disrespect and only suppressed ridicule because of my manner of thinking. For that very reason I have conceived these pages all the more gladly in order to note at this opportunity that during the writing of this letter, I have exhibited an at least not disdainful strength of mind, since for me the harsh and sharper commands irrefutably affecting me: Not to have a say about such subjects! were partly on my mind, partly often glaringly enough evident and about to disconcert me while I was looking up things during the work. What always cheered me up again I have already cited previously, namely, that I may once and for all consider myself exempt. Truly, I am honestly convinced of it and know furthermore from personal experience that wherever we do not exempt personally, but on the contrary, have just this person in mind as we discharge our animosity in general and are fired up by imagining this person, and yet don't intend him specifically with our animosity because we deeply and vividly feel that with regard to this matter, it may be yet a different matter. Give me the same in return, my dear Fichte, and excuse me, as I excused you if you should perhaps find that in one or the other passage of this letter I might have expressed myself too spiritedly. I have intentionally sketched harshly and applied the loudest colors, so that what was to stand out would surely stand out and what between us is only misunderstanding, and what is truly a contrary manner of thinking, would emerge as clearly as possible.

May it go well with you! That I sincerely wish just as sincerely as I am your friend and true admirer.

March 21, 1799   F. H. Jacobi

Translated by Diana I. Behler

On Faith and Knowledge

To Friedrich Köppen
(First Letter.)[1]

Eutin, August 10, 1802

No, my friend, I have not slept through, but with both of my alert ears heard that academic pereat! brought to me by the gentlemen Schelling and Hegel.[2]

I just could not fully understand that song sung with it because of the excessively loud accompaniment of the Scharrivorri-orchestra beneath the stamping, hissing, grinding, and screaming; beneath the roaring and rattling of stones which aimed amiss at my windows, richocheted off the masonry, flew up again from the pavement, and here and there injured the heads of those who hurled them. What I understood appeared to me extremely suitable to the occasion and entirely appropriate to the circumstances. Nothing, absolutely nothing astonished me, not even "that I am a screamer, even a crier of murder, a boisterous one, but only an idle one (for

---

1. The annotations to these and the following letters have just now been added. One should not forget they were written prior to the Köppen work. Now, however, they are based on it and should be read throughout only following it as a mere supplement to it.

2. "Faith and Knowledge, or the Philosophy of Reflections upon Subjectivity in the Entirety of its Forms as Kantian, Jacobian, and Fichtean Philosophy," *Critical Journal of Philosophy*, edited by Schelling and Hegel, second volume, first part.

who would otherwise accuse me of screaming, even the most boisterous kind? Certainly not those gallant men!). Not that I am a
squabbler, a "blusterer and pounderer devoid of thought"; not "that
I slander, talk nonsense, yes even quote falsely pell mell; that I go on
in my own continuously caustic, spiteful, and because of distortions, virtually malicious way." Also not in the least "that my treatise on a prediction by Lichtenberg is a hearty, endlessly quarreling
and apostrophizing Capucinade, in which the din and squabble of
the essay of the *Contributions* has been prepared for even the dilet-
tantes and served up with sentimentalities to promote bitterness, a
caustic edict, full of a shallow, bitter, peevish mood and serving no
instruction, of decrying defamations of criticism, merely to fill unphilosophical folk with horrifying dread and abhorrence of such a
ghost as the Kantian (!!!) philosophy is; that in both essays there is
continuous babbling on a string of absurdities and balderdash with
an unceasing din, working its way into absurdities, flattering itself
in the preparation of balderdash and completely unruly rappings
and quarrelings." Not even that, not in the least, although it is
almost said "that I preach and present an abominable religion and
an equally abominable morality in my writings; that both are from
Hell, since I teach to honor not God, not the human race, but only
the human being, and if reason erects a temple for the deity
(through Spinoza, Schelling and Hegel), it wants to be sure that the
devil is left his chapel beside it. Didn't I, in a letter to Mendelssohn,
call that which is most alive—fatherland, folk and laws—things?
Things, to which Spartias and Bulis, two Spartans I presented there,
are accustomed as one is accustomed to things? I am said to consider them not as holy things but as common ones *because* with regard
to holy things, there is not a relationship of habituation and dependence, etc. Since with respect to moral beauty I am an offence to its
concept and objectivity, one can only consider aspects in which I
wanted to elucidate my idea of moral beauty; and there one generally finds that in the stead of *moral freedom*, I place the utmost
precision, longing egoism, and moral victory, the utmost subjectivity and inner idolatry, and simultaneously justify it. The damnation
of Hell is to be found in my very person; boredom, impotence of
existence, and fornication with one's self is the reason for the catas-
trophe of the unnovelistic occurrences of the heroes Woldemar and

Allivill, and even the uncatastrophizing virtue of the whole environment of characters is essentially more or less tinged with that Hell, etc. etc. etc.[3]

The same reproaches are repeated countless times in the essay "Faith and Knowledge", without a doubt for the arousing, strengthening, and maintenance of the powers of belief of the readers, probably also of the writers while they were still writing. As is well known, one believes oneself in the end what one has often repeated and increasingly vehemently asserted; and for these others, the repetitions here signify so many witnesses, whose numbers will probably be able to make up for the lack of the occurrence, the matter, the despicable reality and empirical truth.

What could be strange here? You and almost all the rest of my friends and acquaintances know how often I have said that if the men of this school just once overcame the little bashfulness in their intention of making me recant, they would then insult me more fiercely and unrestrainedly as they had never before another. In fact, even now, when it is still just beginning, they did not find enough ready-made invectives at hand, but in their distress and haste they had to scold me with persons too: with Locke and Hume (as "arch- and basic empiricists" p. 117, and already before pp. 16 and 66); with Mendelssohn (p. 66 I am, however, much worse, and on p. 117 come to stand immeasurably beneath them); with Herder, from whom (pp. 93 and 94) I am copiously parodied; with Jean Paul (p. 111); yes even with Grandfather Kant, who is indeed supposed to be avenged through me; and with Father Fichte.[4]

Too severe, indeed! if it had not been necessary, if circumstances had not absolutely demanded it thus. Let us put ourselves impartially into the position of these men. They considered themselves painfully insulted by a man whom they had long thought highly of, frequently praised, and overwhelmed with eulogies. This man had not now really caused or started up anything new; assailed nothing in his latest writings which he had not assailed all along; declared and defended nothing which he had not declared and defended

3. See pp. 18, 92, 93, 95, 96, 99, 100, 101, 103, 105, 107, 108, 111, 113, 114, 117, 120, 121, 128, 129, 130, 134.

4. Pp. 16, 117, and throughout. On the other hand, Kant and Fichte are again scolded just as thoroughly with me and just like me, are also scolded here and elsewhere with Locke and Hume; we are together in the same damnation; the one fares no better than the other in the face of truth.

from the very beginning. He had simply become more of a man with the years, and the times also now permitted him to express himself more clearly, definitively, especially more comprehensively and candidly; it was, according to his conviction, also simultaneously a requisite of the times. But exactly in this conviction lay his fault. Those men had a completely different one, and their expressed thoughts in a reprimand directed to him before the deserved punishment might probably sound like this.

"You are mistaken, you old driveling fool, with your stupid head and stupid eyes![5] Go and be silent. What was once your merit will, if you continue, be punishable today; the times require that you be silent. Eighteen years ago when you appeared, we did not yet exist. You say perhaps that you had prepared the way for us; that we had learned much and various things from you; had eagerly and zealously read and used everything you wrote; impressed not only your thoughts, but also your words, phrases and symbols indelibly upon our memories; that they came to our pens automatically when we wrote (although divinely unconscious), especially to our Schelling[6] It may be; we have certainly not been ungrateful towards you. Still to this hour, we call you clever and repeat it with singular pleasure. We have also testified for you publicly and in secret, in our writings, in our professorial chairs, in our confidential associations and correspondences; all without change and unceasingly as long as we first followed you, thereafter accompanied you, went beside and with you. But now we are ahead, know more, better, and completely otherwise than you have ever known, you paltry one! Learn from us, acknowledge yourself to us! If you refuse to do so, then and as

5. See in the treatise on "Faith and Knowledge," p. 107, the witty and humane notation about that which is called the bulletin of my health.
6. Had I made the above letter public at the time when it was written then I would have thought it necessary to have expressly left out Mr. Hegel at this point. Now since I have again read the third section of "Faith and Knowledge," Fichtean Philosophy, more attentively, I may no longer do so. Fichte, and Kant too, are struck dead with the remains of my two latest recently stoned essays and the somewhat earlier Letter to Fichte in these sections, just like the Philistines of old were struck by Simson with a fresh jaw-bone of a jack-ass which had luckily fallen into his hands. One knows there was a molar tooth in this which was secretly a spring and gave the hero water. By the way, one must do justice to Mr. Hegel that he knows how to beware of Jacobian style and art, and if one excludes the boasting and scolding, he would be just as hardly recognizable in his speech as a pupil of Schelling's. One can therefore assume with confidence that in the composition of the treatise on "Faith and Knowledge," Mr. Hegel guided the pen.

dear as the truth and godliness expressing itself solely through us is, we must out of conscience deny you and say of you and swear: we have never known this person! Never indeed then did we learn anything from you. What was to be learned from you *is* Nothing. Therefore it also *was* Nothing. See how this hand turns itself over if you no longer exist; everything with which you might presume to praise yourself before us is destroyed and erased. Accommodate yourself, conform to the times! Wherever not . . . Then get moving, comrades, the audacious one resists! Up against the seducer, the slanderer and liar, the cowardly as well as malicious adversary of the sole true True, the sole beautiful Beautiful, the sole godly Godly, the sole holy Holy! Out with the traitor, that we may stone him!"

I ask every reasonable and fair person who knows how to place himself into a foreign situation with sufficient impartiality whether the represented disposition of the matter, the totality and the general context of the circumstances, would indeed allow the one to be punished to attain the deserved punishment justly in the general quiet way. An extraordinary legal procedure would necessarily have to occur here. And even this is usual enough; from time immemorial it has been the only agreeable one for the high chiefs and authorities. Never did they like to seek and perhaps not find their rights and their execution on the slow, slavish and mechanical path of instruction; but each time they construed it more boldly for themselves with a free hand, through war or stoning. The ordering of the proceedings of the exceptional legal procedure is called tactics. Knowledge and exact observation of them is of the greatest importance. So according to the latter, with a legal stoning such as the one just presented, the procedure must begin with a bad rumor, with an unclear, confused murmuring of transgressions, secret sins, hidden vices and dangerous intentions of the man who until that time had stood in such good repute; it must be rumored here and there that he is to be summoned, brought up for cross-examination; individual points of the presumed accusation must appear and be brought into circulation with suspicious doubts as to how this man, who has suddenly become so suspect, will possibly answer to this and that reproach. Then just some more ugly and confused murmuring about all of this, and it is enough. Because now suddenly an investigation is no longer necessary. With a wild outcry that only the Diana of the Ephesians is great, the tumult breaks out against the agitator. From whence the tumult, if not from him? Whatever rages and raves and slanders and shouts there, it is his raging and raving and slandering and shouting down. Quiet and peace and friendship would reign everywhere if only *He* did not exist. Away with the destroyer!

The comprehension of one's fate is an excellent means of resigning to it, and I have, as you see, known how to make mine completely clear to myself. Therefore it also cannot occur to me either to revile or to resist it. My dear Köppen, just between us, following my stoning I even feel much relieved. It rather depressed me each time and tormented me whenever I felt compelled to express myself publicly with regard to the doctrines of the school of the solely true True and present myself as their opponent. This school had continually shown me respect and affection, an affection which had to be all the more flattering as it was unique in its related tolerance of my assertions flatly oppositional to the basic doctrines of the school. One honor is still worth the other. There is, however, yet more to be considered which is more serious and decisive. Who would have the courage, even if strong reasons speak for it, readily awaken within, to return demonstrations of respect, of goodwill and trust, with insults which the insulted one now, because of those rebukes he gave loudly and publicly, were hindered from retaliating in accordance with the entire extent of his feeling and as quickly and strongly as his need required? It must be unbearable to every well meaning man to know himself at an advantage and his opponent at a disadvantage of this sort; his relationship must oppress him, inhibit him everywhere; he must wish to be rid of these bonds. I have now had such a release, and what makes my satisfaction complete is that Kant and Fichte have been simultaneously expelled and banished with me. We are brothers in one and the same crime, completely similar sinners and deserving of death. A variation in the execution is produced only incidentally because of secondary reasons.

It is exquisite to read, if one has overcome the admittedly rather sour toil of understanding and the dismay in spite of all patience and applied efforts at still not being able to understand several pages after another initially and even here and there thereafter—it is exquisite to read then how the three sinners are heard preliminarily in the introduction, summarily confronted and neutralized. They integrate and differentiate like the three dimensions of the body. The Kantian is "the objective dimension," the Jacobian "the subjective," and the Fichtean "the synthesis of both."[7]

Through us and in us the formerly scattered sins of the philosophical universe have joined together and become one substance; with one another and together through and in us they have gained "their perfection, their perfected expression." Seen in the daylight, the triune Kantian–Jacobian–Fichtean philosophy is "nothing but completed and idealized empirical psychology, Lockeanism, eudaemonism, enlightenment in its nakedness". But the three persons in that triune form among themselves, like so many different functions, "the totality of the possible forms for that principle." (p. 14, better yet p. 186.) The principle is imperfection itself. Imperfection on the objective side in the first person, imperfection on the subjective side in the second, and consistent imperfection of the synthesis of both in the third. These three imperfections together constitute a perfection of imperfection; with them the entire sphere of non-philosophy is described and closed.

The common principle of imperfection which presents itself in each of the above flaws, the basic principle of all non- and pseudo-philosophy in general, consists (pp. 12, 14, 16) "in the postulating of the absolute opposition of finiteness and infinity, reality and ideality, the material and immaterial, and of existing beyond the truly real and absolute." This postulating of existing beyond was done by the triune philosophy with a clear conscience at first, and for this reason the name faith was assumed by it. With this faith it expressly and obviously (p. 4) "recognized the non-existence of reason and postulated something better than it as a beyond outside of and above it." It hence remains for it (p. 16, also p. 4) "a reason submerged only in finiteness and renouncing observation and knowledge of the eternal." It knows how and is able to fill up the infinitely empty space of knowledge, which originates in it through the eternal left empty for knowing, with nothing but the subjectivity of longing and presentiment, since in its perennial inability, in its limitation, (p. 18) it "does not know how to elevate itself above the barrier into that in itself clear and unyearning area of reason." In this manner, it becomes a system in this ungodly philosophy which,

7. See pp. 14 and 17. These dimensions are also called sides: sides of eudaemonism, of the realism of finiteness, of artificial idealism, of false philosophy.

triune, (p. 18) "aims not at the knowledge of God, but only that of the human being, and sanctifies finiteness, since all true sanctification destroys, after all, precisely this finiteness—what otherwise was considered the death of philosophy: that reason should relinquish all claim to its existence in the absolute, exclude itself from it absolutely and only relate to it negatively; henceforth the highest point of philosophy, and the non-existence of the enlightenment, through the consciousness of the same, as the system."

That a philosophy which is the death of philosophy is brought to death and destroyed just in the nick of time by philosophy is in the strictest sense philosophically just. The triune inventors of even this death will not be able to have anything against it. They will rather, one can think them capable of it, rejoice in such a glorious and meritorious decline. Can the world not now be liberated from it once and for all since they have concluded the totality of error in themselves?[8] They die as redeemers of the human race. Their collective death is the most praiseworthy imaginable.

---

8. This is expressly promised in "Faith and Knowledge," p. 186. The passage is too remarkable not to appear here verbatim once again. The reader should not, however, become immediately impatient, since one already has to begin on the previous page (185): Mr. Hegel is so cohesive everywhere that it is impossible to take out something particular from him. Here, therefore, the whole passage:

> After in this manner, through the totality of the philosophies considered, the dogmatism of being has been recast into the dogmatism of thinking, the metaphysics of objectivity into the metaphysics of subjectivity, and thus through this entire revolution of philosophy the old dogmatism and metaphysics of reflection have at first glance merely taken on the hue of inwardness or the new and fashionable culture, the soul, as thing, transformed into ego as a practical reason in the absoluteness of the personality and the singularity of the subject; the world, however, as thing, transformed into the system of appearances, or of affectations of the subject and believed actualities; the absolute, however, as proper matter and absolute object of reason transformed into an absolute transcendence of rational perception; and this metaphysics of subjectivity, run through the complete cycle of its forms in the Kantian, Jacobian, and Fichtean philosophies, while other forms of it do not count even in this sphere; and thus that which is to be reckoned on the side of formative education, namely, the absolute postulating of the separate dimensions of totality and the elaborating of each of them to a system, completely presented and thereby concluded the formative process, so herein the outside possibility is given that the true philosophy arising out of this education and destroying the absoluteness of its limitations presents itself all at once as perfected appearance with all its richness subordinated to the totality. For just as the perfection of the fine arts depends upon the perfection of mechanical

But even this pride was not to be left to us. After we have been sufficiently divided with and through one another, multiplied, subtracted from one another, and again added up in one another, we find ourselves in the end, with the help of a symbol, suddenly transformed merely into "bats", "which (as is known) belong to neither the species of birds nor animals, to neither the earth nor the heavens." And the unhappy bats don't even have the benefit of a free flight, each its own way between day and dark, but they appear rather speared upon one another with "the stake of absolute opposition which they must carry immutably embedded in themselves". Thus speared together, the true bird who is at the same time a true animal (and insists upon this as the most interesting) holds them in its powerful claws, a double eagle with a name, identity of the finite and the infinite, the temporal and the eternal, of existence and non-existence. He hovers "in the absolute middle," grasps with one of his golden beaks the object, with the other, the subject; makes both indifferent in the swallowing and digests them in the infinity of his intestines, which consumes all finiteness and absolutely unrestricts the restricted, to the absolute Absolute. Yet basically and according to the true Truth, he consumes just as little as he emits; he remains eternally with an empty stomach and eternally satiated; what devours and is devoured there is absolutely the same in him. He is surely producing. But he produces only his doubleness, and because he is necessarily double, so in reality, he also does not produce it. Neither upwards nor downwards, neither on this side nor the other, do his two similarly crowned heads gaze out, but by virtue of their absolutely opposite directions, eternally only directly in front of themselves, doubly and singly simultaneously from the absolute

---

skill, so does the rich appearance of philosophy also depend upon the perfection of formative education; and this perfection has been achieved.

Hereupon there still follows in the conclusion (p. 188) that among the three of us (especially, however, Kant and Fichte, who are for that very reason "directly linked" to the true philosophy), we have re-established the speculative Good Friday, which was otherwise historical, in the whole truth and harshness of its godlessness, "out of which harshness alone the greatest totality can and will resurrect itself in its entire earnestness and from its deepest foundation, simultaneously all-encompassing, and in the most sublime freedom of its form because the serene, the more unfathomable and particular of dogmatic philosophy must disappear, just like that of natural religions."

center. It stretches out, however, first the one and then the other head, somewhat towards the front. Thereby all things (which are all things of absurdity, of finiteness) become the entire creation. The fodder is thus produced for the devourer, the devouring one for the fodder. And the infinitely double creature tells itself that there is no doubled one there: I am who I am Not, and will become who I will never be.

A voice resounds to the transformed ones, however, while the creature of all creatures, the sole double eagle, lets them fall from its claws into the abyss. The voice declares: You have made yourselves foul before the Eternal through your reason which is affected by sensuality, which is merely understanding, and therefore feels a contemptible need to postulate something better than it is as a hereafter in a faith outside of and above itself. Blindly you plunge into the ditch which understanding digs for all people, in that it first tempts it to eudaemonism, then to idolatry. You should have resisted it, destroyed it; this is the first step towards wisdom.[9] For understanding turns everything upside down, that is its nature: a God above and reason below. Inverted, it becomes heaven and the sole true God, a blissful enjoyment of eternal contemplation, the highest bliss constructed as idea. Because of that evil nature of understanding, making nonsense of the reasonable comes so easily to wicked people; for the purely reasonable, mirrored in under-

9. The Schellingian annihilation of understanding is a completed one. For just that reason, it elevates itself above "the incompletion of the Kantian annihilation of understanding" ("Faith and Knowledge," p. 70) and above every uncompleted philosophy. Because "the foremost of philosophy is to recognize the absolute Nothingness, which Fichtean philosophy fails to do to the same degree to which the Jacobian thereby abhors it" (ibid, p. 159). As punishment, both are therefore "in the Nothingness which is opposed to philosophy" (ibid.). The Schellingian philosophy now gains a decisive predominance. By means of the completed annihilation of understanding, the principle of contradiction loses its legislative power. Every case lost according to the principle of contradiction will be won through the appeal to reason. The true philosophy absolutely destroys "the either-or, which is a principle of all formal logic and understanding which abandons reason, in the absolute middle" (ibid., p. 160). If understanding now states: Making either sense or nonsense, one thing or not, there is no third: Reason answers thus: No, there is a third and no absolute contradiction. The true philosophers are everywhere no logicians because one has to begin with the annihilation of understanding; as long as an atom of it still remains, there thus remains a here and hereafter, an insoluble contradiction between the finite and the infinite, the temporal and the eternal; it remains dualism, a nature, and that stupid thing beyond nature, God.

standing, always represents itself as a ridiculous, often as a horrible caricature. One must shatter it, the blasphemous mirror on the threshold of the sanctuary.[10] You have now experienced it: an unknowable God beyond the boundary stakes of reason is a basic error and a basic absurdity; this God does not exist. In vain do you refer to him full of longing melancholy in a faith which, in itself unreasonable, is called reasonable by you because your reason, restricting itself to absolute opposition of the finite and infinite, recognized in it something higher above itself from which it excluded itself, and with this exclusion, posited its own emptiness and a firm incomprehensibility. Adorned with the superficial color of such a supersensual, or rather merely varnishing your absolute sensuality with it in one place or another, you stood there wretchedly with your reference to a higher being based on faith like painted pictures of saints, tears of vulgarity on the cheeks of your vulgar faces, the stupid eyes directed towards heaven and a melancholy Oh God! on your lips — impotent and too cowardly to elevate yourselves to the divinity itself elevated above longing and melancholy and the *solely true Truth* to make the identity of the finite and the infinite, the absolute center, your own property and eternal heritage. What finiteness is not capable of consuming is not the True. You considered the privation of the True and solely Essential as the True and Essential and complained that you were to be deprived of a privation. If you thereby strived for beauty, morality, understanding, and happiness, it was a vain effort! Since such beauty can never be without ugliness, such morality never without weakness and baseness, such understanding which occurs along with it not without platitude, good fortune and ill fortune, which play a part in it, the former cannot be without vulgarity, the latter without contemptuousness — therefore down with your threefold ugly, threefold vile, threefold trite, vulgar and contemptible; your nocturnal being is detested by the now dawning eternal day; its hostility towards you is identical to yours against it.[11]

10. An idea is, inasmuch as it is viewed from its negative side against imagination or reflection, for that reason idea because it can be transformed from imagination or reflection into an absurdity ("Faith and Knowledge," p. 80). This transformational process occurs by means of the apprehension of the reasonable through reflection and the transformation of this into something understandable, through which it becomes in itself an absurdity" (ibid., p. 101).

11. I have considered it unnecessary, in "The Speech to the Transformed," to add to every remark the page number where it can be found, since one will easily find them

But it doesn't stop at that. We are again called up and pulled from the stake to be more fully contrasted with one another once again, and even to be compared to the stake on which we are to have impaled ourselves upon each other. Yet the main point in the stake's purpose is not so much its comparison with us as with the true bird, which will not be impaled with it, but will devour and digest it before our eyes.

---

together in the short introduction amounting to not fully nineteen pages. It is better that I place before the reader's eyes in the following a portion of the common Hegelian context itself which contains a large portion of the remarks condensed above and, at the same time, gives a conspicuous example of the aesthetic powers of the author. Art, an artist, and a work of art enliven its enunciation with its contemplator in three symbols, and indeed from such an abundance of fantasy that the middle symbol, insufficient to itself, produces yet a second one within itself, the excellent one about the bats. He as much as eliminated some of the difficulties occurring in choices of word and thought even here in the above previously given conceptual content, and I think one now will be able to read everything with pleasure.

Since the fixed standpoint which the all-powerful epoch and its culture has established for philosophy is that of a reason affected by sensuality, philosophy therefore cannot aim at the knowledge of God, but only at what is called the knowledge of the human being. This so-called human being and the human race, taken as a fixed unsurpassable finiteness of reason, constitute philosophy's absolute standpoint; not as reflected splendor of eternal beauty, as spiritual focus of the universe, but as an absolute sensuality, which does, however, have the capacity of faith to touch itself up here and there with a spot of alien supersensuousness. As if art, reduced simply to portraiture, were to express its ideal aspect in depicting, in addition, a longing in the eye of an ordinary face and a melancholy smile on its mouth; while it was strictly forbidden to depict the gods exalted above longing and melancholy, as if the depiction of eternal images were only possible at the expense of humanity. Similarly, philosophy is not supposed to depict the Idea of the human being, but the abstract concept of an empirical human race mingled with limitation, and to carry the stake of the absolute antithesis immutably embedded in it; and during the time it gets clear about its restriction to the sensuous—either analyzing its own abstraction or entirely abandoning it in the fashion of the sentimental and *bel esprit*—philosophy is supposed to adorn itself with the surface color of the supersensuous while pointing, in faith, to something higher.

Truth, however, cannot be deceived by this sort of hallowing of finiteness, which remains what it was, for a true hallowing would have to nullify the finite. If an artist cannot give true truth to actuality by casting an ethereal light upon it and taking it wholly up therein, but is only able to depict actuality in and for itself—which is what is commonly called reality and truth, though it is neither the one nor the other—then he will take refuge in the pathetic remedy against actuality, the remedy of yearning and sentimentality, painting tears on the cheeks of the vulgar and bringing an "Oh God" to

Remember well some additional annotations about this second scene, in which, if I don't appear as the main character (because none of the three of us is it, we are equal), then I am principally meant and have by far the longest role, so that after I have made my appearance, I don't get to exit again, starting from page 63 to page 188. I have written this letter already beyond one week's postal date. I don't dare to continue it into the second, into two weeks.

Meanwhile, check into it if you have not already done so, and indeed most scrupulously and precisely, how examples of my and your false quoting presented in the essay on "Faith and Knowledge" are constituted. This reproach alone should not remain unanswered. If no printing errors have creeped in, then I know that he is irresponsible, and in each specific case, the deliberate chicanery can

---

their lips. Thus his figures will indeed look away beyond the actual situation toward heaven, but they will do so like bats that are neither bird nor beast, and belong neither to earth nor to sky. There can be no such beauty without ugliness, nor such morality without weakness and vileness, nor such intellect as here occurs without platitude; good fortune cannot exist without meanness, nor ill fortune without fear and cowardice, and neither without contemptuousness. In the same way, when philosophy, in its own fashion, takes up the finite and subjectivity as absolute truth in conceptual form, it cannot purify them by connecting subjectivity with an infinite. For this infinite is itself not the truth, since it is unable to consume finiteness. If, however, actuality and the temporal as such disappear within it, this is called cruel dissection which does not leave the human being whole, or violent abstraction which has no truth, and particularly no practical truth; and an abstraction of this kind is conceived of as the painful cutting off of an essential piece from the completeness of the whole. But the temporal and empirical, and privation, are thus recognized as an essential piece and an absolute In-itself. It is as if someone who sees only the feet of a work of art were to complain when the whole work is revealed to his sight that he was being deprived of his deprivation and that the incomplete had been in-completed. Finite knowledge is this sort of knowledge of a part and a singular; if the absolute were put together out of the finite and the infinite, then abstracting from the finite would indeed be a loss. In the Idea, however, the finite and infinite are one, and hence finiteness as such, insofar as it was supposed to have truth and reality in and of itself, has disappeared. But only that which was negation in it has been negated, and thus the true affirmation posited. The highest abstractum of this absolutized negation is the Ego-ness, just as the thing is the highest abstraction of the position. Each of them is only a negation of the other. Pure being like pure thinking—an absolute thing and absolute Ego-ness are, in the same manner, finiteness made into an absolute. Eudaemonism and Enlightenment stuff belong to the same level—not to mention other manifestations, just like the Kantian, Jacobian, and Fichtean philosophies, to which detailed confrontation with one another, we shall now proceed.

certainly be made apparent.[12] The work which I require from you is vexing but not difficult, since all my proofs are clear and decisive, and I have expressed nothing that I was not in a position to justify doubly and threefold through such totally complete proofs but Kantian doctrine. A totally peculiar coincidence of circumstances has made it possible for me, and could only make it possible for me, to arm the few sheets of my essay as they are armed. For nearly ten years I stood there, the only anti-Kantian of my kind, because compared with the other opponents of this school, I was myself a Kantian. My objections to the transcendental idealism in the discourses of David Hume and the specific discussion of that in the appendix which, ten years later, has so often been cited and emphatically praised, made no noticeable impression at the time of its appearance. It was the same with the treatises and additions composed in the same spirit in the new edition of the letters on the doctrine of Spinoza. Kantian philosophy gained more and more adherents and elevated itself to a virtually unlimited dominion. Under such conditions, there remained for me no other help against the quaking of distrust against me than to procure for myself a certainty elevated above all doubt, so that I see through not only the system, but also the conviction of the inventor and his disciples as to the truth and irrefutability of it. To this end, I have checked and calculated, in the strictest sense, the major Kantian works more than once, until I had placed myself, through perfect equations, into

12. In the supposedly false citation, which Mr. Hegel ("Faith and Knowledge," p. 121) quotes as the main example: "to which malicious distortions blind hatred against the destruction of temporal life and sacred zeal for the good cause of actual things propels;" Köppen, in his refutation, neglected the Schelling-Hegelian self-refutation. It concerns the assertion that the ideas about reason in the Kantian system have no reality. Mr. Hegel looked it up in Kant and found that we had maliciously distorted. We looked it up in Hegel and find the following declarations with him. "According to Kant, the highest idea does not, at the same time, have reality" (p. 4). "The Kantian philosophy hits upon ideas incidentally, which it soon enough drops as merely hollow thoughts" (p. 22). "The hollow unity as practical reason shall again become constitutive, bring forth from itself, and give itself a content: the idea of reason will, in the end, be again established as pure, but again destroyed and postulated as an absolute hereafter in the unreasonableness of faith, as something hollow for knowledge" (p. 42). "That reason as pure unity without contemplation is hollow, Kant recognizes completely and everywhere" (p. 42). "The Kantian dissolution of the dynamic antinomies is a complete trampling down of reason, about which the understanding has its jubilation while declaring itself as the absolute" (p. 47), etc.

such a certain possession of the main factors of the entire contents which produce all products, that I could now effortlessly calculate in the most varied ways and as often as I wished, the former out of the latter, and the latter out of the former, and into one another again. The essay in the Rheinholdian Contributions provides an extract of this work of many years; and nothing in the world can be more ridiculous than the screaming, slandering, rumbling and rapping, etc. etc., which the gentlemen Schelling and Hegel claim to have read in it. There is truly nothing to read there but the serene courage and tone of a man for whom his material is familiar, for whom it becomes a game with his treatment that he diversely turn, amplify, and represent it with ease. But just this diversity of turns of expression, this repeated exposing and dismembering, representation of a basic error which the Schelling system has in common with the Kantian, is the bitter and the bad, the screaming and the shouting, which the wicked essay in the Contributions does, and the "Kapucinade" in paperback is apparently maliciously inclined to spread even more among the people. If those reproaches had even only one basis, then thereby alone would everything already be decided against me; I would not have to be judged first; I would already be judged by myself. Because where truth is, there is peace; where there is no peace but rather mere turbulence, there is reliably no truth. I am pleased to assert this happily. I have sought the truth with the first thought to remain in my consciousness and later strove for it with all my thoughts; but just as then, at no subsequent time either, not out of a merely conceited desire just to adorn myself with it as with something discovered by me or what had first emerged from me. I needed a truth which would not be my creature, but whose creature I was. It was to give fullness to my emptiness, bring light to the night surrounding me, to let it dawn before me and within me as I found it promised within my interior. I proceeded from these promises, and was not indifferent with a view to what might come to my knowledge as long as it were knowledge everywhere. I may therefore not boast about that pure curiosity, which according to the opinions of the great men of this time is the only true spirit of philosophy, just like its each time merely deceptive satisfaction, displacing itself into infinity, is its total intention; but of this alone, that I have proven myself more distrustful of my own prejudices than of any others and everywhere more impartial in testing than the merely curious philosophers have proven. Is it asking too much of them if one wants to have them impartial? Completely uninterested with a view to the object, must not the subject make everything infinite to them, just as impartiality on that side makes complete and partiality, on the other, infinite? Perhaps, however, the newest discovery will bring about a difference here, since according to it, mere curiosity is no longer satisfied in a highly imperfect, merely temporal and transitory, for it indeed completely inadequate, impure manner as before; but in a perfect, absolutely eternal, and also for it totally adequate and completely pure manner, and so to speak, a true appeasing of it has finally occurred. Will not impartiality on the part of the object now be able to consume and destroy partiality on the side of the subject just as absolute infinity has already done with absolute finiteness?

It is indeed so; and that one need only correctly apply the newest discovery to find the right seat between the two chairs of the object and the subject in the absolute middle of an absolute indifference of both, a seat upon which one immediately resembles the fearless and hopeless gods and experiences the whole secret of their all-contentedness, indifference, frugality, inexpressible bliss, serenity, and majesty.

I wish that from all of these, sublimity and majesty alone would appear to me at first—just once! How sheer, mere curiosity could ever gain sublimity and majesty by means of a pure satisfaction created out of itself (however much one still had to admire art!) is incomprehensible to me.—The fable of the frog always occurs to me, and how much less likely must it be possible for a human being to inflate himself to a god.

Farewell! In the next week I hope to embark upon a second written flight to you.

August 16   Jacobi

Translated by Diana I. Behler

ANONYMOUS AUTHOR

The Oldest Systematic Program
of German Idealism

An ethics. Since all metaphysics will henceforth fall into *morals* — for which Kant, with both of his practical postulates has given only an *example* and *exhausted* nothing, so this ethics will contain nothing other than a complete system of all ideas, or what is the same, of all practical postulates. The first idea is naturally the conception *of my self* as an absolutely free being. Along with the free, self-conscious being an entire *world* emerges simultaneously — out of nothingness — the only true and conceivable *creation out of nothingness* — Here I will descend to the fields of physics; the question is this: How should a world be constituted for a moral being? I should like to give our physics, progressing laboriously with experiments, wings again.

So whenever philosophy provides the ideas, experience the data, we can finally obtain physics on the whole, which I expect of later epochs. It does not seem as if present-day physics could satisfy a creative spirit such as ours is or should be.

From nature I come to *man's works.* The idea of the human race first — I want to show that there is no idea of the *state* because the state is something *mechanical*, just as little as there is an idea of a *machine.*

Only that which is the object of *freedom* is called *idea*. We must therefore go beyond the state! — Because every state must treat free human beings like mechanical works; and it should not do that; therefore it should *cease*. You see for yourself that here all the ideas, that of eternal peace, etc., are merely *subordinate* ideas of a higher idea. At the same time I want to set forth the principles for a *history of the human race* here and expose the whole miserable human work of state, constitution, government, legislature—down to the skin. Finally the ideas of a moral world, deity, immortality—overthrow of everything ((superstition)) pseudo doctrines, persecution of the priesthood, which recently poses as reason, come through reason itself.—(The) absolute freedom of all spirits who carry the intellectual world within themselves, and may not seek either God or immortality *outside of themselves.*

Finally the idea which unites all, the idea of *beauty*, the word taken in the higher platonic sense. I am convinced that the highest act of reason, which, in that it comprises all ideas, is an aesthetic act, and that *truth and goodness* are united like sisters *only in beauty*—The philosopher must possess just as much aesthetic power as the poet. The people without aesthetic sense are our philosophers of the letter. The philosophy of the spirit is an aesthetic philosophy. One cannot be clever in anything, one cannot even reason cleverly in history—without aesthetic sense. It should now be revealed here what those people who do not understand ideas are actually lacking—and candidly enough admit that everything is obscure to them as soon as one goes beyond charts and indices.

Poetry thereby obtains a higher dignity; it becomes again in the end what it was in the beginning—*teacher* of (*history*) *the human race* because there is no longer any philosophy, any history; poetic art alone will outlive all the rest of the sciences and arts.

At the same time we so often hear that the great multitude should have a *sensual religion*. Not only the great multitude, but even philosophy needs it. Monotheism of reason and the heart, polytheism of the imagination and art, that is what we need!

First I will speak about an idea here, which as far as I know, has never occurred to anyone's mind—we must have a new mythology; this mythology must, however, stand in the service of ideas, it must become a mythology of *reason*.

Until we make ideas aesthetic, i.e., mythological, they hold no interest for the *people*, and conversely, before mythology is reasonable, the philosopher must be ashamed of it. Thus finally the enlightened and unenlightened must shake hands; mythology must become philosophical, and the people reasonable, and philosophy must become mythological in order to make philosophy sensual. Then external unity will reign among us. Never again the contemptuous glance, never the blind trembling of the people before its wise men and priests. Only then does *equal* development of *all* powers await us, of the individual as well as of all individuals. No power will be suppressed any longer, then general freedom and equality of spirits will reign—A higher spirit sent from heaven must establish this religion among us, it will be the last work of the human race.

Translated by Diana I. Behler

FRIEDRICH WILHELM JOSEPH SCHELLING

Ideas on a Philosophy of Nature as an Introduction to the Study of This Science

Second Edition, 1803

Introduction

What is philosophy? This question will not yield a ready answer. If reaching agreement on a definite concept of philosophy were so simple, we would need only to analyze this concept in order to find ourselves in full possession of a universally valid philosophy. But the issue is this: philosophy is not something that originally and naturally resides within spirit with no effort on the part of spirit. It is entirely a work of freedom. Philosophy is only what each person has made it for himself; for this reason the idea of philosophy is only the result of philosophy itself, which, as an infinite science, is also the science of itself.

Rather than presupposing an arbitrary concept of philosophy in general or of the philosophy of nature in particular in order to break it down into its parts, I will endeavor to let this concept *arise* before the eyes of the reader.

Yet since I must begin somewhere, I shall presume for the moment that a philosophy of nature *should* derive the possibility of a nature, i.e., of the whole world of experience, from principles. But I shall not treat this concept analytically or presume its correctness and draw conclusions from it; rather I shall first of all investigate whether reality can in any sense be attributed to it, and whether it gives expression to something that can be *put into effect.*

On the Problems to be Solved by a Philosophy of Nature

Whoever is occupied with the study of nature and the mere enjoyment of its riches will not ask whether nature and experience are possible. It is enough that nature exists for him; through the *deed* itself he has made it actual. Only the man who does not believe he holds actuality in his *hand* will ask what is possible. Entire ages have passed while nature was being studied, and still it has not become tiresome. A few individuals have spent their lives at this occupation, and they have not ceased to worship the veiled goddess either. Great spirits have lived in their own world, untroubled by the principles of their inventions—and of what measure is all the fame of the most keen-witted doubter against the life of a man who bore a world in his mind and all of nature in his imagination?

We owe it to *philosophy* that we can ask how a world outside ourselves, how nature and experience are possible, or rather, *with* this question philosophy arose. Prior to this man had lived in a (philosophically) natural state. At that time man was still at one with himself and with the world around him. This state still hovers in the dark memories of even the most misguided thinkers. Many never left this state and would have been content in themselves had not a disagreeable example led them astray; for nature releases no one freely from her tutelage, and no one is a son of freedom *from birth.* Indeed, how man ever left that state would be sheerly incomprehensible if we did not know that his spirit, whose element is *freedom* strives to make *itself* free. It must cast off the fetters of nature and its provision and entrust itself to the uncertain fate of its own strength in order to return one day as victor by its own merit to that state in which it spent the childhood of its reason in ignorance of itself.

As soon as man sets himself in opposition to the external world (how he does this will be discussed later), he takes the first step towards philosophy. For with this separation reflection first begins. Henceforth he separates what nature had forever united: object from intuition, concept from image, and finally, by becoming his own *object*, he separates himself from himself.

But this separation is only a *means*, not an *end*. For man's being lies in activity. The less he reflects upon himself, the more active he is; his purest activity ceases to know itself at all. As soon as he makes himself the object, the *whole* person no longer acts; he has annulled part of his activity in order to reflect on the rest of it. Man was not born to waste his spiritual force battling against the phantasms of an imagined world, but rather to exercise all his forces over against a world that has influence on him, that lets him feel its power, and upon which he can reciprocally act. Thus no gulf may be fixed between him and the world; contact and interaction must be possible between them, for only then will man become human. Originally there is an absolute equilibrium of forces and consciousness in man. But through freedom he can annul this equilibrium in order to reestablish it through freedom. However health lies only in the equilibrium of forces.

Thus *mere* reflection is a mental disorder in man, and when it takes control of the whole person it kills the seed of his higher existence and the root of his spiritual life, which proceeds only from identity. Reflection is an evil that accompanies man throughout his life and destroys all his intuition, even for the baser objects of contemplation. Reflection not only rends assunder the world of appearances, but by separating the spiritual principle from this world it fills the intellectual world with chimeras against which no battle can be done, since they lie beyond all reason. Reflection makes the separation between man and the world permanent by viewing the latter as a thing-in-itself, attainable neither by intuition nor imagination, neither by understanding nor reason.

Opposite reflection stands true philosophy, which views reflection simply as a means. Philosophy *must* presuppose that original separation, because without it there would be no need to philosophize.

For this reason philosophy assigns reflection only a *negative* value. It takes that original separation as a point of departure in order to reunite through *freedom* what was originally and *necessarily* united in the human spirit, i.e., in order to annul that separation forever. And insofar as philosophy itself was made necessary by that separation, was itself only a necessary evil, a corrective of reason gone astray, it works in this sense towards its own annihlation. That philosopher who would spend all or part of his life following reflective philosophy into its endless divisions in order to annul it in its last ramifications would, with this accomplishment (which should be respected as highly as any other, even if it serves only to negate) have gained a place of highest honor for himself, even if he were denied the pleasure of seeing philosophy in its absolute form revive from reflection's rending it asunder. The most simple expression of a complicated problem is always the best. Whoever first noticed that he could distinguish between himself and external things, and thus between his representations and objects, and vice versa, this person was the first philosopher. He first interrupted the mechanism of his thinking and annulled the equilibrium of his consciousness in which subject and object are most intimately united.

When I represent an object, the object and the representation are one and the same. And it is only this inability to separate the object from the representation while one is representing it that convinces common understanding of the reality of external things, which in fact make themselves known to it only through representations.

The philosopher annuls the identity of object and representation by asking: how do representations of external things arise in us? With this question we transfer the things *outside* ourselves, we presume them to be independent of our representations. Yet there is supposed to be a connection between them and our representations. We know of no other *real* connection between *different* things than that of *cause* and *effect*. Thus philosophy first attempts to establish a relationship of cause and effect between object and representation.

But now we have explicitly posited things *independent of us*. We feel *ourselves*, on the other hand, to be dependent upon these objects. For our representation is *real* only to the extent that we are constrained to assume concordance between it and things. Therefore we cannot make things the effects of our representations. We have no choice but to make representations dependent on things, viewing the latter as causes, the former as effects.

But we can immediately see that with this attempt we have not achieved what we wanted to. We wanted to explain how it was that object and representation are inseparably united in us. For only in this unity lies the reality of our knowledge of external things. And it is precisely this reality that the philosopher is to demonstrate. But if things are the *causes* of representations, then they *precede* representations. And with that, the separation between them becomes permanent. But our desire was that after we had separated object and representation through freedom we would reunite them both through freedom; we wanted to know that *originally* there is no separation between them, and why this is so.

Furthermore, we know things only in and through our representations. We have no concept of what they are insofar as they precede our representations and thus are not represented.

Furthermore, by asking how it is that I represent, I raise myself *above* the representation; I become, *with* this question, a being that feels originally *free* as it views all representing, seeing the faculty of representation itself and the whole connection of its representations *beneath* it. With this question I become a being that has *being in itself* independent of external things.

Thus with this question I step outside the sequence of my representations, I dissociate myself from the connection with things, I attain a position where no external power can reach me. Only now do the two hostile essences, *spirit* and *matter*, part. I transfer each of them to two different worlds, between which no connection is possible. By stepping out of the sequence of my representations even *cause* and *effect* become concepts that I see beneath me. For both arise only in the necessary succession of my representations, from which I have dissociated myself. How can I submit again to these concepts and allow things outside myself to influence me?[1]

Or let's try it the other way around: allow external things to influence us and then explain how, in spite of this, we come to ask how representations are possible in us?

In fact it is utterly incomprehensible how things can act on *me* (a free being). I comprehend only how things act on things. But insofar as I am *free* (and this I *am* when I raise myself above the connection of things and ask how this connection itself became possible), I am not a *thing*, not an *object*. I live in my own world, a being existing not for other beings, but *for itself*. Deed and action alone can be in me, effects alone can *proceed* from me. There can be no

---

1. This was the objection given right from the start by several clever Kantian philosophers. This philosophy allows all concepts of cause and effect to arise only in our mind, in our representations, and yet the representations, in turn, are *effected* by external things according to the law of causality. No one wanted to hear this then; but one will have to hear it now.

passivity in me, for passivity exists only where there is effect and counter-effect, and these exist only within the connection of things, above which I have raised myself. This is the case except if I am a *thing* which itself is caught up in the sequence of causes and effects; except if I, together with the whole system of my representations, am a mere result of the manifold influences that come to me from outside; in short, except if I myself am a mere product of a mechanism. But whatever being is caught up in a mechanism cannot step outside it and ask how all this is possible. *Here* in the midst of the sequence of appearances absolute necessity shows it its place. If it leaves this place it no longer is this being, and it is incomprehensible how any external cause could still influence this autonomous being that is whole and perfect in itself.

Thus one must be *capable* of asking this question with which all philosophy begins in order to be able to philosophize. This is not one of those questions that one can repeat after others with no effort on one's own part. It is a freely produced, self-assigned problem. *That* I am able to raise this question is proof enough that as such I am independent of external things, for otherwise how could I have asked how these things themselves are possible *for me* in my faculty of representation? One should think, then, that whoever raises this question would immediately cease to explain his representations in terms of the influence of external objects. But this question fell among people who were completely incapable of addressing it to themselves. In their mouths it acquired another meaning, or rather it lost all sense and meaning. *They* are beings who know nothing more of themselves than to what extent the laws of cause and effect hold complete sway over them. By posing this question *I* have raised myself above these laws. *They* are caught up in the mechanism of their thought and representations; *I* have broken through this mechanism. How should they understand me?

Whoever is nothing more for himself than what things and circumstances have made of him; whoever, having no control over his own representations, is caught and swept away by the current of causes and effects, how should he know where he comes from, where he is going, and how he has become what he is? Does the wave that sweeps him away in the current know this? He does not even have the right to say that he is the result of the combined effects of external things; for in order to be able to say this he must presume that he knows *himself*, that he is something *for himself*. But he is not. He exists only for other rational beings, not for himself; he is a mere *object* in the world, and it is in his own and science's best interest that he never hear or imagine it to be otherwise.

The most everyday sort of people have ever refuted the greatest philosophers with things that were comprehensible even to children. One hears, reads, and wonders that such great men were unaware of such common things and that such recognizably insignificant people could master them. No one considers that perhaps these men knew all that, too, for how else could they have swum against the current of evidence? Many are convinced that if Plato could only read Locke, he would walk away abashed; some believe that even Leibnitz, if he were resurrected from the dead to be schooled by Locke for an hour, would be converted; and how many children have not struck up their songs of triumph over Spinoza's grave?

What was it, you ask, that drove these men to abandon the manner of representation common to their age and to invent systems opposed to everything the great masses had always believed and fancied? With one free bound they were raised into a sphere where *you*, too, no longer understand their task, even as much became incomprehensible to them that seems most simple and comprehensible to you.

It was impossible for them to associate or establish contact between those things that nature and mechanism have forever united in you. They were equally incapable of denying that there was a world outside them or a spirit within them, and yet there seemed to be no possible connection between the two. But when you consider this problem, you do not care that you transform the world into a play of concepts or the spirit within you into a lifeless mirror of things.

For a long time the human spirit (still youthfully strong and fresh from the gods) had lost itself in mythologies and poems about the origins of the world; religions of entire peoples were based on that battle between spirit and matter before a fortunate genius—the first philosopher—found those concepts with which all generations after him grasped and held fast the two extremities of our knowledge. The greatest thinkers of antiquity did not dare to go beyond this opposition. Plato still set matter in opposition to God. The *first* man to see spirit and matter with full consciousness as one, and thought and extension simply as modifications of this same principle, was *Spinoza*. His system was the first bold sketch of a creative imagination that grasped the finite immediately in the idea of the infinite, purely as such, and found the former only in the latter. *Leibnitz* came and took the opposite path. The time has come when we can reinstitute his philosophy. His spirit despised the fetters of a school; no wonder that he lived on among us in so few kindred spirits and became a stranger long ago among the rest. He belonged to the few who also treat science as a free work. He had within him the universal *spirit of the world*, which reveals itself in the most diverse forms, giving forth life wherever it goes. Hence it is doubly insufferable that we purport to have found the right concepts for his philosophy only now, and that the Kantian School forces its fabrications upon him, putting words into his mouth that constitute the exact oppposite of his teachings. Leibnitz could not have been further from that speculative phantasm of a world of *things*-in-themselves that cannot be known or intuited by any spirit, but that nevertheless acts on us and produces all our representations. His first assumption was that " . . . the representations of external things arose in the soul by virtue of its own laws, *as if in a separate world*, as if nothing but God (the infinite) and the soul (the intuition of the infinite) were present." In his last writings he still maintained the absolute impossibility of an external cause acting on the interior of a spirit; accordingly, he also maintained that all changes, all alterations of perceptions and representations within a spirit could proceed only from an inner principle. When Leibnitz said this he was speaking to philosophers. Today people have forced their way into philosophy who have sense for everything else but this. Thus when someone among us says that no representation can arise in us through external influence, there is no end to the amazement. Now it is valid in philosophy to believe that the monads have windows through which things climb in and out.[2]

It is certainly possible to drive even the most decisive proponent of things-in-themselves as the effecters of representations quite into a corner with all kinds of questions. One can say to him, I understand how matter acts on matter but not how one in-itself acts on another, since in the realm of the intelligible there can be no cause and effect, nor how this law can be extended from one world into such a different—indeed an opposite—world. You would have to admit that if I am dependent on external impressions, then I am no

2. Leibnitz's *Princip. Philosoph.* §7.

more than matter, a sort of lens in which the lightbeam of the world refracts. But the lens does not see by itself; it is only a means in the hand of a rational being. And what is that within me which judges there to have been an impression made upon me? Again it is I myself who, insofar as I judge, am active, not passive; thus there is something within me that feels free from impressions and yet is aware of them, apprehends them, and raises them to consciousness.

Furthermore, while one is intuiting no doubt arises as to the reality of the external intuition. But then the understanding enters and proceeds to divide, and divides into infinity. If matter outside you is actual, then it must *consist* of infinitely many parts. If it does consist of infinitely many parts, then it must be assembled from these parts. But our imagination has only a finite measure for this assembling. Thus infinite assembling must occur in finite time. Or the assembling began somewhere, i.e., there are final particles of matter, and I must come upon these final particles in the process of dividing. But in fact I only find more and more of the same kinds of bodies and never get further than the surface. The real seems to flee from me or to slip out from under my hand, and matter, that first foundation of all experience, becomes the most insubstantial thing we know.

Or does this controversy perhaps exist only in order to enlighten us as to our own selves? Is intuition perhaps only a dream that deludes all rational beings with reality, and has understanding been given to them only in order to awaken them from time to time, to remind them of what they are, so that their existence be divided between sleeping and waking (for it is clear enough that we are intermediate beings)? But I do not comprehend an original dream of this sort. For then all dreams are shadows of actuality, "memories from a bygone world." If one wanted to assume that a higher being effected these shadowy images of actuality within us, then here, too, the question of the real possibility of the concept of such a relationship would return (since in this region I know of nothing that occurs according to cause and effect). And since this being produces what it imparts to me out of itself, then assuming—as is necessary—that it could not have a transitive effect on me, the only possibility would be that I receive these shadowy images merely as limitations or modifications of its absolute productivity, i.e., through production again and again within these limits.

Matter is not insubstantial, you say, because it possesses original *forces* that cannot be destroyed through division. "Matter has forces": I know that this expression is very common. But how? "Matter has": here matter is assumed to be something that exists for itself and independently of its forces. Then these forces would be only accidental to it? Because matter exists *outside you*, it must owe its forces to an external cause. Are they implanted in it by a higher hand, as some Newtonians say? But you have no concept of influences through which forces are *implanted*. You only know how matter acts, i.e., as force against force; how something that originally is not a *force* could be acted upon, we cannot comprehend at all. One can make such a statement, it can be passed from one mouth to another, but it has never actually gotten into anyone's head because no human mind is able to think such a thing. Thus you cannot think of matter without force.

Furthermore, these forces are forces of attraction and repulsion. "Attraction and repulsion": do these occur in empty space, do not they themselves require filled space, i.e., matter? Thus you must admit that neither forces without matter nor matter without forces is representable. But matter is the last substratum of your knowledge, beyond which you cannot proceed; and since you cannot explain these forces in terms of matter, you cannot explain them empirically, i.e., as something *outside yourselves*, which you would have to do according to your system.

Nevertheless, in philosophy the question is raised as to how matter *is possible* outside ourselves, thus also how these forces are possible outside ourselves. One can renounce all philosophizing (would to God that those who were inept here would fancy doing just that), but if you do wish to philosophize, this question cannot be dismissed. Yet you cannot make at all intelligible what a force independent of yourselves might be. For force makes itself known only to your *feeling*. But feeling alone gives you no objective concepts. Yet you make objective use of these forces. For you explain the motion of the heavenly bodies—the law of gravity—with the forces of attraction, and purport to have an absolute principle for these appearances with this explanation. In your system, however, the force of attraction counts for nothing more or less than a *physical* cause. Since matter exists independently outside you, you can know only through experience which forces are attributable to it. But as the ground of a physical explanation, the force of attraction is nothing more or less than an obscure quality. But let us first see if empirical principles are at all sufficient to explain the possibility of a system of the world. The question negates itself, for the most we know from experience is that a universe exists; with this statement the limits of our experience are given. Or rather, that a universe exists is itself only an *idea*. So much the less, then, can the universal equilibrium of world forces be something that you obtained from experience. You cannot derive this idea, if it is always to be an idea, from experience for a single system. And the idea is projected onto the whole only by means of analogical inferences. But such inferences yield only probability, while ideas such as universal gravity must be true in themselves, thus must be products of something or be based on something that is itself absolute and not dependent on experience.

Thus you must concede that this idea extends into a region higher than mere natural science. Newton, who never abandoned himself wholly to natural science, and who himself inquired into the *effective cause of attraction*, saw all too clearly that he was standing at the limits of nature, that here two worlds parted. Rarely have great spirits lived at the same time without working towards the same purpose from completely different angles. Whereas Leibnitz based the system of the spiritual world on a preestablished harmony, Newton found in the equilibrium of world forces the system of a material world. But if there is unity in the system of our knowledge, and if we will ever succeed in uniting even its greatest extremes, then we must hope that even here, where Leibnitz and Newton parted ways, a comprehensive spirit will one day find the center around which the *universe of our knowledge* (those two worlds between which our knowledge is now divided) moves, and Leibnitz's preestablished harmony and Newton's gravitational system will appear as one and the same, or as different aspects of one and the same knowledge.

I shall go further. Crude matter, i.e., matter insofar as it is conceived as simply filling space, is only the solid ground and foundation upon which the framework of nature is first constructed. Matter is supposed to be something real. What is real can be perceived only through sensation. How is sensation possible in me? To say, as you do, that I am acted on from the outside is not sufficient. There must be something within me that has *sensations*, and between this something and what you presume to be outside me no contact is possible. Or if what is external acts on me as matter acts on matter, then I can have a reciprocal effect only on what is external (for instance with a repulsive force), but not *on myself*. And yet this is supposed to occur; for I am supposed to have *sensations* and to raise them into my consciousness.

What your sensations perceive of matter you call its *quality*, and only insofar as it has a determined *quality* do you call it *real*. It is *necessary* that matter has quality *as such*, but to you it appears *accidental* that matter has a *determined* quality. If this is so, then matter cannot have one and the same quality, but there must be a manifold of *qualities*, all of which you know through mere sensation. Now what is it that effects sensation? "Something *inward*, an inner quality of matter." But these are words, not things. For where is this inner quality of matter? You may divide into infinity and still you will get no further than the surface of the body. All this was evident to you long ago. For this reason you have long since declared that whatever is perceived merely by sensation has its ground merely in your sensation. Yet this is only the least of the matter. For to say that nothing should exist outside you that is sweet or sour in itself, does not make the sensation any more comprehensible. For you always assume a real *cause* outside yourselves that effects this sensation within you. Supposing we were to grant you an external influence; what, then, would colors, odors, etc., or the causes of these sensations have in common with your spirit? Indeed, with great acumen you examine how the light reflecting off bodies acts on your optic nerves, and, too, how the image, inverted on the retina, appears upright, not inverted, in your soul. But what is it within you that looks at this image on the retina again and investigates how it could have entered the soul? Obviously something that to this extent is completely independent of the external impression, and yet to which the impression is not unknown. How did the impression get to *this* region of your soul where you feel entirely free and independent of impressions? You can insert as many intermediate members as you like between the affection of your nerves, your brain, etc., and the representation of an external thing. Yet you deceive only yourselves; for according to your own representations the transition from body to soul cannot be continuous, but must be made in a leap, which you purport to wish to avoid.

Furthermore, one mass acts on another sheerly by means of its motion (through inpenetrability): this is called its impact or *mechanical* motion.

Or matter acts on matter without the condition of previously acquired motion, so that motion proceeds from rest: this through attraction, which you call *gravity*.

You think of matter as *inert*, i.e., as something that does not move through self-activation, but can be moved only through an external cause.

Furthermore, you equate gravity, which you ascribe to bodies, with the quantity of matter as its specific weight (without considering its volume).

But now you find that one body can impart motion to another without being moved itself, i.e., *without* acting on it through *impact*.

You recognize, furthermore, that two bodies can mutually attract each other completely independent of the relation of their masses, i.e., *independent* of the laws of *gravity*.

You thus assume that the ground of this attraction could be sought neither in gravity nor on the surface of a body moved in this manner, but that the ground must lie within, dependent upon the *quality* of the body. But you have never explained what you mean by "*within* the body." Furthermore, it has been proven that quality pertains only to your sensation. But here the issue is not your sensation but an objective fact occurring outside yourselves that you apprehend with your senses and that your understanding wants to translate into intelligible concepts. Suppose we concede that quality is something whose ground lies not merely in your sensation but also in the body outside yourselves. What does it mean to say that one body attracts another by its qualities? For what is *real* in this attraction, i.e., what you are able to intuit, is merely—the body's motion. Motion, however, is a purely mathematical quantity that can be determined purely phoronomically. How is this external motion related to an inner quality? You borrow pictorial expressions such as kinship from the sphere of living beings, but you would be at a loss to transform this image into an intelligible concept. Furthermore, you pile elements upon elements, but these are nothing more than so many asylums for your ignorance. What do you think they are? Not matter itself, carbon, for instance, but something contained within this matter which, as if hidden, first imparts these qualities to matter. But where is this element in the body? Have you ever found it through division or analysis? You still have not been able to give a sensorial description of even one of these substances. Suppose we concede their existence—what is won? Has the quality of matter been explained? I conclude that either the quality the elements impart to bodies is attributed to the elements themselves, or it is not. In the first case nothing is explained, because precisely this was the question: how do qualities arise? In the second case again nothing is explained, for how one body (mechanically) strikes another and thus can impart motion to it, this I can understand; but how a body completely stripped of qualities can impart qualities to another body, this no one understands, and no one will ever make it intelligible. For you still have not been able to offer any objective concept of quality, although you make objective use of it (at least in chemistry).

These are the elements of our empirical knowledge. For if we may presuppose matter and its forces of attraction and repulsion, also an infinite manifold of matter, all distinguished by different qualities, then, according to the table of categories, we have the following:

1. *quantitative* motion, which is proportional to the quantity of matter alone: *gravity*;
2. *qualitative* motion, which corresponds to the inner qualities of matter: *chemical* motion;
3. *relative* motion, which is imparted to bodies by an external influence (impact): *mechanical* motion.

The entire system of the study of nature can arise and become from these three possible kinds of motion.

The division of physics which deals with the *first* is called *statics*; the one dealing with the *third* is called *mechanics*. The latter is the main division of physics, for basically the whole of physics is nothing but applied mechanics.[3] The division which deals with the *second* kind of motion serves only auxiliarily in physics: *chemistry*,

---

3. Mechanics can at once include the general properties of bodies, such as elasticity, hardness, and density, insofar as they influence *mechanical* motion. However the *general* study of motion is not part of the empirical study of nature. I believe that by this division physics is given a far simpler and more natural coherence than in most textbooks to date.

whose proper object is to derive the specific differences in matter, is the science which first provides mechanics (in itself a completely formal science) with content and diverse applications. It costs little effort to derive the primary objects of physics' investigations (with regard to their mechanical and dynamic motion) from the principles for chemistry. For example, one can say that in order for chemical attraction between bodies to occur, a material that extends them and counteracts their inertia—light and heat—is required, as are materials that mutually attract each other, as is *one* element that attracts all others in order that greatest simplicity be possible. And since nature itself requires many chemical processes for its continuation, these conditions for chemical processes must be present everywhere: hence vital air, as a product of light and this element. And because this air encourages the power of fire all too much and exhausts the strength of our organs too greatly, it is mixed with an opposite kind of air: hence atmospheric air, etc.

This is more or less the way the study of nature comes to completion. But it is not our task here to portray such a system, once it exists, but rather to find how such a system could exist at all. The question is not whether or how this connection of appearances and the sequence of causes and effects (that we call the course of nature) has become actual *outside us*, but *for us*. The question is how this system and this connection of appearances have found their way to our spirit, and how they have acquired in our faculty of representation the necessity with which we are plainly constrained to think of them. For we presuppose as an undeniable fact that the representation of a succession of causes and effects outside ourselves is as necessary for our spirit as if it belonged to our spirit's being and essence. To explain this necessity is a (the) primary problem of all philosophy. The question is not whether this problem should exist in the first place, but rather how this problem, once it exists, should be solved.

First, what does it mean that we must conceive of a succession of appearances that is plainly *necessary*? Obviously this: these appearances can follow each other only in a *determined succession*, and conversely, this succession can continue only with these *determined* appearances.

That our representations follow each other in this determined order, that, for instance, lightning precedes thunder and does not follow it, of such things we do not seek the ground *in ourselves*.

How we allow the representations to succeed each other is not up to *us*. The ground must lie in the *things*, and we maintain that this determined succession is a succession of the *things themselves*, not merely of our representations of them. Only insofar as the appearances *themselves* follow each other in this and no other manner, are *we* constrained to represent them in this order; only because and insofar as this succession is *objectively* necessary is it also *subjectively* necessary.

From this we see that this determined succession cannot be separated from these determined appearances; the succession must become and arise simultaneously with the appearances, and, conversely, the appearances with the succession. Thus succession and appearance are in a reciprocal relationship with each other, each is mutually necessary in relation to the other.

We may analyze only the most common judgments that we constantly make with regard to the connection between all appearances in order to find that these presuppositions are contained in all of them.

Now if neither the appearances can be separated from their succession, nor, conversely, the succession from its appearances, then only the following two cases are possible:

Either succession and appearances both arise simultaneously and unseparated *outside* us;

Or succession and appearances both arise simultaneously and unseparated *within* us.

Only in these two cases is the succession that we represent to ourselves an actual succession of things and not merely an ideal succession of our representations.

The first assertion is held by common human understanding, and even the sceptical philosophies of Reid, Beattie, and Hume have thoroughly opposed it. In this system the things-in-themselves succeed one another, and we are mere observers; but how the representation of this succession has entered us is a question that lies far beyond this system. Now we do not wish to know how the succession is possible outside us, but how this determined succession, since it proceeds independent of us, is represented by us *as such*, and to this extent with absolute necessity. This system takes no heed of this question. It is therefore unfit for any philosophical critique. It has not a single point in common with philosophy from which one could investigate, test, or refute it, for it does not even know of the question which philosophy has truly been given to solve.

We would first have to make this system philosophical before we could even test it. But then we run the risk of fighting against a mere fabrication, for common understanding is not all that consistent, and a system as consistent as common understanding's would be has in fact never existed in any human mind. For as soon as we attempt to render it in philosophical terms, it becomes completely unintelligible. It speaks of a succession that is supposed to occur *independent* of me, *outside me.* How a succession (of representations) occurs *within me,* this I understand; but a succession that proceeds in the things themselves, independent of finite representations, is completely unintelligible to me. For if we posit a being that is not finite, i.e., not bound to the succession of representations, but rather embraces all of the present and the future in one intuition, then for a being of this sort there would be no succession in the things outside it, for there is succession only under the condition of the finitude of the faculty of representation. But if the succession were also based in the things-in-themselves independent of all representations, then there would have to be a succession for a being of the sort we assumed above, which is a contradiction.

For this reason all philosophers up till now have unanimously maintained that succession cannot be thought of independent of the representations of a finite spirit. But we have established that if the representation of a succession is necessary, then it must arise simultaneously with the things and vice versa; succession must be as little possible without things as the things without succession. If, then, succession is something that is possible only in our representations, we have a choice between two options:

Either we continue to maintain that things exist outside us independent of our representations — with this we declare the objective necessity with which we imagine a determined succession of *things* to be a mere deception, in that we deny that the succession occurs in the things themselves.

Or we decide to assert that even the appearances themselves become and arise simultaneously with the succession only in our representations, and that only to this extent is the order they follow a truly objective order.

The first assertion obviously leads to the most outlandish system that has ever existed, and which even a few in our time have upheld, although they themselves were not aware of this. *Here* is the place to completely annihilate the principle that things act on us from the outside. Suppose we should ask what the external things were independent of these representations? First we must strip them of everything belonging to the idiosyncracies of our faculty of representation. This includes not only succession, but also every concept of cause and effect. And if we want to be consistent it also includes the representation of space and extension, both of which are unrepresentable without time, from which we have removed the things-in-themselves. Nevertheless, these things-in-themselves, although completely inaccessible to our intuitive faculty, are still actually present—we do not know how or where—probably in some Epicurean *intermundium*; and these things must *act* on me and give rise to my representations. Granted, no one has ever been willing to discuss which representation one would truly make oneself of such things. To say they cannot be represented amounts to an evasion that is easily cut short. If someone talks about something, he must have a representation of it, or else he is not speaking as he should. One has a representation even of nothing; one can at least think of it as absolute emptiness, as something purely formal, etc. One might think that the representation of the thing-in-itself would be a similar representation. However, the representation of nothing can still be sensualized through the schema of empty space. The things-in-themselves, however, are expressedly removed from time and space, since the latter belong only to that manner of representing peculiar to finite beings. Thus all that is left is a representation that hovers midway between something and nothing, i.e., that does not even have the credit of being absolutely nothing. It is indeed incredible that such a preposterous composite of things that, robbed of all sensual determinations, but still having to act as sensual things, has ever entered the human mind.[4] Indeed, if one has already annulled all of what belongs to the representations of an objective world, what remains that I could understand? Obviously only *myself*. Thus all representations of the external world would have to be developed out of *myself*. For if succession, cause, effect, etc., are first attributed to things in my faculty of representation, then one

---

4. The truth is that the idea of the things-in-themselves had come to Kant through tradition, but as it had been handed down, it has lost all meaning.

comprehends neither what these concepts could be without the things, nor the things without these concepts. Hence the outlandish explanation of the origin of the representations that this system is constrained to give. A mind is posited opposite the things-in-themselves, and this mind contains within itself certain forms *a priori* that are superior to the things-in-themselves only insofar as they, at least, can be represented as absolutely empty. Things are apprehended in these forms when we represent them to ourselves. Thereby the formless object receives shape, the empty forms content. But as to how it comes about that things are represented at all, here we find profound silence. It is sufficient that we represent things outside us to ourselves and that we first project time and space, as well as the concepts of substance and accident, cause and effect, etc., onto them in our faculty of representation; thus the succession of our representations arises in us, indeed, a necessary succession, and this self-made succession, first produced with consciousness, is called the course of nature.

This system hardly needs refutation. To portray it is to topple it to the ground. Far superior to this, indeed, incomparably so, is *Hume*'s scepticism. Hume (remaining faithful to his principles) leaves the question of whether things outside us correspond to our representations completely undecided. He must assume in any case that the *succession* of appearances occurs only in our representations; but that we consider precisely this determined succession to be *necessary*, he declares is a mere deception. Yet we can rightly require of Hume that he at least explain the origin of this *deception*. For he cannot deny that we actually think of the succession of cause and effect as necessary, and that upon this rest all our empirical sciences, natural science, and history (of which Hume himself was such a great master). Whence this deception? Hume replies: "Out of habit: *since appearances have always succeeded one another in this order*, the imagination acquired the habit of expecting the same order in the future, and finally this expectation has become *a second nature* to us, as does every longstanding habit." But this explanation is circular. For he was supposed to explain *why things have always succeeded one another in this order* (*that* this is so Hume does not deny). Was this succession perhaps in the things outside us? But outside our representations there is no succession. Or if it was merely the succession of our representations, then there must also be a ground for the constancy of this succession. What exists independent of me I cannot explain; but the ground for what occurs only *inside me* must also be able to be found inside me. Hume can say this is the way it is, and that is enough for me. But that is not called philosophizing. I do not say that a *Hume should* philosophize, but when someone *purports* to philosophize, then the question, "Why?" can no longer be dismissed.

We have no choice but to attempt to derive the necessity of a succession of representations from the *nature* of our spirit, i.e., of the finite spirit as such, and to let the things themselves arise in the spirit simultaneously with the succession, so that this succession is truly *objective*.

Of all previous systems I know of only two, Spinoza's and Leibnitz's, which not only make this attempt, but whose whole philosophy consists in nothing other than this attempt. Since there is still much doubting and discussion concerning the relationship between these two systems — whether they contradict each other, or how they are connected — it would seem useful to submit some preliminary remarks on this topic.

Spinoza, as it appears, was troubled very early on by the connection between our ideas and the things outside us; he could not bear the separation that had been established between them. He recognized that the ideal and the real (thought and object) are most intimately united in our nature. He could explain that we have representations of things outside us and that our representations themselves extend *beyond* them, only on the basis of our *ideal nature*; but that actual *things* correspond to these representations, he had to explain on the basis of *affections* and *determinations* of the ideal within us. We could not become conscious of the real except as the opposite of the ideal, and of the ideal only as the opposite of the real. Consequently, no separation could occur between actual things and our representations. Concept and object, thought and extension thus were one and the same, both merely modifications of one and the same ideal nature.

But instead of descending into the depths of his self-consciousness and observing from that point the emergence of two worlds within us — the ideal and the real — he passed over himself; instead of explaining on the basis of our nature how the finite and the infinite, originally united within us, proceed reciprocally from each other, he immediately lost himself in the idea of an infinity outside us. In this infinity affections and modifications arose, or rather originally were — whence one did not know — and with these an endless series of finite things. For because there was no transition from the infinite to the finite in his system, the beginning of *becoming* was as incomprehensible to him as the beginning of *being*. But that this endless succession is represented by me and is *necessarily* represented, resulted from the things and my representations being originally one and the same. I myself was only a thought of the infinite, or rather was myself but a constant succession of representations. But how I myself became conscious of this succession, Spinoza could not make intelligible.

For as he penned it, Spinoza's system is the most unintelligible that has ever existed. One must have taken this system into oneself, have placed oneself at the locus of his infinite substance in order to know that the infinite and the finite do not *arise* but rather *exist* originally unseparated and simultaneously — not *outside us* but rather — *within us*; and that precisely upon this original unity the nature of our spirit and our entire spiritual existence rests. For we know only our own being immediately, and we are intelligible only to ourselves. I do not understand how affections and determinations are or could be in an absolute outside me. But that nothing *infinite* could be within me without there being something *finite* at the same time, this I understand. For that necessary unity of the ideal and the real, of the absolutely active and the absolutely passive (which Spinoza transferred to an infinite substance outside me) is originally *within me* with no effort on my part, and it is precisely this that constitutes *my nature*.[5]

Leibnitz took this path, and it is at this point that he differs from Spinoza and is also related to him. It is impossible to understand Leibnitz without bringing oneself to this same point. *Jacobi* demonstrated that his entire system proceeds from and returns to the concept of *individuality*. What all other philosophy divides — the positivity and negativity, the activity and passivity of our nature — is originally united in the concept of individuality alone. Spinoza

---

5. Closer observation will teach everyone that all positing-in-myself of the absolute identity of the finite and the infinite, as well as the positing-outside-myself, is once again only *my* positing, thus this identity *in itself* is neither an in-myself nor an outside-myself.

could not make intelligible how *determinations* could be in an infinity outside us, and in vain he sought to avoid a transition from the infinite to the finite. Only where the finite and the infinite are *originally* united will this transition not be found, and this *original* unity is nowhere else but in the essence of an individual nature. Thus Leibnitz passed neither from the infinite to the finite nor vice versa, but for him both were made actual at once — as if through one and the same development of our nature—through one and the same activity of spirit.

It is the necessary result of our finitude that these representations *succeed* one another; but the *endlessness* of succession proves that it proceeds from a being in whose nature finitude and infinity are united.

The *necessity* of this succession in Leibnitz's philosophy follows from this: things arise simultaneously with representations sheerly by virtue of the laws of our nature, according to an inner principle within us, as if in a separate world. Leibnitz considered that *representing beings* alone were originally real and actual *in themselves*; for only in these was that *unity* original from which everything else that we call actual *develops* and *proceeds*. For everything that is actual outside ourselves is finite, hence unthinkable without something positive to give it reality and something negative to set its limits. This union of positive and negative activity is *original* nowhere else but in the nature of the individual. External objects *were* not actual *in themselves*, but only *became* actual through the manner of representation in spiritual natures; but that being alone from whose nature all existence first *proceeds*, i.e., the representing being, had to be something that carried the source and origin of its existence within itself.

If the entire succession of representations arises from the *nature* of finite spirit, then the whole sequence of our experiences must be able to be derived from it. For that all beings of our kind represent the appearances of the world in the same necessary succession, can be comprehended only on the basis of our common nature. But to explain this concordance within our nature on the basis of a preestablished harmony does not actually explain it at all. For this word indicates only *that* such concordance occurs, but not how and why. But it lies in Leibnitz's system itself that this concordance would follow from the *essence* of finite natures. If this were not the case, then spirit would cease to be the absolute *self-ground* of its knowledge and cognition. It would then have to seek the ground of its representations *outside itself*, and we would have returned to the point from which we began, that the world and its order was *accidental* for us and the representation of it came to us only from the outside. But then we inevitably roam beyond those limits within which alone we can understand ourselves. For if a higher hand has put us together in such a way that we are constrained to represent a world of this sort and an order of appearances of this sort, then, disregarding that this hypothesis is completely unintelligible to us, this entire world once again becomes a deception; one sleight of that hand can snatch it away from us or transport us into a completely different order of things. It even becomes completely dubious whether beings like ourselves (with the same representations as ours) exist outside ourselves. Thus Leibnitz could not have associated his preestablished harmony with the idea normally associated with it. For he explicitly states that no spirit could have *arisen*, i.e., the concepts of cause and effect cannot be applied to a spirit. Spirit is the absolute self-ground of its being and knowledge, and simply by being, it is *what* it is, i.e., a being to whose *nature* this determined system of the representations of external objects belongs. Philosophy is nothing other than a *natural science of our spirit*. Henceforth all dogmatism is inverted from the ground up. We contemplate the system of our representations not in its *being*, but in its *becoming*. Philosophy becomes *genetic*, i.e., it allows the entire necessary sequence of our representations to arise and take its course before our eyes. Henceforth there is no more separation between experience and speculation. The system of nature is at the same time the system of our spirit, and now that this great synthesis is completed, our knowledge returns to analysis (to *research* and *experimentation*). But this system is not yet here. Many timid spirits despair prematurely, for they speak of a system of *our nature* (whose dimensions they do not know) as if it were nothing but a doctrinal structure[6] of our *concepts*.

---

6. In the texts and translations from the earliest period of German purism one often finds these expressions: *doctrinal structure* of beings, *doctrinal structure* of *nature*. It is unfortunate that our newer philosophy has allowed this expression to fall into disuse.

The dogmatician who presupposes that all things are originally *present* outside ourselves (not *becoming* and *arising out of* ourselves) must at least offer to explain what is *outside* ourselves on the basis of *external* causes. He will succeed as long as he finds himself within the connection of cause and effect, disregarding that he can never make comprehensible how this connection of causes and effects *itself* arose. As soon as he raises himself above particular appearances his whole philosophy is finished; the limits of mechanism are also the limits of his system.

But this mechanism by no means constitutes all of nature. For as soon as we step into the sphere of *organic nature* every mechanical connection between cause and effect ceases for us. Every organic product exists *for itself*, its existence is dependent upon no other existence. Now the cause is never *the same* as the effect; only between completely *different* things is a relationship of cause and effect possible. But the organization produces *itself*, arises *from itself*; each particular plant is but a product of an individual of *its own kind*, and so each particular organization produces and reproduces only *its own species* into infinity. Thus no organization *progresses* but always returns to *itself* into infinity. Accordingly, an organization as such is neither the *cause* nor the *effect* of a thing outside itself; it in no way engages in the connection of the mechanism. Every organic product bears the ground of its existence within *itself*, for it is its own cause and effect. No single part could *arise* except *in* this whole, and this whole exists only in the *interaction* of the parts. In every other object the parts are *arbitrary*, they exist only insofar as I *divide*. Only in an organized being are they *real*; they are there with no effort on my part, because there is an *objective* relationship between them and the whole. Thus every organization is based on a *concept*; for wherever there is a necessary relationship of the whole to the parts, and of the parts to the whole, there is a *concept*. But this concept dwells within *the organization itself* and cannot be separated from it. It *organizes itself*, and is not simply a work of art whose concept is present *outside* itself in the understanding of the artist. Not its form alone, but its *existence* is purposive. It could not organize itself without already being organized. The plant nourishes and sustains itself through the assimilation of external substances, but it cannot assimilate anything without first being organized. The sustenance of a living body is bound to respiration. The vital air that it inhales is broken down by its organs so that it can flow through the nerves as electrical fluid. But in order that this process be made possible, the organization must already exist, which in turn is not sustained without this process. Hence organization is formed only by organization. For this reason form and matter are inseparable in the organic product; this determined matter could become and arise only with this determined form, and vice versa. Thus every organism is a *whole*; its *unity* lies *within itself* and does not depend on our volition, on whether we think of it as one or many. Here cause and effect are transitory, evanescent, mere *appearance* (in the usual sense of the word). The organization, however, is not mere appearance, but is *itself* an object, a self-sustaining, indivisible object, whole in itself; and because in it form and matter are inseparable, the *origin* of an organization as such can no more be explained mechanically than the origin of matter itself.

Thus if the purposiveness of organic products is to be explained, the dogmatician finds himself totally abandoned by his system. Here it is of no use to separate concept and object, form and matter, as we please. For *here*, at least, both are originally and necessarily united, not in our faculty of representation, but in the *object* itself. I wish that one of those who considers philosophy to be a game with concepts, and phantasms of things to be actual things would venture to meet us here on *this* ground.

First you must concede that we speak of a *unity* that cannot be *explained* on the basis of *matter* as such. For it is a unity of the *concept*; this unity exists only in relation to an intuiting and reflecting being. For this is a *judgment*: that absolute individuality is in an organization, that its parts are possible only through the whole, and that the whole is possible, not by assembling the parts, but through their interaction; and this judgment cannot be made except by a spirit that reciprocally relates the part and the whole, form and matter, each to the other. Only in and through this relating does all purposiveness and concordance arise and become as a whole. What do these mere material parts have in common with an *idea* that is originally foreign to matter and yet with which the parts are to accord? No relationship is possible here except through a third principle to whose representations both matter and concept belong. But only an intuiting and reflecting spirit is a third principle of this sort. Thus you must concede that organization is possible only in relation to a *spirit*.

Even those who allow that organic products arise from a wondrous collision of atoms concede this point. For when they derive the origin of these things from blind chance, they annul all purposiveness within them, and with this all concepts of organization as well. This is called consistent thinking. For since purposiveness is representable only in relation to a judging understanding, then the question of how organic products arise independent *of me* must be answered as if there were no relationship between them and the judging understanding, i.e., as if there were no purposiveness in them anywhere.

The first point you concede, then, is that every concept of purposiveness can arise only in an understanding, and only in relation to an understanding of this sort can any object be called purposive.

Yet you are no less constrained to concede that the purposiveness of natural products dwells *within them*, that they are *objective* and *real* and thus do not belong to your *arbitrary*, but to your *necessary* representations. For you can certainly differentiate between what is arbitrary and what is necessary in the connections among your concepts. As often as you subsume things that are spacially separated under a *single* number, you act completely freely. The unity that you give them is simply projected from your thoughts onto them; in the *things themselves* there is no ground that compels you to think of them as one. In that you think of every plant as an individual in which everything accords with one purpose, you must seek the ground for this in a *thing outside yourselves*. You feel forced to make this judgment, and thus you must concede that the unity with which your judgment is thought is not merely *logical* (in your thoughts), but rather *real* (actual outside yourselves).

Now you are required to answer this question: how is it that an idea that obviously can exist only within you and that can have reality only in relation to you, still must be intuited and represented as something actual outside yourselves?

There are philosophers who have *one* universal answer for all these questions; they repeat this answer at every opportunity and never tire of repeating it. That which is form in things, they say, is something we first project onto them. But this is precisely what I have long demanded to know: how can you do this; what are the things without the form you first project onto them; or what is form without the things onto which you project it? You must admit that *here*, at least, form and matter, concept and object, are utterly inseparable. Or if it is your volition that decides whether the idea of purposiveness is projected onto things outside you or not, how is it that you project this idea only onto *certain* things, but not *all*; furthermore, that you feel not *free* but altogether constrained to represent these purposive products? You cannot give a reason for either, except that to certain *things* outside yourselves this purposive form simply is attributed originally and with no effort on the part of your volition.

Given this, what held true previously also holds true now: the form and matter of these things can never be separated; both can become only simultaneously and reciprocally through each other. The concept upon which this organization is based has no reality *in itself*, and, conversely, this determined matter is *organized matter* only through the indwelling *concept*, and not *as matter*. Thus this determined object can only arise simultaneously with this concept and this determined concept only simultaneously with this determined object.

All previous systems can be judged according to this principle.

In order to comprehend this union of concept and matter, you assume a higher, divine understanding which planned its creations with ideals and produced nature in accordance with these ideals. But a being in whom concepts *precede* the deed, and the plan its execution, cannot *produce*, but can only shape and form matter that already exists, can only press the stamp of understanding and purposiveness upon matter from the outside; what it produces is not purposive *within itself*, but only accidentally, only in relation to the artist's understanding, not *originally* and *necessarily*. Is not the understanding a lifeless faculty, and does it serve any other purpose but to apprehend and comprehend actuality when it exists, and does not the understanding first borrow its own reality from the actual itself instead of creating the actual, and is it not the sheer enslavement of this faculty—its capacity to describe the *outlines* of actuality—that establishes the mediation between it and actuality? But here the question is how the *actual* arises, and with it the ideal (the purposive) unseparated from it. Not that natural things as such are purposive just as every work of art is, but rather that this purposiveness is something that could not have been imparted to them from the outside, that they are originally purposive *through themselves*—this is what we want explained.

You take refuge in the *creative* capacity of a deity from whom actual things arose and came forth simultaneously with their ideas. You recognized that you had to let the actual arise simultaneously with the purposive, and purposive simultaneously with the actual, if you wished to assume that things outside yourselves were purposive in and through themselves.

But let us assume, for a moment, what you maintain (although you are unable to make this intelligible); let us assume that through the creative power of a deity the whole system of nature and with it the whole manifold of purposive products arose outside ourselves. Does this get us even one step further? Do we not find ourselves at the same point where we began? I did not in the least demand to know how organized products became actual outside of and independent of myself, for how could I make a clear concept of this even for myself? The question was how the *representation* of purposive products outside myself entered *into me*, and how *I* am constrained to think of this purposiveness as something *actual and necessary outside myself, although it is attributed to things only in relation to my understanding.* You have not answered this question.

For as soon as you view natural things as actual outside yourselves, and thus as the work of a creator, purposiveness cannot dwell within them, since purposiveness pertains only to *your* understanding. Or do you want to presuppose concepts of purpose, etc., in the creator of things as well? But as soon as you do this, he ceases to be the creator and becomes a mere artist or at most an architect of nature; and you *destroy* every idea of *nature* as soon as you make purposiveness come into nature from the outside by passing out of some being's understanding. As soon as you make the idea of the creator *finite*, he ceases to be creator; but if you extend this idea to *infinity*, then all concepts of purposiveness and understanding are lost and you are left only with the idea of an absolute power. Henceforth everything finite is a mere modification of the infinite. But you no more comprehend how a modification of the infinite is at all possible than you comprehend how these modifications of the infinite, i.e., the whole system of finite things, entered your faculty of representation; or how the unity of things, which in the infinite being can only be *ontological*, has become *teleological* in your understanding.

You could try to explain this on the basis of the peculiar nature of a finite spirit. But if you do this, you no longer need the infinite as something outside yourselves. Henceforth you can let everything become and arise in your spirit. For even if you presuppose things *outside* of and independent of yourselves that are purposive *in themselves*, yet you still must explain how your *representations* accord with these external things. You must take refuge in a preestablished harmony; you must assume that within the external things themselves a spirit rules that is analogous to your own. For only in a spirit with creative capability can concept and actuality, the ideal and the real, so interpenetrate each other, so unite themselves, that between them no separation is possible. I cannot help but think that Leibnitz thought of substantial form as a governing *spirit indwelling* organized beings.

This philosophy must therefore assume that there is a hierarchy of life in nature. Even in mere organized matter there is *life*, albeit life of a limited kind. This idea is so old and has been so steadfastly maintained in the most diverse forms even to our own day (even in the most ancient times the whole world was thought to be penetrated by an animating principle called the world soul, and later Leibnitz's age would give every plant a soul), that one can easily suppose in advance that there must be some ground for this natural belief within the human spirit itself. And so it is. The whole enchantment that surrounds the problem of the origin of organized bodies rests on the intimate unity of necessity and accident in these things: *necessity*, because their *existence* and not only their form (as in works of art) is *purposive*; *accident*, because this purposiveness is actual only for an intuiting, reflecting being. For this reason the human spirit was led early on to the idea of *self*-organizing matter, and, because organization is representable only in relation to a spirit, to an original unity of the spirit and the matter within these things. Man saw himself constrained to seek the ground of these things on the one hand in nature itself, and on the other hand in a principle higher than nature; and so very early on he came to think of spirit and nature as one. Here the ideal essence in which man thinks of concept and deed, a plan and its execution as one, first emerged from its holy darkness. Here man was first confronted with a presentiment of his own nature, in which intuition and concept, form and object, the ideal and the real are originally one and the same. Hence the peculiar aura surrounding this problem, an aura that mere reflective philosophy, being concerned only with *separation*, could never unfold, while pure intuition, or rather the creative imagination, had long since found a symbolic language that one need only interpret to find that nature speaks the more intelligibly to us, the less we think merely reflectively about it.

Yet it is no wonder that this language, when it was used dogmatically, itself soon lost its sense and meaning. As long as I am *identical* to nature I understand what a living nature is as well as I understand my own life, I comprehend how general life in nature reveals itself in the most manifold forms, in hierarchical developments, gradually approximating freedom. But as soon as I separate myself from nature, and with myself all of the ideal, I am left with nothing but a dead object, and I cease to comprehend how *life* is possible *outside* myself.

If I ask common understanding, it believes to see *life* only where there is *free motion*. For the faculties of an animal's organs—sensibility, irritability, etc.—presuppose an impulsive principle without which the animal would be unable to counteract external irritations, and only through this free reaction of its organs does the stimulus become an irritation and an impression. Here we find fullest interaction: only through external irritation is the animal determined to produce motion, and, conversely, only through this capacity to produce motion within itself does the external impression become an irritation. (Thus irritability is not possible without sensibility, nor sensibility without irritability.)

But all these faculties of the organs taken merely as such cannot give a sufficient explanation of *life*. For we could indeed think of a composition of fibers, nerves, etc., in which free motion is produced through external irritation (as, for example, the nerves of a destroyed organic body through electricity, metallic irritation, etc.), without our being able to ascribe *life* to this assembled thing. One can perhaps retort that the concordance of *all* these movements effects life; yet to life belongs a higher principle that we cannot explain on the basis of matter itself, a principle that orders and integrates each particular movement and thus creates and brings forth a whole out of a manifold of movements that accord with each other, reciprocally producing and reproducing each other. Thus once again we encounter the absolute union of nature and freedom in one and the same being: the animated organization is to be a produce of *nature*; but an ordering, integrating *spirit* is to rule in this product of nature. Both of these principles are not to be separated, but rather most intimately united within it. In the intuition no differentiation between them is to be allowed; no *before* or *after* is to occur between them, only simultaneity and interaction.

As soon as philosophy annuls this union, two completely opposing systems arise, neither of which can refute the other, because both destroy from the ground up every idea of life, which flees all the further from them the closer they believe they are coming to it.

I do not speak of that so-called philosophy which makes even thought, representation, and will arise in us, now from an accidental collision of already organized corpuscles, now from a truly artistic composition of muscles, fibers, membranes, and hamuli which hold the body together and fluids that flow through it. But I maintain that we can no more empirically comprehend *life outside ourselves* than consciousness *outside ourselves*; that neither the one nor the other can be explained in physical terms; that, seen from this viewpoint, it is of no consequence whether the body is viewed as an accidental aggregate of organized corpuscles, or a hydraulic machine, or a chemical laboratory. Supposing, for example, that all movements of animated matter could be explained on the basis of changes in the mixture of its nerves and fibers or of the fluids believed to be circulating through them, then we must not only ask how these changes are effected, but also what principle harmoniously integrates them. Or if some philosophical view of nature as a system that is never static but constantly moves forward finally discovers that nature with its animated matter goes beyond the bounds of lifeless chemistry, and thus that there must be a principle within living bodies releasing them from chemical laws (since otherwise chemical processes would be inevitable in the body, for a dead body is destroyed by true chemical decomposition); and if this principle is called a *vital force*, then I would state to the contrary that a vital force (as familiar as this expression might be), taken in this sense, is a completely contradictory concept. For we can think of a force only as something finite. But a force is never finite according to its *nature*, except insofar as it is limited by an opposing force. Whenever we think of a force (as in matter), we must also think of an *opposing* force. Between opposing forces we can only think of a dual relationship. Either the forces are in *relative* equilibrium (absolute equilibrium would completely annul both forces), and then they are thought to be *at rest*, as in matter, which we therefore call "inert;" or they are thought to be in a constant, never-ending conflict, alternately prevailing and succumbing, but then there must be a third principle which sustains this conflict and maintains the work of nature in this conflict of alternately prevailing and succumbing forces. This third principle cannot be yet another force, for then we would return to the previous alternative. Thus it must be something higher than *force*. But *force* is the final principle to which all our physical explanations must return (as I shall demonstrate later): thus this third principle would have to be something lying completely beyond the bounds of the empirical investigation of nature. Now according to common representation there is nothing known above or beyond nature that is higher than spirit. But if we wished to comprehend the vital force as a spiritual principle, we would annul this concept altogether. For what we call *force* can be placed, at least as a *principle*, at the pinnacle of natural science, and although it cannot be depicted, it can be determined by physical laws according to its *effects*. But how a spirit could have physical effects, of this we do not have even the vaguest concept; thus a spiritual principle cannot be called a *vital force*, since by this expression one intimates at least the hope that this principle can be made to work according to physical laws.[7]

But if we abandon this concept (of a vital force) as we are constrained to do, then we are constrained to flee to a completely opposite system in which spirit and matter suddenly oppose each other again (disregarding that we can no more comprehend how spirit acts on matter than how matter acts on spirit).

Spirit, when thought of as a principle of life, is called the *soul*. I will not reiterate the objections that have been raised long ago against dualistic philosophy. Up to the present it has been contested largely on the basis of principles having as little substance as the contested system itself. The question is not how the union of body and soul is at all possible (an illegitimate question, since the one asking it does not understand it himself), but rather—and this question can be understood and must be answered—how the representation of such a union entered *into us* in the first place. That I think, represent, and will, and that this thinking, etc., cannot be a result

---

7. One sees this very clearly in the statements of several advocates of the *vital force*. For example, Mr. *Brandis* (in his *Essay on the Vital Force*, §81) asks, "Should electricity (which seems to be at work in all phlogistic processes) also take part in the phlogistic processes of life (which the author presumes), or should *electricity* be *the vital force itself*? I consider this to be more than a *probable*."

of my body, but rather that this body itself only becomes *my* body through these very faculties of thought, will, etc. — of this I am well aware. Moreover, the distinction between the principles of the mover and the moved, the soul and the body shall be permitted in the meantime for the sake of speculation, disregarding that as soon as the discussion turns to action this distinction is completely forgotten. From all these presuppositions this much is obvious, that if life and soul (the latter seen as distinct from the body) are in me, then I can become certain of both only through *immediate* experience. I must know that I *am* (think, will, etc.) if I am to know anything at all. Thus I understand how a representation of my own being and life enters into me because I must understand this if I am to understand at all. Because I am also immediately conscious of my own being, the inference that there is a soul within me rests upon at least *one* indubitable premise (even if the inference should be false): that I *am, live, represent, will.* But how do I come to project *being, life,* etc., onto things *outside myself?* For as soon as this happens, my immediate knowledge becomes *mediate.* But I maintain that only *immediate* knowledge of being and life is possible, and that whatever *is* and *lives* only is and lives to the extent that it exists first and foremost *for itself,* becoming conscious of its life only through its own life. Supposing that an organized, free-moving being enters my intuition; then I am well aware that this being *exists,* that it exists *for me,* but not that it exists *for itself* and *in itself.* For life can no more be represented outside life than consciousness outside consciousness.[8] Thus an empirical conviction of something living outside me is also altogether impossible. For the idealist can state: the fact that you represent organized, free-moving bodies to yourself can be due solely to the necessary characteristics of your faculty of representation; and indeed philosophy itself, which animates everything outside me, does not allow the representation of this life outside me to enter into me from the *outside.* But if this representation arises only *within me,* how can I be convinced that it corresponds to something outside me? It is also evident that I can be convinced only *practically* of a life and an autonomous being outside myself. I must be practically *constrained* to recognize those beings outside myself which are my equals. If I were not constrained to enter into society with other people, and into all the practical

8. Jacobi's *David Hume*, p. 140.

relationships associated with it; if I did not know that beings whose external shape is similar in appearance to my own had no *more* reason to recognize freedom and spirituality in me than I did in them; finally, if I did not know that my moral existence first receives purpose and determination from the existence of other moral beings outside myself, then, abandoned to mere speculation, I could, of course, doubt whether humanity dwelled behind every face, and freedom in every breast. All this is confirmed by our most common judgments. Only from beings outside myself who are on equal footing with me in life, where receiving and giving, passivity and activity, are completely reciprocal between them and me, do I recognize that they are of a spiritual nature. Conversely, if someone asks inquisitively whether animals also are given a soul, a person with common understanding becomes obstinate, because by assenting he believes himself to be conceding something that he cannot know immediately.

If, finally, we return to the original source of dualistic belief—that at least within *me* there dwells a soul distinct from the body—then what is that within me which judges that I consist of body and soul, and what is this *I* that is supposed to consist of body and soul? Obviously, there is something higher here which, free and independent of the body, gives the body a soul, unifies body and soul in its thought, and yet itself does not enter into this union—a higher principle, it would seem, in which body and soul once again are identical.

Finally, if we insist on this dualism we come into closest proximity with the opposition that was our starting point: spirit and matter. For that same incomprehensibility—how connection is possible between spirit and matter—still oppresses us. One can hide the cutting edge of this opposition with deceptions of all sorts, one can insert as much intermediate matter between spirit and matter as one likes, letting it become ever more subtle, but sooner or later one must come to the point where spirit and matter are one, or where the enormous leap that for so long we wished to avoid becomes unavoidable, and here one theory is the same as the next. Whether I allow animal spirits, electrical substances or gases to flow through or fill the nerves, and then allow external impressions to be transmitted to the sensorium through them, or whether I follow the soul into the extreme (and beyond this, problematical) humors of the brain (an experiment that at least deserves credit for having gone to *extremes*) is of no consequence in view of the *issue* at hand. It is clear that our critique has completed its circular path, but not that we are the least bit wiser than we were at the beginning with regard to the opposition that was our starting point. We leave man behind as that visible, vagrant problem of all philosophy, and our critique ends at the same extremes at which it began.

If we gather nature together as a whole, then *mechanism*, i.e., a descending sequence of causes and effects, stands in opposition to *purposiveness*, i.e., independence from mechanism, simultaneity of causes and effects. By uniting both extremes the idea of a purposiveness of the *whole* arises in us, nature becomes a circle that returns to itself, a system closed within itself. The sequence of causes and effects ceases altogether and a reciprocal relationship of *means* and *ends* arises; the particular cannot become *actual* without the whole, nor the whole without the particular.

This absolute purposiveness of the whole of nature is an idea that we think of not arbitrarily, but *necessarily*. We feel ourselves compelled to relate every particular to such a purposiveness of the whole. When we find something in nature that seems to be purposeless or even at odds with purposiveness, then we believe that the whole connection of things has been torn asunder, or we do not rest until even this apparent anti-purposiveness has become purposiveness again in a new context. Thus it is a necessary maxim of the reflective reason that connection always be presumed to follow purpose and means in nature. And although we do not immediately transform this maxim into a constitutive law, yet we obey it so steadfastly, so unabashedly, that we evidently presuppose that nature will freely meet us half way, as it were, in our endeavor to discover absolute purposiveness within her. In the same manner we proceed from particular, subordinate laws to general, higher laws with complete trust in the concordance between nature and the maxims of our reflective reason; and even when we proceed from appearances which stand isolated in the sequence of our knowledge, we do not cease to presuppose *a priori* that *these*, too, are connected to each other through some common principle. And only where we see a manifold of effects and a unity of the means do we believe in a nature outside ourselves.

What is the mysterious bond that connects our spirit with nature, or the secret organ through which nature speaks to our spirit, or our spirit speaks to nature? To begin with, we grant you all your explanations of how a purposive nature of this sort has become actual *outside ourselves*. For to explain this purposiveness by saying that its originator is a divine understanding is not to philosophize but to piously meditate. You have explained as much as nothing; for we demand to know not how a nature of this sort arises outside ourselves, but how the *idea* of a nature of this sort has entered *into us*; which is not to ask how we have arbitrarily produced it, but how and why it is the original and *necessary* foundation of all that our race has ever thought about nature. For the existence of a nature of this sort *outside myself* by no means explains the existence of this nature *within me*: for when you assume a preestablished harmony to occur between them, you have stated the very object of our question. Or when you maintain that we merely *project* this idea onto nature, then not even a hint of what nature is and should be to us has ever come into your soul. For we wish not that nature coincide *accidentally* with the laws of our spirit (for instance through the mediation of a *third principle*), but that *nature itself* necessarily and originally not only *express*, but *itself realize* the laws of our spirit, and that it be nature and be called nature only to the extent that it does this.

Nature shall be visible spirit, and spirit invisible nature. *Here* in the absolute identity of spirit *within* us and nature *outside* us the problem of how a nature outside us is possible must be solved. Thus the final goal of our further investigations will be this idea of nature. If we succeed in reaching this goal, then we can be certain that we have done justice to the problem.

These are the main problems. To solve them shall be the purpose of this text.

But this text does not begin *from above* (with the putting forth of principles), but *from below* (with the experiences and with the examination of previous systems).

Only when I have arrived at the goal I set for myself will I be allowed to retrace my path in the reverse direction.

Translated by Priscilla Hayden-Roy

Deduction of a Universal Organ
of Philosophy, or Main Propositions
of the Philosophy of Art According to
Principles of Transcendental Idealism

1. Deduction of the Art Product
in General

The postulated intuition should comprehend what exists separated in the appearance of freedom and in the intuition of the
product of nature, namely, *identity of conscious and unconscious in
the ego and consciousness of this identity.* The product of this
intuition will thus be contiguous on the one side with the product of
nature and on the other side with the product of freedom, and it
will have to unite within itself the characteristics of both. If we
know the product of intuition, then we also know the intuition
itself. We therefore need only deduce the product in order to deduce
the intuition.

The product will have in common with the product of freedom
the fact that it is produced with conscious intent, and with the
product of nature that it is produced unconsciously. In the first
respect it will consequently be the inverse of the organic product of
nature. If unconscious (blind) activity is reflected as conscious by
the organic product, then inversely by the product here discussed
conscious activity will be reflected as unconscious (objective); or, if

the organic product reflects for me unconscious activity as determined by conscious activity, then inversely, the product which is here deduced will reflect conscious activity as determined by unconscious activity. More briefly: nature begins unconscious and ends conscious; its production is not purposive but its product indeed is. The ego, in the activity here discussed, must begin with consciousness (subjectively) and end in the unconscious, or *objectively*; the ego is conscious as regards production, unconscious as regards the product.

How shall *we*, however, explain transcendentally for ourselves an intuition of this nature, in which unconscious activity, as it were, works its way through conscious activity to perfect identity with it? We reflect first on the fact that the activity is supposed to be a conscious one. Now it is plainly impossible that something objective should be produced with consciousness, which nevertheless is here required. Only what arises unconsciously is objective; the genuinely objective element in that intuition therefore cannot be introduced by means of *consciousness*. On this point we may appeal immediately to the proofs that have already been adduced in regard to free action, namely, that the objective element in free action arises in it by force of something independent of freedom. The difference is merely this: (a) that in free action the identity of both activities must be annulled precisely in order that the action should thereby appear as free; here, on the other hand, in *consciousness* itself, and without the negation of consciousness, both should appear as one. Also (b) the two activities in free action can *never* become absolutely identical. Hence, again, the object of free action is necessarily an *infinite* one, never fully realized; for were it fully realized, then the conscious and the objective activity would collapse into one, i.e., the appearance of freedom would vanish. Now what was simply impossible through freedom is to be possible through the action here postulated, which, however, just on this account, must cease to be a free action and become one in which freedom and necessity are absolutely united. But the production was to have occurred with consciousness, which is impossible unless both the activities are separated. Here, therefore, is a clear contradiction. I shall set it forth once more. Conscious and unconscious activity are to be absolutely one in the product, just as they are also in the organic product; but they are to be one in a different way—both are to be one *for the ego itself*. But this is impossible unless the ego is conscious of the production. But if the ego is conscious of the production, then the two activities must be separate, since this is a necessary condition for consciousness of production. The two activities must therefore be one, for otherwise there is no identity; the two must be separate, for otherwise there is identity, but not for the ego. How is this contradiction to be resolved?

Both activities must be separated for the sake of the appearance, the objectivation of production, just as they must be separated in free action for the sake of the objectivation of intuition. But they cannot be separate *to infinity*, as in free action, because the objective phase would then never be a complete representation of the relevant identity. The identity of the two was to have been broken up only for the sake of consciousness, but the production is to end in unconsciousness. Hence there must be a point where both fall together into one; and conversely, where both fall together into one, the production must cease to appear free.

Once this point in the production is arrived at, the productive process must cease absolutely, and it must be impossible for the producer to continue to produce. For the condition of all producing is just the opposition of conscious and unconscious activity, whereas these are here supposed to meet absolutely; so that in intelligence all strife is ended, all contradiction resolved.

Intelligence will thus terminate in full recognition of the identity expressed in the product, as one whose principle lies in itself, i.e., it will terminate in a complete self-intuition. Now since it was the free tendency to self-intuition in this identity that originally brought about the self-estrangement of intelligence, the feeling that accompanies this intuition will be a feeling of infinite satisfaction. The whole productive drive comes to rest with the completion of the product; all contradictions are resolved, all riddles unraveled. Since the production proceeded from freedom, i.e., from an infinite opposition of the two activities, intelligence will not be able to ascribe to *freedom* the absolute unification of the two in which the production ends. For simultaneously with the completion of the product all appearance of freedom is removed; intelligence will feel itself surprised and *blessed* by that unification, i.e., it will regard it as though it were a freely bestowed favor of a higher nature that has by means of it made the impossible possible.

But this unknown, which here brings objective and conscious activity into unexpected harmony, is none other than that Absolute which contains the universal ground of the pre-established harmony between the conscious and the unconscious. If, then, this absolute is reflected from the product, it will appear to intelligence as something above it and which itself, in opposition to freedom, adds the element of purposelessness to that which was begun with consciousness and purposeful intention.

This unchangeable identity, which cannot arrive at consciousness and is only reflected from the product, is for the producer exactly what destiny is for the actor, i.e., an obscure unknown power that adds the element of perfection, completion, or objectivity to the fragmentary work of freedom. And, as the power that realizes non-intended ends by means of our free action without our knowledge is called destiny, so the incomprehensible principle which adds the objective to the conscious without the co-operation of freedom and in a certain way in opposition to freedom, in which what is united in the above-mentioned production eternally flees from itself, is signified by the obscure concept of *genius*.

The postulated product is none other than the product of genius, or, since genius is possible only in art, the *product of art*.

The deduction is finished and we now have nothing to do but show by a complete analysis that all the characteristic traits of the postulated production converge in the aesthetic process.

That all aesthetic production rests on an opposition of activities may properly be inferred from the declaration by all artists that they are involuntarily impelled to the creation of their works, that they merely satisfy an irresistible impulse of their nature through such production. For if every impulse originates in a contradiction in such a way that, given the contradiction, the free activity occurs involuntarily, then the artistic impulse must also proceed from such a feeling of an inner contradiction. But this contradiction, since it sets into motion the whole man with all his powers, is without doubt a contradiction that seizes upon the *ultimate in him*, the root of his entire existence. It is as though in the rare persons who are, above all others, artists in the highest sense of the word, the immutable identity, on which all existence rests, has put off the raiment with which it clothes itself in others and now, just as it is immediately affected by things, with equal immediacy reaffects everything.

Consequently it can only be the contradiction between the conscious and the unconscious in free action that sets the artistic impulse into motion, just as, once more, it can only be given to art to satisfy our infinite striving as well as to resolve the ultimate and most extreme contradiction in us.

Just as aesthetic production starts from the feeling of an apparently irresolvable contradiction, so, according to the testimony of all artists and of all who participate in their inspiration, it comes to a close in the feeling of an *infinite* harmony. That this feeling, which accompanies the closure, is at the same time an *emotion* (a being *moved*), already demonstrates that the artist ascribes the complete resolution of the contradiction which he discovers in his work not [alone] to himself but to a spontaneous gift of his nature, which, however inexorably it sets him into contradiction with himself, with equal grace removes the pain of this contradiction from him. For just as the artist is driven to production involuntarily and even against his inner resistance (hence the maxims among the ancients: pati Deum, etc., and hence in general the image of being inspired by a breath from without), so the objective element comes about in his production as though without his co-operation, i.e., itself in a purely objective way. Just as the fateful man does not accomplish what he intends or has in view but rather what he must, by an incomprehensible destiny under whose influence he stands, so the artist, however purposeful he may be, nevertheless, in regard to what is truly objective in his creation, seems to stand under the influence of a power that sets him apart from all other men and compels him to express or represent things he does not himself fully see through and whose meaning is infinite. Now since that absolute confluence of the two mutually fleeing activities is not at all further explicable, but is merely an *appearance*, which, though incomprehensible, cannot be denied, art is the sole and eternal revelation that exists and the miracle which, even if it had existed only once, must have persuaded us of the absolute reality of that highest principle.

Moreover, if art is brought to completion by two thoroughly different activities, then genius is neither the one nor the other but that which is above both. If we must seek in one of these two activities, namely conscious activity, for what is usually called *art*, but which is merely one part of art, namely, the part that is practiced with consciousness, deliberation, and reflection, which can also be taught and learned, received from others, and attained by one's own practice, then, on the other hand, we must seek in the unconscious, which also enters into art, for that in art which cannot be learned, cannot be attained by practice or in any other way, but can only be inborn by the free gift of nature, and which is what we may call in one word the *poetry* in art.

Obviously, then, it would be utterly futile to ask which of the two constituents is prior to the other; for in fact either without the other has no value and only the two in conjunction can bring forth the highest. For though that which cannot be achieved by practice but is native with us is generally considered the nobler of the two, the gods have so firmly tied the exercise of that original power to painstaking human effort, to industry and deliberation, that without art, poetry, even where it is innate, produces only products that appear lifeless, in which no human understanding can take delight, and which repel all judgment and even intuition by the completely blind force at work in them. On the contrary, it is rather to be expected that art might be able to accomplish something without poetry than poetry without art, partly because a person can hardly be by nature devoid of poetry, while many have no art, and partly because persistent study of the ideas of the great masters can to some degree compensate for an original lack of objective power. Still, only a semblance of poetry can arise in this way, which is easily distinguishable by its superficiality, in contrast with the inexhaustible depth which the true artist, though he works with the greatest presence of mind, puts into his work involuntarily and which neither he nor anyone else is able to penetrate completely. There are also many other characteristics by which such mere semblance of poetry is distinguishable, e.g., the great value it places on the merely mechanical features of art, the poverty of the form in which it moves itself, etc.

It is evident also that as neither poetry nor art can produce a perfected work singly each by itself, so the two existing in separation cannot produce such a work. Consequently, because the identity of the two can only be original, and is absolutely impossible and unattainable through freedom, the complete work of art is possible only through genius, which for this reason is for aesthetics what the ego is for philosophy, namely, that which is highest, absolutely real, which itself never becomes objective but is the cause of everything objective.

2. Character of the Art Product

A) The work of art reflects for us the identity of conscious and unconscious activity. But the opposition of the two is infinite, and it is removed without any contribution of freedom. The basic character of the work of art is thus an *unconscious infinity* [synthesis of nature and freedom]. The artist seems to have presented in his work, as if instinctively, apart from what he has put into it with obvious intent, an infinity which no finite understanding can fully unfold. To make this clear to ourselves merely by one example, Greek mythology — of which it is undeniable that it includes within itself an infinite meaning and symbols for all Ideas — arose among a people and in a manner both of which make it impossible to assume any thoroughgoing intentionality in its discovery and in the harmony with which everything is unified into a single great whole. So it is with every true work of art: each is susceptible of infinite interpretation, as though there were an infinity of intentions within it, yet we cannot at all tell whether this infinity lay in the artist himself or whether it resides solely in the art-work. On the other hand, in a product that merely simulates the character of a work of art, intention and rule lie on the surface and appear so limited and bounded that the product is nothing other than a faithful impression of the conscious activity of the artist and is altogether merely an object for reflection, but not for intuition, which loves to immerse itself in what it intuits and can come to rest only in the infinite.

B) Every aesthetic production starts from the feeling of an infinite contradiction. Hence also the feeling that accompanies the completion of the art product must be the feeling of such a satisfaction, and this feeling must in turn go over into the work of art itself. The outward expression of the work of art is therefore the expression of repose and of quiet grandeur, even where the greatest tension of pain or of joy is to be expressed.

C) Every aesthetic production starts from an intrinsically infinite separation of both activities, which are separated in every free production. Since, however, both these activities are to be presented in the product as united, an infinite will be finitely presented by this product. But the infinite finitely presented is beauty. The basic character of every work of art, which comprehends within itself both of the foregoing characters, is therefore *beauty*, and without beauty there is no work of art. For although there are sublime works of art as well, and beauty and sublimity are in a certain respect opposite (in that a natural scene, for instance, can be beautiful without thereby being sublime, and conversely), still the opposition between beauty and sublimity is one that occurs only in regard to the object and not in regard to the subject of intuition. For the difference between a beautiful and a sublime work of art rests only on the fact that where beauty exists the infinite contradiction is resolved in the object itself, whereas where sublimity exists the contradiction is not unified in the object itself but is merely raised to a level at which it involuntarily removes itself in the intuition, which then is as good as if it were removed from the object. It can also be shown easily that sublimity rests on the same contradiction as beauty. For whenever an object is called sublime, a magnitude is apprehended by unconscious activity which cannot be apprehended in conscious activity; the ego is thereby set into a conflict with itself which can end only in an aesthetic intuition that places both activities in an unanticipated harmony. However, the intuition, which lies here not in the artist but in the intuiting subject itself, is completely involuntary, because the sublime (quite unlike the merely marvelous, which likewise poses the imagination with a contradiction which, however, it is not worth the effort to resolve) sets all the powers of the mind in motion in order to resolve the contradiction that threatens one's entire intellectual existence.

Now that the characteristics of the work of art have been derived, its *difference* from all other products has also been brought to light.

For the work of art distinguishes itself from the organic product of nature chiefly by the fact that a) the organic being presents still unseparated what aesthetic production presents after separation but united; b) organic production does not start out from consciousness, hence also not from an infinite contradiction, which is a condition of aesthetic production. The organic product of nature will therefore also not necessarily be beautiful if beauty is exclusively the resolution of an infinite contradiction; and if it is beautiful, then its beauty will seem simply accidental, because the condition of its existence cannot be thought of as existing in nature. From this the altogether unique interest in natural beauty—not insofar as it is beauty in general, but insofar as it is definitely *natural beauty*—can be explained. Our view regarding the imitation of nature as the principle of art becomes clear from the foregoing. For far from its being the case that a merely accidentally beautiful nature should give the rule to art, what art produces in its perfection is the principle and the norm for judging the beauty of nature.

It is easy to determine what the distinction is between the aesthetic product and the *ordinary art product*. In its principle, all aesthetic production is absolutely free, since the artist can indeed be impelled to produce by a contradiction, but only by one that lies in the highest region of his own nature, whereas all other production is occasioned by a contradiction that lies outside the real producer and hence all such production has its end outside itself. From its independence of external ends there springs the sanctity and purity of art. This goes so far that it excludes not only affinity with everything that is merely sensuous enjoyment (to demand which of art is the peculiar characteristic of barbarism), or with the useful (to demand which is possible only to an age that places the highest efforts of the human spirit in economic discoveries), but even affinity with everything that belongs to morality. Indeed, it leaves far below it science itself, which in view of its disinterestedness borders most closely upon art, merely because it is always directed to a goal beyond itself and in the end must itself serve as a mere means for the highest (art).

As for the relation of art to science in particular, they are both so opposed in tendency that, were science ever to have accomplished its whole task as art always has accomplished its, both would have to converge and become one — which is the proof of completely opposite tendencies. For although science, in its highest function, has one and the same problem as art, yet this problem, because of the manner of its solution, is an infinite one for science. We can thus say that art is the model for science, and wherever art may be, there science must first join it. From this we can see why and to what extent there is no genius in the sciences, not because it would be impossible for a scientific problem to be solved in a "genial" way, but because the very problem whose solution can be discovered by genius is also soluble mechanically. Of such a sort, e.g., is the Newtonian system of gravitation, which could have been a "genial" discovery — and in its first discoverer, Kepler, really was — but could equally well have been a wholly scientific discovery, as it became through Newton. Only what art produces is possible solely and alone through genius, because in every task that art has fulfilled an infinite contradiction has been resolved. What science produces *can* be produced by genius, but it is not necessarily so produced. Genius, therefore, is and remains problematic in science, i.e., one can always definitely say where it is not, but never where it is. There are only a few characteristic traits from which we can infer to genius in science. (That we have to infer to it already demonstrates a wholly unique state of affairs here.) E.g., genius is certainly not present where a whole, such as a system, arises part by part and as if by composition. Conversely, genius would have to be presupposed wherever it is clear that the idea of the whole has preceded the individual parts. For, since the idea of the whole cannot grow distinct except by unfolding itself in the individual parts, while, again, the individual parts are possible only through the idea of the whole, there appears to be a contradiction here which is possible only through an act of genius, i.e., through an unexpected confluence of unconscious and conscious activity. Another reason for imputing genius in science would be if someone were to say and assert things whose meaning he could not have wholly penetrated (whether in view of the time in which he lived or in comparison with his other utterances), where he thus expressed something apparently with consciousness which, nevertheless, he could only have expressed unconsciously. Yet that these grounds of imputation can be highly deceptive can easily be demonstrated in a number of ways.

Genius is differentiated from everything that is mere talent or skill by the fact that it resolves a contradiction which is absolute and resolvable by nothing else. In all production, even in the most ordinary everyday variety, an unconscious activity works together with conscious activity; but only a production whose condition was an infinite opposition of both activities is aesthetic and is possible *only* through genius.

3. Corollaries

Having derived the nature and character of the art product as fully as was required for the present investigation, nothing remains but to give an account of the relation in which the philosophy of art stands to the whole system of philosophy in general.

1. Philosophy as a whole starts from, and must start from a prin-

ciple that, as the absolute identity, is completely nonobjective. How then is this absolutely nonobjective principle to be evoked in consciousness and understood, which is necessary if it is the condition of understanding the whole of philosophy? No proof is needed of the impossibility of apprehending or presenting it by means of concepts. Nothing remains, therefore, but that it be presented in an immediate intuition; yet this itself seems incomprehensible and, since its object is supposed to be something absolutely nonobjective, even self contradictory. If, however, there were nevertheless such an intuition, which had as object that which was absolutely identical, in itself neither subjective nor objective, and if on behalf of this intuition, which can only be an intellectual intuition, one were to appeal to immediate experience, by what means could this intuition be established as objective i.e., how could we establish beyond doubt that it does not rest on a merely subjective illusion, unless there were an objectivity belonging to the intuition which was universal and acknowledged by all men? This universally acknowledged and thoroughly undeniable objectivity of intellectual intuition is art itself. For aesthetic intuition is precisely intellectual intuition become objective.[1] The work of art merely reflects to me what is otherwise reflected by nothing, that absolutely identical principle which has already divided itself in the ego. Thus what for the philosopher divides itself already in the first act of consciousness, and which is otherwise inaccessible to any intuition, shines back to us from its products by the miracle of art.

But not only the first principle of philosophy and the first intuition from which it proceeds, but also the whole mechanism that philosophy deduces and on which it itself rests, becomes objective for the first time through aesthetic production.

Philosophy starts out from an infinite dichotomy of opposed ac-

1. Philosophy as a whole proceeds, and must proceed, from a principle that, as the absolute principle, is also at the same time the simply identical. An absolutely simple, identical entity cannot be apprehended or communicated by description or, in general, by concepts. It can only be intuited. Such an intuition is the organ of all philosophy. But this intuition, which is not sensuous but intellectual and which has for its object not the objective or the subjective but the absolutely identical, the in-itself neither subjective nor objective, is itself merely something inward which cannot again become objective for itself: it can become objective only through a second intuition. This second intuition is aesthetic intuition. [Alternate version by Schelling.]

tivities; but all aesthetic production rests on the same dichotomy, which latter is completely resolved by each artistic representation. What then is the marvelous faculty by which, according to the assertions of philosophers, an infinite opposition annuls itself in productive intuition? We have until now been unable to make this mechanism fully comprehensible because it is only the faculty of art that can fully disclose it. This productive faculty under consideration is the same as that by which art also attains to the impossible, namely, to resolve an infinite contradiction in a finite product. It is the poetic faculty which, in the first potency, is original intuition, and conversely it is only productive intuition repeating itself in the highest potency that we call the poetic faculty. It is one and the same thing that is active in both, the sole capacity by which we are able to think and comprehend even what is contradictory—the imagination. Hence also it is products of one and the same activity that appear to us beyond consciousness as real and on the hither side of consciousness as ideal or as a world of art. But precisely this fact, that under otherwise entirely identical conditions of origin, the genesis of one lies beyond consciousness and that of the other on this side of consciousness, constitutes the eternal and ineradicable difference between the two.

For while the real world proceeds wholly from the same original opposition as that from which the world of art must proceed (bearing in mind that the art world must also be thought of as a single great whole, and presents in all of its individual productions only the one infinite), nevertheless the opposition beyond consciousness is infinite only to the extent that an infinite is presented by the objective world as a *whole* and never by the individual object, whereas for art the opposition is infinite in regard to *each individual object*, and every single product of art presents infinity. For if aesthetic production proceeds from freedom, and if the opposition of conscious and unconscious activity is absolute precisely for freedom, then there exists really only a single absolute work of art, which can to be sure exist in entirely different exemplars but which yet is only one, even though it should not yet exist in its most original form. To this view it cannot be objected that it would be inconsistent with the great freedom with which the predicate "work of art" is used. That which does not present an infinite immediately or at least in reflection is not a work of art. Shall we, e.g., also call poems works of art that by their nature present merely what is individual and subjective? Then we shall also have to apply the name to every epigram that records a merely momentary feeling or current impression. Yet the great masters who worked in these literary types sought to achieve objectivity only through the *whole* of their writings, and used them only as means whereby to represent a whole infinite life and to reflect it by a many-faceted mirror.

2. If aesthetic intuition is only intellectual intuition become objective, then it is evident that art is the sole true and eternal organon as well as document of philosophy, which sets forth in ever fresh forms what philosophy cannot represent outwardly, namely, the unconscious in action and production and its original identity with the conscious. For this very reason art occupies the highest place for the philosopher, since it opens to him, as it were, the holy of holies where in eternal and primal union, as in a single flame, there burns what is sundered in nature and history and what must eternally flee from itself in life and action as in thought. The view of nature which the philosopher composes artificially is, for art, original and natural. What we call nature is a poem that lies hidden in a mysterious and marvelous book. Yet if the riddle could reveal itself, we would recognize in it the Odyssey of the spirit which, in a strange delusion, seeking itself flees itself; for the land of fantasy toward which we aspire gleams through the world of sense only as through a half-transparent mist, only as a meaning does through words. When a great painting comes into being it is as though the invisible curtain that separates the real from the ideal world is raised; it is merely the opening through which the characters and places of the world of fantasy, which shimmers only imperfectly through the real world, fully come upon the stage. Nature is nothing more to the artist than it is to the philosopher; it is merely the ideal world appearing under unchanging limitations, or it is merely the imperfect reflection of a world that exists not outside but within him.

What is the derivation of this affinity of philosophy and art, despite their opposition? This question is already sufficiently answered by the foregoing.

We conclude therefore with the following observation. A system is completed when it has returned to its starting point. But this is precisely the case with our system. For it is just that original ground of all harmony of the subjective and the objective which could be presented in its original identity only by intellectual intuition, that was fully brought forth from the subjective and became altogether objective by means of the work of art, in such a way that we have conducted our object, the ego itself, gradually to the point at which we ourselves stood when we began to philosophize.

But now, if it is art alone that can succeed in making objective with universal validity what the philosopher can only represent subjectively, then it is to be expected (to draw this further inference) that as philosophy, and with it all the sciences that were brought to perfection by it, was born from and nurtured by poetry in the childhood of science, so now after their completion they will return as just so many individual streams to the universal ocean of poetry from which they started out. On the whole it is not difficult to say what will be the intermediate stage in the return of science to poetry, since one such intermediate stage existed in mythology before this seemingly irresolvable breach occurred. But how a new mythology (which cannot be the invention of an individual poet but only of a new generation that represents things as if it were a single poet) can itself arise, is a problem for whose solution we must look to the future destiny of the world and the further course of history alone.

Translated by Albert Hofstadter

Philosophical Investigations into the Essence of Human Freedom and Related Matters

Foreword

The author finds only few comments to make on the following treatise.

Since reason, thought, and knowledge are the first to be accounted to the essence of the spiritual nature, the opposition between nature and spirit was rightly first seen from this point of view. The formulation of this viewpoint is adequately justified by the firm belief in a purely human reason, the conviction that all thought and knowledge are completely subjective, and that nature is entirely without reason and thought, and also by the mechanistic manner of representation which prevails everywhere, since the dynamic principle newly revived by Kant simply returned to a higher mechanism, and was in nowise recognized in its identity with the spiritual. But that root of opposition has now been torn up, and the establishment of a more correct perception can easily be left to the universal progress towards better knowledge.

The time has come for the higher, or rather the real opposition to come to the fore: the opposition of necessity and freedom, in which the innermost center of philosophy first comes to view.

The author has limited himself exclusively to investigations into the philosophy of nature after the first general presentation of his system (in the *Journal for Speculative Physics*), the continuation of which was unfortunately interrupted by external circumstances. Following the beginning made in the essay *Philosophy and Religion*, which remained vague, to be sure, because of its faulty presentation, the present treatise is the first in which the author has set forth his concept of the ideal portion of philosophy with complete clarity. Therefore, if the first presentation was to have had any importance, the author must now place the present treatise by its side, which, according to the nature of the object of investigation, must contain more profound disclosures of the whole of the system than all more partial presentations.

Although the author has, with the exception of the one essay *Philosophy and Religion*, previously never explained his views on the main points discussed in this treatise, i.e., freedom of the will, good and evil, personality, etc., this has not prevented certain opinions entirely inappropriate to the content of this text — which seems, in fact, to have been quite ignored — from being ascribed to the author according to someone else's good pleasure. Moreover, it may well be that unappointed, so-called disciples have brought forth, supposedly in accordance with the author's principles, a number of wrong statements having to do with these as well as other matters.

It would seem that only a finished, concluded system should be able to have disciples in the true sense of the word. Up to now the author has established nothing of the kind, but has shown only specific aspects of such a system (and this often only in a specific — for instance a polemical — context). Thus he has declared his texts to be fragments of a whole, the perception of whose coherence would require a finer talent for observation than one is accustomed to find in importunate disciples, and more good will than is to be had in opponents. Because the one scientific presentation of his system was not completed, its true tendency was understood by no one, or only by the very fewest. Immediately following the appearance of this fragment the slandering and falsifying began on the one hand, and the annotating, revising, and translating on the other, the worst genre of which being those translations into a supposedly more genial tongue (since at that same time minds had been possessed of an utterly unrestrained poetic delirium). Now it appears that a healthier age is again wanting to enter. Faithfulness, diligence, and sincerity are again being sought. The emptiness of those who have strutted about with the maxims of the new philosophy like heroes of French theater, or have struck the poses of tight-rope dancers, is beginning to be generally recognized for what it is. At the same time those others who snatched up the latest pieces and sang them in all the marketplaces as if to a hurdy-gurdy have aroused such general disgust, that soon there will be no audience for them to find; especially if there were not critics, otherwise not malevolent sorts, who say of every incomprehensible rhapsody that combines a few of some well-known writer's expressions, that it is composed according to his principles. Let them rather treat all such writers as originals, which is what they want to be after all, and in a certain sense is what many of them are.

Thus may this treatise serve to quell some prejudices on the one hand, and much loose, light-minded gossip on the other.

Finally we wish that those who have attacked the author out of prejudice, whether openly or underhandedly, might set forth their opinion just as candidly as has been done here. If complete mastery of one's material makes its free artistic formulation possible, then polemic's artificial convolutions cannot be the form of philosophy. But even more do we desire that the spirit of a common endeavor be increasingly established, and that the sectarian spirit that all too often rules over Germans not impede the acquisition of a knowledge and viewpoint which Germans have ever seemed destined to bring to complete formation, and which was perhaps never closer to them than now.

Munich, March 31, 1809

Philosophical investigations into the essence of human freedom can in part concern themselves with the correct concept of freedom; for as immediately as the feeling of freedom is impressed on all people, the fact of freedom lies by no means so close to the surface that there would not be more than common clarity and profundity of meaning required simply to express it in words. In part such investigations can touch upon the connection of this concept with the whole of a scientific world view. However, both aspects of the investigation coincide here, as everywhere, since no concept can be defined individually, and the demonstration of its

connection with the whole is provided only by the final completion
of science. This must be the case above all for the concept of freedom, which, if it is to have any reality at all, must be not merely a
subordinate or secondary concept, but one of the predominant centers of the system. According to an ancient, but by no means si-
lenced myth, the concept of freedom is supposed to be incongruous
with any system, and every philosophy that lays claim to unity or
totality should lead to the denial of freedom. It is not easy to dispute
general affirmations of this sort; for who knows what limiting notions have already been associated with the word "system," so that
the assertion states something which is true, but also very common-
place. Or if one is of the opinion that the concept of freedom
contradicts the concept of system as such and in itself, then it is
curious that since individual freedom must in some way be connected with the universe (no matter if the latter is thought of realistically
or ideally), some system must be present at least in the divine understanding, with which freedom coexists. To make the general assertion that this system could never come to be perceived by the human
understanding, again is to assert nothing, since the statement can be
true or false, according to how it is understood. It depends on how
the principle by which man can know anything is defined. In pre-
suming such knowledge one should make use of what Sextus said
with regard to Empedocles: the grammarian and the ignorant man
can consider the presumption of such knowledge to have arisen
from boastfulness and elevation of self over others, qualities that
should be foreign to all those who have even a bit of practise in
philosophy. But whoever takes the theory of physics as his point of
departure and knows that it is a very ancient doctrine that like is
known by like (which purportedly originates with Pythagoras, although found in Plato, but was expressed far earlier by Empedocles), will understand that the philosopher asserts such (divine)
knowledge because he alone, keeping the understanding pure and
unobscured by darkness, comprehends the God outside himself
with the God within himself.[1] But those who are ill-disposed towards science customarily consider it to be knowledge like basic
geometry, completely abstract and lifeless. It would be briefer or
more decisive to deny this system even in the will or understanding

1. *Sext. Empir. adv. Grammaticos* L. I, c. 13, p. 238, ed. Fabric.

of the original being, to say that there are only individual wills, each of which constitutes a center for itself, and, to use Fichte's expression, that each I is absolute substance. Yet the reason, which presses towards unity, as well as feeling, which demands personality and freedom, is constantly rebuffed by a mere decree that prevails for a while, and then finally is undone. Thus Fichte's doctrine had to attest to its recognition of unity, even if only in the paltry form of a moral world order, whereby however, it fell into contradictions and inadmissible statements. Thus it seems that while much can be brought forward in defense of this assertion from a strictly historical standpoint, i.e., from previous systems (we could find no basis for this in the essence of reason and knowledge), yet the connection of the concept of freedom with the whole of a world view will probably always remain the object of a necessary task, without whose solution the concept of freedom itself would be mutable, and philosophy would be wholly without value. For this enormous task is the unconscious and invisible mainspring of all striving for knowledge, from the lowest to the highest. Without the contradiction of necessity and freedom, not only philosophy but every higher volition of the spirit would sink to the death peculiar to those sciences that have no use for it. But to withdraw from the dispute by renouncing reason looks more like flight than victory. By the same right someone else could turn his back on freedom in order to throw himself into the arms of reason and necessity, without there being cause for triumph on either side.

This same opinion was more clearly expressed by the statement: the only possible system of reason is pantheism; but pantheism inevitably is fatalism.[2] Such general labels by which entire points of view are designated, are undeniably an excellent invention. Once one finds the right label for a system, the rest follows of its own accord, and one is spared the trouble of investigating its peculiarities with any greater precision. Even the ignorant man can pass judgment over the most intricate thought with the help of such labels, as soon as they are but given to him. Nevertheless, in this sort of extraordinary assertion everything depends on the closer definition

2. Assertions made previously to this effect are well-known. Whether Friedrich Schlegel's remark in his text *On the Language and Wisdom of the Indians*, p. 141: "Pantheism is the system of pure reason," could perhaps have a different meaning, we leave unanswered.

of the concept. For it certainly could not be denied that if pantheism designated no more than the doctrine of the immanence of things in God, every rational view would have to be attracted to this doctrine in some sense. But in just what sense—this makes all the difference here. That a fatalistic sense can be combined with pantheism is undeniable; but that they are not essentially combined is evident, since so many people are driven to the pantheistic view precisely by the liveliest feeling of freedom. Most people, were they to be honest, would admit that because of the nature of their representations, individual freedom seemed contradictory to nearly all attributes of a highest being, for instance to omnipotence. In freedom a power is asserted, unconditional in principle, which is outside of or beside divine power—but these very concepts make this inconceivable. As the sun in the firmament extinguishes all the celestial lights, even so and yet much more does the infinite power cancel every finite power. Absolute causality in one being leaves nothing but unconditional passivity for all others. This leads to the dependency of all the world's beings upon God, so that even their sustenance is but a constantly renewed creation in which the finite being is produced not as an undetermined generality, but as this determined, particular being, having these and no other thoughts, strivings, and actions. To say that God restrains his omnipotence so that man can act, or that he permits freedom, explains nothing: if God withdrew his power for an instant, man would cease to be. Since freedom in contradiction to omnipotence is inconceivable, is there any other alternative to this argument except to save man with his freedom in the divine being itself, to say that man is not outside God, but in God, and that his activity itself belongs to the life of God? Starting at this very point, mystics and religious minds of all times have come to believe in the unity of man and God, which seems to appeal as much to one's deepest feeling as it does to reason and speculation, or perhaps even more so. Indeed in this very consciousness of freedom Scripture itself finds the seal and earnest of the belief that we live and have our being in God. How, then, can *this* doctrine, maintained by so many in view of man in order to save freedom, necessarily be at odds with freedom?

Another explanation, usually thought to be even more to the point, maintains that pantheism consists in a complete identification of God with all things, a mingling of the creator with the creature. From this explanation a great many difficult and intolerable assertions are derived. Yet one can scarcely imagine a more total differentiation between all things and God than is found in Spinoza, who is taken to be the classic representative of this doctrine. God is that which is in itself and is comprehended solely through itself; the finite, however, which necessarily is in something other, is comprehended only through this other. Obviously as a result of this differentiation things are distinguished from God not merely in degree or by their limitations, as it might seem according to a superficial view of the doctrine of modifications, but rather *toto genere*. Whatever their relationship to God beyond this might be, they are absolutely separated from God because they can be only in and after another (i.e., God), and because their concept is derivative and would not be at all possible without the concept of God. The latter, by contrast, is the only autonomous and original concept, alone affirming itself; to it all else can be related only as something affirmed, as the consequence is related to the ground. Only given this presupposition are other attributes of things valid, for instance their eternality. God is eternal according to his nature; things are so only in him, as a consequence of his existence, i.e., derivatively. Precisely because of this difference, all particular things taken together cannot constitute God, as is usually claimed. For whatever is derived according to its nature cannot, through any kind of summation, pass over to what is by nature original; just as little as the individual points of a periphery taken together can constitute the latter, since the periphery as a whole is necessarily prior to the points in terms of the concept. Still more fatuous is the inference that in Spinoza even the individual object must be equal to God. For even if the strong statement that each object is a modified God were found in his writings, the elements of the concept are so contradictory, that it breaks down even as it is being assembled. A modified, i.e., a derivative God, is not God in the truly eminent sense; because of this one addition the object steps back to its position, eternally separated from God. The reason for such misinterpretations, which other systems have also experienced in full measure, lies in the general misunderstanding of the law of identity or of the meaning of the copula in judgment. A child might readily be made to understand that in no possible statement which according to accepted explanation states the identity of subject and predicate, will this uniformity or even a mere immediate connection between the two be expressed — as, for example, the statement: "This body is blue," does not mean that this body in or by its being a body is also blue; but means only that that same thing which this body is, is also blue, although not in the same regard. However, this supposition [of identity], which demonstrates complete ignorance of the essence of the copula, is constantly being made in our own times in relation to the higher application of the law of identity. If, for example, the statement is put forth, "The perfect is the imperfect," then its meaning is: the imperfect is not imperfect in or by its being imperfect, but by virtue of the perfect that is in it. But in our own time it means: the perfect and the imperfect are one and the same, everything is equal, the worst and the best, folly and wisdom. Or take the statement, "God is evil." This wishes to say that evil does not have the power to be by virtue of itself; the being within it is the good (viewed in and of itself). But it is interpreted thus: the eternal difference between right and wrong, virtue and vice, is denied, since both are logically the same. Or if in another phrase the necessary and the free are declared to be one, the sense of which is: the essence of the moral world is the same (in the final instance) as the essence of nature; then it is understood to mean: the free is nothing but natural force, a mainspring that, like all others, is subject to mechanism. The same thing occurs in the statement that the soul is one with the body, which is interpreted to mean: the soul is material — air, ether, nervous fluid, and the like. The opposite interpretation, that the body is soul, or in the previous statement that what is apparently necessary is free in itself, although just as easily drawn from the statement, is deliberately discarded. Such misunderstandings, which, if not intentional, require a degree of dialectical immaturity that Greek philosophy left behind practically in its infancy, make the recommendation of a thorough study of logic an urgent duty. Ancient, profound logic differentiated between subject and predicate according to what preceded and what followed (*antecedens et consequens*), and thereby expressed the real sense of the law of identity. This relationship remains even in the tautological statement, if it is not perhaps to be entirely meaningless. Whoever says, "The body is a body," consistently thinks of something different by the subject than by the predicate of the statement, namely by the former the unity, by the latter the particular qualities contained in the concept of body, which are related to it as the antecedent to the consequent. This is the very meaning of a more ancient explanation, according to which subject and predicate are opposed as the enveloped to the unfolded (*implicitum et explicitum*).³

Yet the defenders of the above assertion will now say that the point of pantheism is not that God is all (which is not easily avoided given the customary representation of his attributes), but rather that things are nothing, that this system annuls all individuality. Certainly this new definition seems to contradict the former one; for if things are nothing, how is it possible to mingle God with them? There would be nothing but pure, unclouded divinity then. Or if

3. Mr. Reinhold, who wished to recreate all of philosophy through logic, but who apparently does not know what Leibnitz, in whose footsteps he imagines himself treading, has already said on the meaning of the copula in the context of Wissawatius' objections (Opp. T. I ed. Dutens, p. 11), is still toiling in this labyrinth, in which he mistakes identity for sameness. In a paper that lies before us we find the following passage written by him: "According to Plato's and Leibnitz's requirements, the task of philosophy lies in the demonstration of the subordination of the finite to the infinite; according to the requirements of Xenophanes, Bruno, Spinoza, and Schelling, in the demonstration of the unconditional unity of the two." Insofar as this opposition obviously suggests that unity is to signify equality here, I assure Mr. Reinhold that he finds himself in error, at least with regard to the last two persons. Where is a more pointed expression of the subordination of the finite to the infinite to be found than in the one by Spinoza cited above? The living must protect those no longer present from calumniations, as we expect those living after us will do in the same circumstances out of respect for us. I speak only of Spinoza, and ask what one should call this practise, by which one blithely announces what one finds good in systems without knowing them thoroughly, as if it were a mere trifle to ascribe this, that, or the other thing to them. In normal, moral society it would be called *unconscionable*. According to another passage in the same paper, the fundamental error of all newer philosophy, as well as the older, lies for Mr. Reinhold in failing to differentiate between (confusing, mistaking) unity (identity) and connection (nexus), as well as between differentness (diversity) and difference. This is not the first instance of Mr. Reinhold's finding in his opponents the same errors he imposes on them. This seems to be the way he uses the needed *medicina mentis* for himself, as there are said to be cases of persons possessing an excitable imaginative faculty who recuperated through the medications they had others take for them. For who, with respect to the older and newer philosophy, commits this error of mistaking what he calls unity (but what is sameness) with connection more decisively than Mr. Reinhold himself, who interprets the comprehension of all things in God as Spinoza's assertion of their *equality*, and who generally considers non-differentness (with respect to substance or essence) to be non-difference? If Spinoza is actually to be understood as Mr. Reinhold interprets him, then the well-known statement that the thing and the concept of the thing are one would have to be understood to mean that, for example, one could beat the enemy with the concept of an army instead of an army, etc., consequences that the serious and thoughtful man will certainly find himself above drawing.

there is nothing outside God (not only *extra*, but also *praeter Deum*), how can he be all, except in word only, so that the whole concept seems to dissolve and waft off into nothing? In any case one must ask if much is gained by resurrecting such general labels, which may well deserve to be held in honor in the history of heresies, but which seem to be far too crude handholds for the products of the spirit, where, as in nature's most delicate appearances, subtle distinctions cause essential changes. One could also doubt if the last mentioned distinction could even be applied to Spinoza. For if he recognizes nothing beyond (*praeter*) substance except mere affections, which are declared to be things, then this concept is purely negative, expressing nothing essential or positive. It serves merely to determine the relation of things to God, but not what they might be when considered in themselves. One cannot conclude from the deficiency of this determination that things contain nothing positive, even if only derivatively. Spinoza's most difficult expression is certainly the following: the individual being is substance itself, considered in one of its modifications, i.e., one of its consequences. If we posit that infinite substance = A, and infinite substance considered in one of its consequences = $\frac{A}{a}$; then the positive in $\frac{A}{a}$ is certainly A. But it does not therefore follow that $\frac{A}{a}$ = A, i.e., that infinite substance considered in its consequence *is the same* as infinite substance considered as such; in other words, it does not follow that $\frac{A}{a}$ is not a separate, particular substance (even though the consequence of A). Of course this is not stated in Spinoza's writings. But our primary concern here is pantheism as such, so the only question is whether the given view is incompatible with Spinozism *per se*. One would be hard-pressed to assert this, since it has been admitted that Leibnitz's monads, which are entirely the same as what is expressed by $\frac{A}{a}$ above, are not a decisive remedy against Spinozism. Without an added explanation of the above sort a number of Spinoza's statements remain enigmatic, for example that the essence of the human soul is a living concept of God; this concept is explained in terms of being eternal (not transitory). Thus even if substance dwelled in its other consequences, $\frac{A}{b}$, $\frac{A}{c}$ . . . , only transitorily, it would still dwell eternally in this consequence, the human soul = a, and thus substance as $\frac{A}{a}$ would be divided from itself as A in an eternal and undying manner.

If one wished, furthermore, to explain the true character of pantheism in terms of the denial, not of individuality, but of freedom, then a great number of systems would be contained within this concept which otherwise are essentially different from it. For up to the discovery of idealism a true concept of freedom was lacking in all more recent systems: in Leibnitz's as well as Spinoza's. And freedom as it has been thought of by many among us—who further-more can boast of the liveliest feeling of freedom, according to which it consists in the sheer domination of the intelligent principle over the sensual principle and the desires—a freedom of this sort can still be derived from Spinoza, not with difficulty, but rather quite easily, and even with greater definitude. Thus the denial or the assertion of freedom in general appears to be based on something entirely other than the assumption or non-assumption of pantheism (the immanence of things in God). For if at first glance it seems as if freedom, unable to maintain itself in opposition to God, were de-stroyed in the identity, still one can say that this semblance is merely the consequence of an imperfect and empty representation of the law of identity. This principle does not give expression to a unity which, revolving in a circle of sameness, would be unprogressive, and thus insensitive or unalive. The unity of this law is immediately creative. In the relation of the subject to the predicate we have already shown the relation of the ground to the consequent, and the law of [sufficient] reason is therefore just as original as the law of identity. For this reason the eternal must also be a ground in an immediate manner, just as it is in itself. That of which the eternal by its essence is ground, is, to this extent, a dependent, and from the viewpoint of immanence, is also comprehended in the eternal. But dependence does not annul autonomy or even freedom. It does not determine essence, but merely says that the dependent, whatever it might be, can only be as a consequent of that upon which it is dependent; it does not say what it is, and what it is not. Each organic individual, as something which has become, has its being only through another, and to this extent it is dependent in terms of becoming, but not at all in terms of being. It is not incongruous, says Leibnitz, that he who is God is at the same time begotten, or vice versa; as it is no more a contradiction that he who is the son of a man is himself a man. On the contrary, if the dependent or conse-quent were not autonomous, this rather would be contradictory. This would be dependence without a dependent, consequence without a consequent (*consequentia absque consequente*), and thus would not be an actual consequence, i.e., the whole concept would annul itself. The same holds true for the comprehension of one thing in another. The individual member, such as the eye, is possible only in the whole of an organism; nevertheless it has a life for itself, indeed a kind of freedom, the obvious proof of which is disease, which lies within the eye's capability. If what is comprehended in another were not itself alive, then there would be comprehension without something being comprehended, i.e., nothing would be comprehended. A much higher point of view is afforded by considering the divine being itself, the idea of which would totally contradict any consequence other than engenderment, i.e., the positing of something autonomous. God is not a God of the dead, but of the living. It is incomprehensible how the most perfect being could delight in a machine, even the most perfect one possible. However one might think of the manner of consecution of beings from God, it can never be mechanical, never a mere effecting of positing, where what is effected is nothing for itself. Nor can it any more be emanation, in which case what flows out remains the same as that from which it flowed, and thus is nothing of its own, nothing autonomous. The consecution of things from God is a self-revelation of God. God can reveal himself only in what is like him, in free beings that act by themselves, for whose being there is no ground except God, but who are as God is. He speaks, and they are there. Even if all the world's beings were only thoughts in the divine mind, for this very reason they would have to be living. Thus thoughts are certainly engendered by the soul; but the engendered thought is an independent power, continuing to act by itself, indeed growing to such an extent in the human soul that it vanquishes its own mother and subjugates her. Yet divine imagination, which is the cause of the specification of the world's beings, is not like human imagination, which imparts mere ideal actuality to its creatures. The divinity's representations can be only autonomous beings; for what limits our representations other than our seeing the limited? God looks at the things-in-themselves. But only the eternal is in itself, resting in itself; it alone is will and freedom. The concept of a derivative absoluteness or divinity is so little contradictory, that it is far more the central concept of all philosophy. A divinity of this sort is attributed to nature. Immanence in God so little contradicts freedom, that only the free, and only insofar as it is free, is in God, and the unfree, insofar as it is unfree, is necessarily outside God.

As unsatisfactory as such a general deduction is in itself for those who see more deeply, yet it at least illuminates that the denial of formal freedom is not necessarily implicit in pantheism. We do not expect anyone to oppose us with Spinozism. It takes a lot of cheek to assert that a system, however it has been composed in some person's head, is the system of reason *kat' exochēn*, eternal and unchanging. What is understood by Spinozism? Perhaps the whole doctrine as it is presented in the man's writings, thus also his mechanistic physics, for instance? Or according to what principle would divisions and sections be made, where everything is supposed to be so replete with extraordinary and singular consistency? It shall forever remain a striking phenomenon in the history of German intellectual development, that at any time the assertion could be made that the system which mingles God with things, the creature with the creator (thus it was understood), and which subjects all to blind, mindless necessity, is the only system of reason possible, the only one that can be developed from pure reason! In order to comprehend this we must recall the prevailing spirit of an earlier age. At that time mechanistic thought, which rose to the peak of its atrocity in French atheism, had taken possession of nearly all minds. In Germany, too, one began to look at this manner of thinking and to hold it for the only true philosophy. Since, however, the originally German mind could never be in union with the consequences of this thought, at that time the schism between mind and heart characteristic of the philosophical literature of more recent times first arose. One abhorred the consequences of this manner of thinking without being able to free oneself from its ground or to rise to better thought. The wish was to express these consequences, and since the German mind could apprehend mechanistic philosophy only in its (supposed) highest expression, in this manner the dreadful truth was uttered: all philosophy, absolutely all, that is purely rational, is or becomes Spinozism! Now all men were warned of the abyss; it had been laid bare before all eyes. The one remedy that still seemed viable was seized; this bold word was able to give rise to the crisis and frighten Germans quite away from that pernicious philosophy, leading them back to the heart, inner feeling, and faith. Nowadays, since this manner of thinking has long since passed and the higher light of idealism shines upon us, the same assertion would not be comprehensible to the same degree, nor would it hold the same consequences.[4]

And now, once and for all, our definite opinion of Spinozism! This system is not fatalism because it allows things to be conceived in God, for as we have shown, pantheism does not make formal freedom, at least, an impossibility. Thus Spinoza must be a fatalist for reasons quite different from and independent of this. The error of his system lies by no means in the positing of things *in God*, but rather in that there are *things* in the abstract concept of the world's beings, instead of infinite substance itself, which in fact is also a thing for him. Thus his arguments against freedom are entirely deterministic, and in nowise pantheistic. He treats the will, too, as a thing, and then very naturally proves that it must be determined in its every action by another thing, which, in turn, is determined by yet another, etc., into infinity. Hence the lifelessness of his system: the mindlessness of its form, the impoverishment of its concepts and expressions, the unyielding acerbity of its definitions — this all being superbly compatible with the abstract point of view; hence also, with complete consistency, his mechanistic view of nature. Or is there any doubt that with the dynamic representation of nature the fundamental views of Spinozism must be essentially changed? If the doctrine of the comprehension of all things in God is the ground of the whole system, then this doctrine must at least first be animated and wrested from abstractions before it can become the principle of a system of reason. How general is the expression that finite beings are modifications or consequences of God! What a gulf must be filled in here, and what questions must be answered! One could view Spinozism in its rigidity as Pygmalion's statue: it needed to be given a soul by the warm breath of love. But this comparison is

4. In a review of Fichte's more recent writings in the *Heidelberg Annuals of Literature* (Vol. 1, No. 6, p. 139), Mr. Friedrich Schlegel advises Fichte to hold exclusively to Spinoza in his polemical undertakings, because only in the latter would he meet with a system of pantheism completely perfect in form and consistency — which, according to the above statements, would at once be the system of pure reason. While this advice may otherwise offer certain advantages, yet it becomes strange insofar as Mr. Fichte is doubtless of the opinion that Spinozism (as Spinozism) has already been refuted by his *Doctrine of Science* wherein he is also quite correct. Or perhaps idealism is not a work of reason? And perhaps the supposedly sad honor of being a system of reason remains only for pantheism and Spinozism?

imperfect, since Spinozism much rather approximates a work sketched in only its barest outlines, whose many missing or unexecuted features would first be noticed if it were given a soul. It should rather be compared to the most ancient images of the divinities, which appeared the more mysterious the less their features were expressed with individuality and liveliness. In a word, Spinozism is a one-sidedly realistic system, an expression which sounds less condemnatory than pantheism, to be sure, but which indicates its peculiarity much more correctly — and which also is not being used for the first time here. It would be tedious to reiterate the many explanations that can be found on this point in the author's first writings. The interpenetration of realism and idealism was the explicit intent of his endeavors. The fundamental concept of Spinozism, spiritualized through the principle of idealism (and changed on one essential point), acquired a living basis in the higher view of nature and in the recognized unity of the dynamic with the mental and spiritual. Out of this grew the philosophy of nature. While it could stand alone as mere physics, it was always considered to be only one part with respect to the whole of philosophy, namely the real part. Only after it is completed by the ideal part, in which freedom dominates, is it able to be raised to the true system of reason. In freedom, it was asserted, is found the final potentiating act through which all of nature is transfigured into sensation, intelligence, and finally into will. In the final and highest instance there is no being other than will. Will is original being, and to it alone all predicates of being apply: groundlessness, eternality, independence of time, self-affirmation. All philosophy strives only to find this highest expression.

It is to this point that philosophy, through idealism, has been raised in our times; and only from here can we truly take up the object of our investigation. For it could by no means be our intent to give consideration to all the difficulties which can be raised against the concept of freedom from the one-sidedly realistic or dogmatic system, and which have long since been raised. Yet as far as idealism has brought us in this regard, and as certainly as we have it to thank for the first perfect concept of formal freedom, in itself it is anything but a completed system. As soon as we wish to deal more precisely or specifically with the doctrine of freedom, it nevertheless leaves us perplexed. In this regard we note that in idealism which has been developed into a system, it is by no means sufficient to assert that,

"Activity, life, and freedom alone are true actuality," whereby even Fichte's subjective idealism (which misunderstands itself) can remain standing. Rather the demand is made that the converse be demonstrated as well: that all actuality (nature, the world of things) has activity, life, and freedom as its ground, or in Fichte's words, that not only is the I all, but conversely, all is I as well. The thought of making freedom the single, all-inclusive principle of philosophy set the human spirit completely free — and this not merely with reference to itself — and has achieved in all divisions of science a more emphatic about-face than any previous revolution. The idealistic concept is the true initiation into the higher philosophy of our times, particularly into its higher realism. Would that those who judge or appropriate this realism bear in mind that its innermost presupposition is freedom; in what a different light they would regard and apprehend it! Only he who has tasted of freedom can sense the desire to make everything its analogue, to spread it throughout the whole universe. Whoever does not come to philosophy by this path merely follows and imitates what others do, without feeling why they do it. But it will forever remain a curiosity that Kant, after he had first only negatively differentiated things-in-themselves from appearances by making them independent of time, and later, in the metaphysical discussions of his *Critique of Practical Reason*, actually had treated freedom and independence of time as correlative concepts, did not proceed to think of transferring this solely possible positive concept of In-itself to things, whereby he immediately would have risen to a higher point of view, above the negativity characteristic of his theoretical philosophy. But on the other hand, if freedom is the positive concept of In-itself as such, then the investigation of human freedom is again thrown back into the general, since the intelligible, upon which freedom alone was grounded, is also the essence of the things-in-themselves. Thus idealism is insufficient for demonstrating the specific difference, i.e., the distinctness of human freedom. Likewise it would be wrong to suppose that pantheism has been annulled and destroyed by idealism; this opinion could arise only by mistaking pantheism for one-sided realism. For whether individual things are comprehended in an absolute substance, or just as many individual wills are comprehended in an original will — to pantheism, as such, it is all the same. In the first case it is realistic, in the second idealistic, but the basic concept remains the same. From this we can already see that the most profound difficulties lying in the concept of freedom can no more be solved by idealism, taken by itself, than by any other partial system. For the concept of freedom idealism offers is, on the one hand, only the most general one, and on the other, merely formal. The real and living concept, however, has freedom as the capability for good and for evil.

In the entire doctrine of freedom this is the point of profoundest difficulty, and it has been felt at all times, bearing upon not just a few systems, but more or less on all of them.[5] Certainly it bears most strikingly on the concept of immanence; for either actual evil is allowed, so that evil is unavoidably placed within infinite substance or within the original will itself, whereby the concept of a supremely perfect being is utterly destroyed; or the reality of evil must somehow be denied, whereby the concept of freedom disappears at the same time. No smaller is the difficulty, however, when even the remotest connection is presumed between God and the world's beings. For even if this is restricted to mere *concursus*, as it is called, or to the necessary cooperation of God in the creature's activity (which must be assumed because of the essential dependence of the latter on God, even if freedom is also being asserted), God still undeniably appears as co-originator of evil, since the permission given to an entirely dependent creature [to do evil] is not much better than co-causation; or the reality of evil must again be denied in some manner. The statement that everything positive in creatures comes from God must also be asserted in this system. Now if it is assumed that something positive is in evil, then this positive, too, came from God. Against this can be raised the objection that the positive in evil, insofar as it is positive, is also good. Evil does not thereby disappear, although it is not explained either. For if what has *being* within evil is good, where does that *within* which this being is come from, the *basis* which truly constitutes evil? Altogether different from this assertion (although often mistaken for it, even recently) is the following: there is never anything positive in evil, or in other words, evil does not exist at all (not even

5. In his work on India, and in several other instances, Mr. Friedrich Schlegel has the credit of bringing this difficulty to bear especially upon pantheism, although one can only regret that this keen-witted scholar has thought it well not to impart his own view of the origin of evil and its relationship to the good.

with or alongside some other positive). Rather all actions are more or less positive, and the difference between them is a mere plus or minus of perfection, whereby no opposition is established, and evil disappears altogether. This is the second assumption one could possibly make in relation to the statement that everything positive comes from God. In this case, the power that shows itself in evil would indeed be comparatively less perfect than that in the good, but viewed in itself or beyond the comparison, would itself be a perfection, which, like all other perfections, must be derived from God. Whatever we call evil in that power is but a lesser degree of perfection; it appears as a defect only in our comparison, but is not one in nature. It cannot be denied that this is Spinoza's true opinion. Someone could attempt to avoid this dilemma by replying: the positive, which derives from God, is freedom, which in itself is indifferent to evil and good. However if he thinks of this difference not merely in negative terms, but as a living, positive capability for good and for evil, then it is incomprehensible how a capability for evil could be a consequence of God, who is viewed as pure goodness. From this it becomes evident, to mention only in passing, that if freedom really is what it must be in consequence of this concept (which it infallibly is), then the above attempted derivation of freedom from God probably is not correct either; for if freedom is a capability for evil, then it must have a root independent of God. Hereby compelled, one might be tempted to throw oneself into the arms of dualism. But this system, if it actually is thought to be the doctrine of two absolutely different and mutually independent principles, is but a system of the self-laceration and despair of reason. However if the evil principle is thought to be in any sense dependent upon the good principle, then while the whole difficulty of the descent of evil from the good is concentrated on one being, still the difficulty is thereby more increased than decreased. Even if it is assumed that this second being was initially created good and fell from original being through fault of its own, the initial capability for a deed opposed to God still remains inexplicable in all previous systems. Thus if one wished, finally, to annul not only the identity, but also every connection between the world's beings and God, and to view their entire present existence, and thus the world's as well, as a departure from God, the difficulty would only be pushed back a step, but not annulled. For in order to have been able to emanate

from God, the world's beings must already have existed in some manner. Hence the doctrine of emanation can be opposed least of all to pantheism, since it presupposes an original existence of things in God, and thus also pantheism. But as an explanation of this departure one could assume only the following: it is either an involuntary departure on the part of things, but not on God's part, in which case they were cast out by God into the state of misfortune and wickedness, and God is the originator of this state; or the departure is involuntarily caused by both sides, perhaps through the superfluity of being, as some express it — an entirely untenable fancy; or it is voluntary on the part of things, a breaking loose from God, thus the consequence of guilt, upon which follows ever deeper lapsing, in which case this initial guilt itself is already evil, and thus offers no explanation of its origin. While this ancillary thought explains evil in the world, it also completely extinguishes the good and introduces pandemonism instead of pantheism; but without it all true opposition between good and evil disappears in this very system of emanation. The good is lost in infinitely many intermediate stages through its gradual diminution to what no longer has any semblance of the good, much as Plotinus[6] shrewdly but insufficiently describes the transition of original good into matter and evil. That is to say, through continued subordination and departure [from the good] an ultimate emerges, beyond which nothing else can become, and precisely this (that which is incapable of further production) is evil. Or if something comes after what is first, then something must be last, as well, in which nothing of the first remains, this being matter and the necessity of evil.

In light of these observations it simply does not seem right to throw the whole weight of this difficulty onto a single system, especially since the supposedly higher system opposed to it is so insufficient. The generalities of idealism cannot provide any assistance here either. Nothing whatsoever can be accomplished with such abstract concepts of God as *actus purissimus*, the likes of which earlier philosophy established, nor with the ones newer philosophy continually produces in its concern to put a goodly distance between God and nature. God is something more real than a mere moral world order, and has within himself completely other, more

6. *Ennead*. I, L. VIII, C. 8.

lively powers of movement than are ascribed to him by the impover-
ished subtlety of abstract idealists. The abhorrence of everything
real, the belief that every contact with the real contaminates the
spiritual, must naturally make one blind to the origin of evil as well.
Idealism, if it does not receive a living realism as its basis, becomes
just as empty and abstract a system as the Leibnitzian, the Spino-
zian, or any other dogmatic system. All new European philosophy
since it began with Descartes has this common defect, that nature
does not exist for it and that it lacks a living ground. Thus Spinoza's
realism is as abstract as the idealism of Leibnitz. Idealism is the soul
of philosophy, realism is its body; only both together constitute a
living whole. The latter can never provide the principle, but must be
the ground and the means by which the former actualizes itself and
assumes flesh and blood. If a philosophy lacks this living foundation—which usually is a sign that its ideal principle, too, was originally only weakly effective—then it becomes lost in those systems
whose abstract concepts of aseity, modifications, etc., stand in
sharpest contrast to the force of life and the fullness of actuality.
However, when the ideal principle actually acts powerfully to a high
degree, but cannot find the reconciling, mediating basis, it engenders a turbid and wild enthusiasm, which erupts in self-castigation
or, as in the case of the priests of the Phrygian goddess, in self-
emasculation; in philosophy this is accomplished by surrendering
reason and science.

It seemed necessary to begin this treatise by correcting those essential concepts that have ever been confused, especially of late. The
previous remarks thus are to be considered a mere introduction to
our true investigation. We have just explained that only from the
principles of a true philosophy of nature can a view be developed
which is completely sufficient for the task at hand. We do not
thereby deny that this correct view has been present in individual
minds for a long time. But these were also the very ones who,
without fear of those slanderous words—materialism, pantheism,
etc.—ever useful against all realistic philosophy, sought the living
ground of nature, who were natural philosophers (in both senses of
the word), as opposed to the dogmaticians and abstract idealists,
who cast them out as mystics.

The current philosophy of nature first established in science the
distinction between a being insofar as it exists, and a being insofar

as it is merely the ground of existence. This distinction is as old as its first scientific presentation.[7] Despite the fact that at this very point the philosophy of nature most definitely parts ways with Spinoza, in Germany one could still assert up to the present day that its metaphysical principles are the same as Spinoza's. And although it is this very distinction that yields the most definite distinction between nature and God, yet this did not prevent its being accused of mingling God with nature. Since it is this very distinction upon which the present investigation is based, let the following be given as commentary.

Since nothing is prior to or outside of God, he must have the ground of his existence within himself. All philosophies say this, but they speak of this ground as of a mere concept, without making it something real and actual. This ground of his existence which God has within himself is not God viewed absolutely, i.e., insofar as he exists; for it is only the ground of his existence, it is *nature* — in God, a being which, though inseparable from him, still is distinguished from him. This can be illustrated with the analogous relationship between gravity and light in nature. Gravity precedes light as its eternally dark ground; it is not *actu* itself, and flees into the night when light (that which exists) dawns. Even light does not fully break the seal beneath which gravity lies enclosed.[8] Therefore gravity is neither pure essence nor the actual being of absolute identity, but is only a consequence of the nature of absolute identity;[9] or it *is* absolute identity viewed in a specific potential. Moreover, that which appears as something existing with reference to gravity, itself belongs to the ground; hence nature in general is everything that lies beyond absolute identity.[10] As far as this precedence is concerned, it is to be thought of neither as precedence in time, nor as priority of being. In the circle out of which all things become, it is not a contradiction that what engenders one thing is itself regenerated by it. Here there is no first and last, because all things mutually presuppose each other; nothing is the other, and yet nothing is without the other. God has within himself an inner ground of his existence

7. See the *Journal for Speculative Physics*, Vol. II, No. 2, § 54, also note 1 to § 93, and the explanation on page 114.
8. Ibid, pp. 59, 60.
9. Ibid, p. 41.
10. Ibid, p. 114.

which to this extent precedes him in his existence; yet God is just as much prior to the ground insofar as the ground, also as such, could not be if God did not exist *actu*.

The view that proceeds from things also leads to this same distinction. First the concept of immanence must be discarded altogether insofar as it is supposed to express a dead comprehension of things in God. Instead we recognize that the concept of becoming is the only one commensurate to the nature of things. But they cannot become in God viewed absolutely, since they are *toto genere*, or, to say it more correctly, infinitely different from God. In order to be divided from God, they must become in a ground that is different from him. But since nothing can have being outside of God, this contradiction can be resolved only by things having their ground in that which is in God, but *is not God himself*,[11] i.e., in that which is the ground of his existence. If we wish to speak of this being in terms more accessible to man, then we can say it is the longing felt by the eternal one to give birth to itself. This longing is not the [eternal] one itself, but is eternal with it. It wishes to give birth to God, i.e., to unfathomable unity, but to this extent the unity is not yet within itself. Hence, viewed in itself it is also will, but will in which there is no understanding, and which therefore is not autonomous and perfect will, since understanding is the true will in willing. Nevertheless this longing is a willing of the understanding, namely its longing and desire; it is not a conscious but a presentient will, whose presentiment is understanding. We speak of the essence of this longing viewed in and of itself, of what must indeed be seen although it has long since been supplanted by the superior one which has risen from it, and even though we cannot apprehend it with the senses, but only with the mind and the thoughts. Following the eternal act of self-revelation, all is rule, order, and form in the world as we now see it. But the ruleless still lies in the ground as if it could break through once again, and nowhere does it appear as though order and form were original, but rather as if something initially ruleless had been brought to order. This is the incompre-

---

11. This is the only correct dualism, i.e., the one that at the same time allows unity. We spoke above of modified dualism, according to which the evil principle is not coordinated with, but subordinated to the good principle. It is hardly to be feared that the relationship established here would be mistaken for the dualism in which the subordinate is always an essentially evil principle and for this very reason remains completely incomprehensible with respect to its origin in God.

hensible basis of reality in things, the indivisible remainder, that which with the greatest exertion cannot be resolved in the understanding, but rather remains eternally in the ground. From this non-understanding is born understanding in the true sense. Without this preceding darkness there is no reality of the creature; the gloom is its necessary inheritance. God alone—the existing one himself—dwells in pure light, for he alone is from himself. Man's self-conceit balks at this origin from the ground and even searches for moral grounds against it. Yet we know of nothing more able to impel man to strive towards the light with all his might than consciousness of the deep night from which he was raised to existence. The effeminate complaints that this would make non-understanding the root of understanding, and night the beginning of light, while they rest in part on a misunderstanding of the issue (since they do not comprehend how the conceptual priority of understanding and essence can be maintained in this view), nevertheless express the true system of today's philosophers, who would gladly make *fumum ex fulgore*, to which end, however, even the most violent Fichtean precipitation is insufficient. All birth is a birth from darkness into light; the seed must be buried in the earth and die in darkness, so that the lovelier figure of light might arise and unfold itself in the rays of the sun. Man is formed in his mother's womb, and from the darkness of non-understanding (from feeling, longing, the glorious mother of knowledge) lucid thoughts first grow. Thus we must represent original longing to ourselves in this manner: it directs itself towards the understanding, which it yet does not know, as we in our longing desire an unknown, nameless good, and it moves presentiently like an undulating, surging sea, similar to Plato's matter, following a dark, uncertain law, incapable of forming something lasting by itself. But this longing, which as the still dark ground is the first rousing of divine existence, has as its counterpart a reflexive representation engendered in God, through which, since it can have no other object but God, God beholds himself in his own image. God, viewed absolutely, is actualized for the first time in this representation, although only in himself; it is in the beginning with God, and is the God begotten *in* God himself. This representation is at the same time the understanding—the *word* of this longing.[12] Eternal spirit, feeling the word within itself and at the same time the infinite

---

12. In the sense that one says: the word of [the solution to] a riddle.

longing, and moved by the love which it itself is, utters the word, which now, with understanding and longing together, becomes freely creating, omnipotent will, giving form in initially ruleless nature as in its own element or instrument. The first effect of the understanding in nature is the division of forces, since only thereby is the understanding able to unfold the unity which is contained unconsciously but necessarily in nature as in a seed. Thus in man light enters the dark longing to create something when in the chaotic jumble of his thoughts—all connected, although each hinders the other from coming forth—the thoughts divide and the all-inclusive unity lying hidden in the ground arises. Likewise in the plant it is only in relation to the unfolding and extension of forces that the dark bond of gravity is loosed, and the unity hidden in the divided material is developed. For because this essence (initial nature) is nothing other than the eternal ground of God's existence, it must contain within itself, although locked up, the essence of God as a gleaming spark of life in the darkness of the deep. But longing, aroused by the understanding, strives henceforth to contain the spark of life apprehended within itself, and to lock itself within itself in order that a ground always remain. Thus when the understanding, i.e., the light placed in initial nature, rouses longing, which is striving to return to itself, to divide the forces (to surrender darkness) and in this very division raises up the unity locked up in what is divided, the hidden light—in this manner something comprehensible, something singular first arises. This occurs not through external representation, but through true *imagination*, whereby what arises is imaged into nature; or, more correctly, through awakening, whereby the understanding raises up the unity or the idea hidden in the divided ground. The forces separated (but not completely dispersed) in this division are the material out of which the body is later configured; but the living bond which arises as the center of the forces in the division, which arises from the depths of nature's ground, is the soul. Because original understanding raises up the soul from a ground independent of itself as something internal, the soul itself remains independent of original understanding as a particular being sustained in itself.

It is easy to see that with the resistence longing provides—which is necessary for perfect birth—the most inward bond of forces is loosed in an unfolding that occurs only by degrees, and at every stage of the division of forces a new being arises from nature whose soul must be the more perfect, the more it contains in divided form what is still undivided in other beings. It is the task of a complete philosophy of nature to show how each successive process comes closer to the essence of nature, until in the highest division of forces the innermost center emerges. For our present purpose only the following is essential: every being which arose in nature in the manner indicated has a twofold principle within itself, which, however, is fundamentally one and the same, but viewed from two possible aspects. The first principle is the one by which beings are divided from God, or through which they are in the mere ground. But since an original unity occurs between what is in the ground and what is preformed in the understanding, and the process of creation comes to light only through an inner transmutation or transfiguration of the initially dark principle (since the understanding or the light placed in nature truly seeks only the light which is akin to it, which is turned inwards, in the ground); thus the principle which is dark according to its nature is the very one which at the same time is transfigured into light, and both are one in every natural being, although only to a certain degree. To the extent that the principle originates in the ground and is dark, it is the creature's self-will; but to the extent that self-will has not yet been raised to (or does not grasp) perfect unity with the light (as the principle of the understanding), it is mere craving or desire, i.e., blind will. Opposed to this self-will of the creature is the understanding as universal will, which uses the former and subjugates it as a mere instrument. But when through progressive transmutation and the division of all forces the innermost and deepest point of initial darkness is finally transfigured completely into light in one being, then while its will is a particular will insofar as the being is an individual, yet it is one with the original will or the understanding in itself, or as the center of all other particular wills, so that from both a single whole now comes to be. This elevation of the very deepest centers into light occurs in no creatures visible to us except in man. In man is the whole power of the dark principle, and in him, too, the whole force of light. In man are the deepest abyss and the highest heaven, or both centers. Man's will is the seed—hidden in eternal longing—of the God who as yet is present only in the ground; it is the divine spark of life locked up in the depths which God beheld when he decided to will nature. In man alone God loved the world; and this very image of God was apprehended in its center by longing when it came to oppose light. Because man arises from the ground (is creaturely), he has within him a principle relatively independent of God. But because this very principle, without ceasing to be dark in accordance with the ground, is transfigured into light, something higher emerges in him—*spirit*. For eternal spirit spoke unity, or the word, into nature. But the spoken (real) word has its being only in the unity of light and darkness (vowel and consonant). Now both principles are in all things, to be sure, but without complete consonance because of the deficiency of what was raised from the ground. Thus the word which in all other things is still restrained and incomplete, is first spoken completely in man. But in the spoken word is revealed spirit, i.e., *God* as existing *actu*. Now since the soul is the living identity of both principles, it is spirit; and spirit is in God. If the identity of both principles were just as indissoluble in man's spirit as in God, then there would be no difference, i.e., God as spirit would not be revealed. The unity that is indivisible in God must therefore be divisible in man—and this is the possibility of good and evil.

We expressly say the possibility of evil, and for the present seek only to make the divisibility of the principles comprehensible. The actuality of evil is the object of a completely different investigation. That principle which is raised from the ground of nature, and by which man is divided from God, is man's selfhood, but this becomes *spirit* because of its unity with the ideal principle. Selfhood *as* such is spirit; or man as selfish, particular being (divided from God) is spirit; it is precisely this combination which constitutes the personality. But by being spirit, selfhood is raised from the creaturely to the super-creaturely; it is will beholding itself in complete freedom, no longer the instrument of the universal will creating in nature, but above and outside all nature. Spirit is above light, just as in nature it raises itself above the unity of light and the dark principle. Thus by being spirit, selfhood is free from both principles. But selfhood, or self-will, is spirit—and consequently free or above nature—only by being actually transformed into original will (light). Thus while it remains (as self-will) in the ground (since there must always be a ground)—just as matter in a transparent body, having been raised to identity with light, does not therefore cease to be matter (the dark principle)—yet it remains merely as the bearer and container, as it were, of the higher principle of light. But by having spirit—provided it is not the spirit of eternal love—selfhood can separate itself from light, since spirit rules over light and darkness. Or the self-will can strive to be what it is only in identity with universal will, as particular will; and it can strive to be what it is only insofar as it remains in the center (just as the quiet will in the still ground of nature is also universal will, precisely because it remains in the ground), on the periphery, too, or as creature (for the creature's will is indeed outside the ground; but then it is mere particular will, not free but bound). Thereby in man's will there arises a division of spiritualized selfhood from the light (since spirit stands above light), i.e., a dissolution of the principles which are indissoluble in God. If on the contrary man's self-will remains in the ground as the central will, so that the divine relationship of the principles is sustained (just as the will in the center of nature never raises itself above light, but remains beneath it as a basis in the ground); and if instead of the spirit of discord, which wishes to divide the will's own principle from the general one, the spirit of love presides within the will, then it is according to divine manner and order. But that this very raising of the self-will is evil, is clarified by the following. The will that steps out of its supernaturalness in order to make itself, as general will, at the same time particular and creaturely, strives to reverse the relationship of the principles, to raise the ground above the cause, to use spirit, which it received only as the center, outside the center and against the creature, resulting in anarchy within and outside himself. Man's will is to be seen as a bond of living forces; as long as it remains in its unity with the universal will, these powers also are sustained in divine measure and equilibrium. But hardly does the self-will move from its position in the center, and the bond of forces also gives way; in its place a mere particular will rules which can no longer unite the forces under itself as the original will did, and which consequently must strive to form or assemble its own peculiar life from the dispersed forces, from the enraged host of desires and appetites (since every single force is also a craving and appetite). This is possible insofar as the first bond of the forces, the ground of nature, still persists even in evil. But since it cannot be true life, such as can exist only in the original relationship, there arises a life which is indeed its own, but which is a false life, a life of lies, a growth of unrest and corruption. The most fitting comparison is offered by disease, which, as the disorder that enters nature through the abuse of freedom, is the true counterpart of evil or sin. There is never universal disease without the hidden forces of the ground being discharged; it arises when the irritable principle, which is supposed to preside in the stillness of the depths as the innermost bond of the forces, activates itself, or when Archaos is provoked and leaves his quiet dwelling in the center and steps into the surroundings. Thus, on the other hand, all original healing consists in the reestablishment of the relationship of periphery to center, and the transition from sickness to health can truly occur only through its opposite, i.e., through the reassumption of separate and particular life into the inner spark of the being, from which the division (crisis) again results. Even particular disease arises only when what has its freedom or life in order to remain in the whole, strives to be for itself. Just as disease certainly is nothing essential, and is truly only a phantasm of life, a mere meteoric appearance of it—a hovering between being and non-being—even though it announces itself to one's feelings as something very real, so it is with evil.

This solely correct concept of evil, according to which evil rests on a positive reversal or inversion of the principles, has been given prominence again in recent times by Franz Baader, who has illustrated it with profound physical analogies, in particular with that of disease.[13] All other explanations of evil leave the understanding and

13. In his treatise, "On the Assertion that There Can be No Evil Use of the Reason," in the *Morgenblatt*, 1807, No. 197, and in "On Solids and Liquids," in the *Annuals for Medicine as a Science*, Vol. III, No. 2. For the sake of comparison and further commentary let us also cite here the pertinent note found at the end of this treatise, p. 203: "Here an instructive explanation is given by common fire (as a wild, consuming, tormenting heat) as opposed to the so-called organic, beneficial heat of life: in the *latter* fire and water come together in One (growing) ground, or in a conjunction; while in the *former* they separate in discord. But neither fire nor water were as such, i.e., as divided spheres, in the organic process, but the former was there as the center (*mysterium*), the latter openly or as the periphery. Precisely the unlocking, elevation, and inflammation of the former, along with the locking up of the latter resulted in sickness and death. Thus I-hood or individuality is generally the basis, the foundation, or the natural center of every creature's life; but as soon as it ceases to be a serving center and steps into the periphery as ruler, it burns there like a Tantalean rage of selfishness and egoism (of inflamed I-hood). ⊙ now becomes ○— that is, in a single place in the planetary system the dark center of nature is locked up, latent, and serves for this very reason as the bearer of light for the advent of the

moral conscience equally dissatisfied. They are all based on the annihilation of evil as a positive opposite and its reduction to the so-called *malum metaphysicum*, or the negative concept of the imperfection of the creature. It was impossible, said Leibnitz, for God to impart all perfection to man without making him into God. The same holds true for created beings in general: thus different degrees of perfection and all sorts of restrictions had to occur among them. If one asks where evil comes from, the answer is from the creature's ideal nature insofar as it is dependent upon the eternal truths contained within the divine understanding, but not upon God's will. The region of eternal truths is the ideal cause of evil and good, and must be put in the place of the ancients' [concept of] matter.[14] There are indeed two principles, he says in another place, but both are in God: these are the understanding and the will. The understanding yields the principle of evil, although it does not thereby itself become evil. For it represents natures as they are in accordance with eternal truths; it contains within itself the ground for the admission of evil. But the will is directed toward the good alone.[15] This sole possibility was not made by God, since the understanding is not its own cause.[16] If this differentiation of understanding and will as two principles in God—whereby the first possibility of evil is made, independent of the divine will—is in keeping with this man's sensual nature; and if, too, the representation of the understanding (of divine wisdom) as something in which God behaves more passively than actively, points to something more profound, yet, on the other hand, the evil that can originate from this solely ideal ground again ends up being something merely passive: restriction, defect, privation—concepts that are entirely at odds with the true nature of evil. For even the simple consideration that man, the most perfect of all visible creatures, is alone capable of evil, shows that the ground of evil could by no means lie in defect or privation. The devil, accord-

higher system (the irradiation of light, or the revelation of the ideal). Thus for this very reason this place is the open point (sun-heart-eye) in the system—and were the dark center of nature to elevate or open itself here as well, then the point of light would *eo ipso* lock itself up; light would become darkness in the system, or the sun would be extinguished!"
14. *Tentam. theod.* Opp. T. I, p. 136.
15. Ibid., p. 240.
16. Ibid., p. 387.

ing to the Christian view, was not the most limited creature, but the most unlimited.[17] Imperfections in the general metaphysical sense are not the usual character of evil, since evil often manifests itself united with an excellence of individual forces that much more rarely accompanies the good. Thus the ground of evil must lie not only in something positive as such, but rather in the highest positive contained in nature; which of course is the case according to our view, since it lies in the revealed center or original will of the first ground. Leibnitz tries in every way to make comprehensible how evil could arise from a natural deficiency. The will, he says, strives after the good in general, and must desire perfection, the highest measure of which is in God. But if it remains entangled in the voluptuousness of the senses and loses higher goods, then it is precisely this deficiency in further striving which is the privation in which evil consists. Otherwise, he supposes, evil requires a special principle as little as cold or darkness does. The affirmative enters into evil only attendantly, as force and efficacy into cold; freezing water bursts the strongest closed container, and yet cold truly consists in a decrease of motion.[18] Yet since privation by itself is nothing at all, requiring something positive against which it can appear, in order even to become noticeable, here the difficulty arises of explaining the positive that still must be assumed in evil. Since Leibnitz can derive this only from God, he sees himself constrained to make God the cause of what is material in sin, and to ascribe only what is formal in it to the original limitation of the creature. He attempts to illustrate this relationship with the concept discovered by Kepler of the natural force of inertia in matter. This is, he says, the perfect picture of original (i.e., preceding all activity) limitation in the creature. If two different bodies of unequal mass are moved to unequal velocities by

17. In this respect it is striking that it was not the scholastics who first posited evil as mere privation, but rather many of the earlier Church Fathers, above all Augustine. Particularly noteworthy is the passage in *Contr. Jul.* L. 1, C. III: "Quaerunt ex nobis unde sit malum? Respondemus ex bono, sed non summo, ex bonis igitur orta sunt mala. Mala enim omnia participant ex bono, merum enim et ex omni parte tale dari repugnat. — Haud vero difficulter omnia expediet, qui conceptum mali semel recte formaverit, *eumque semper defectum aliquem involvere attenderit*, perfectionem autem omnimodam incommunicabiliter possidere Deum; neque magis possibile esse, creaturam illimitatam adeoque independentem creari, quam creari alium Deum."
18. *Tentam. theod.*, p. 242.

the same impulse, the reason for the slowness of the first body's motion does not lie in the impulse, but rather in the tendency towards inertia that is innate in matter and peculiar to it, i.e., in the inner limitation or imperfection of matter.[19] But here it should be noted that inertia itself cannot be thought of as mere privation, but is something positive indeed, namely the expression of the inner selfhood of the body, the force whereby it seeks to assert itself in its autonomy. We do not deny that in this manner metaphysical finitude can be made comprehensible; but we deny that finitude in itself is evil.[20]

This manner of explanation in fact arises from a lifeless concept of the positive, according to which privation alone can oppose it. But an intermediate concept still remains, which forms a real opposition to it, and which is far removed from the concept of mere negation. This originates from the relationship of the whole to the individual, of unity to multiplicity, or however one wishes to express it. The positive is always the whole or the unity; opposing it is the division of the whole, the disharmony or ataxia of forces. Within the divided whole are the same elements that were in the single whole; what is material is the same in each of them. (From this aspect evil is not more limited or worse than good). What is formal in both is entirely different, and it is derived precisely from the essence or the positive itself. Hence there must necessarily be an essence in evil as in good, but in the former an essence opposed to the good which turns the temperature held within it into distemperature. It is impossible for dogmatic philosophy to recognize this essence, since it has no concept of personality, i.e., of selfhood elevated to spirituality, but only the abstract concepts of the finite and the infinite. Thus if someone wished to reply that it is precisely in disharmony that privation is, namely the privation of unity, the concept itself would still be insufficient, even if the general concept of privation included the concept of the annulment or separation of unity. For the separation of forces in itself is not disharmony; this rather is the false unity of forces, which can be called separation

19. Ibid, P. I, § 30.
20. For this same reason all other explanations of finitude, for example those based on the concept of relations, must be insufficient as explanations of evil. Evil does not come from finitude in itself, but from finitude elevated to autonomous being.

only insofar as it refers to true unity. If unity is entirely annulled, then conflict is thereby also annulled. Sickness is brought to an end by death, and no single note constitutes disharmony by itself. Yet in order to explain this false unity, something positive is required, which accordingly must necessarily be assumed in evil. But it will remain inexplicable as long as a root of freedom is not recognized in the independent ground of nature.

The Platonic view, insofar as we can judge it, can be better discussed in terms of the question of the actuality of evil. The notions of our age — which deals much more leniently with this point, and carries its philanthropism to the point of denying evil — do not have the remotest connection to such ideas. According to them, the sole ground of evil lies in sensuality, or in animality, or in the earthly principle, since they do not oppose heaven to hell, as would be fitting, but rather to earth. This notion is a natural consequence of the doctrine which states that freedom consists in the mere domination of the intelligent principle over the sensual desires and inclinations, and that the good comes from pure reason. One can accordingly understand that there is no freedom for evil (since the sensual inclinations dominate here), or, to speak more correctly, evil is entirely annulled. For while the weakness or inefficacy of the intelligent principle can be a ground for deficiency in good and virtuous actions, it cannot be a ground for positively evil actions and those contrary to virtue. Assuming, however, that sensuality or passive behavior towards external impressions would produce evil actions with a kind of necessity, then man himself would be only passive in doing them, i.e., evil would have no meaning with respect to himself, that is subjectively; and since what results from natural determination cannot be objectively evil either, it would have no meaning whatsoever. But to say that the reasonable principle is ineffective in evil also provides no ground. For why does it not exercise its power? If it wills to be ineffective, then the ground of evil lies in this willing and not in sensuality. Or if it can in nowise overcome the power of sensuality, then mere weakness and deficiency are here, but nowhere evil. Hence according to this explanation there is only one will (if it can be so called), and no twofold will. In this respect adherents of this view could be called by a name taken from Church history — Monothelites — now that such names as Arian have happily been introduced to philosophical criticism, although in a sense different from our own. But just as it is by no means the intelligent principle or principle of light in itself which acts in the good, but this principle combined with selfhood, i.e., raised to spirit, even so evil does not result from the principle of finitude in itself, but from the dark or selfish principle brought into intimacy with the center. And as there is enthusiasm for good, so, too, there is inspiration for evil. While this dark principle is effective in animals, as in all other natural beings, it has not yet been born into light in them as it has in man; it is not *spirit* and understanding, but blind craving and desire. In short, no fall is possible here, no separation of the principles, where there still is no absolute or personal unity. The conscious and the unconscious are united in animal instinct only in a certain and determined manner, which for this reason is unalterable. Thus, precisely because they are only relative expressions of unity, they stand beneath it, and the force working in the ground maintains the unity of principles befitting them ever in the same proportion. Animals can never remove themselves from unity, whereas man can voluntarily rend the eternal bond of the forces. Hence Franz Baader correctly states that it would be desirable that man's depravity go only as far as animalization; but unfortunately man can only stand above or beneath animals.[21]

We have sought to derive the concept and the possibility of evil from first grounds, and to uncover this doctrine's general foundation, which lies in the differentiation between what exists and what is the ground of existence.[22] But the possibility does not yet include the actuality, and truly the latter is the greatest object of our investigation. Moreover, what has to be explained is not, for instance, how evil becomes actual in the individual man alone, but rather its universal effectiveness, or how it was able to burst forth from creation as an unmistakable general principle, battling everywhere against the good. Since it is undeniably actual, at least as a general opposite, already there can be no doubt that it was necessary for the

21. In the above-cited treatise in the *Morgenblatt*, 1807, p. 786.
22. Augustine says in opposition to emanation that nothing can proceed from God's substance but God; therefore creation was created out of nothing, which is the source of its corruptibility and deficiency (*De lib. arb.* L. I, C. 2). This "nothing" has long since been the cross of the understanding. An expression from Scripture provides an insight: man is created *ek tōn mē ontōn*, out of that which does not exist, just as the famous *mē on* of the ancients, which, like creation out of nothing, might receive a positive meaning by the above distinction.

revelation of God; in fact this can be drawn from what was said earlier as well. For if God as spirit is the indivisible unity of both principles, and this same unity is actual only in man's spirit, then if it were just as indissoluble in him as in God, there would be no difference between man and God. Man would be absorbed in God, and there would be no revelation and no movement of love. For every being can be revealed only in its opposite: love only in hate, unity only in conflict. Were there no division of principles, unity could not demonstrate its omnipotence; were there no discord, love could not become actual. Man is placed on the pinnacle where he has the source of self-movement towards good and evil equally within him; the bond of principles within him is not a necessary but a free one. He stands at the junction; whatever he chooses, that will be his deed. But he cannot remain in indecision, because God must necessarily reveal himself and because in creation nothing whatsoever can remain ambiguous. Nevertheless, it seems he cannot remove himself from his indecision either, precisely because it is indecision. Hence there must be a general ground for the solicitation, the temptation to do evil, even if it were there only to enliven the two principles in him, i.e., to make him conscious of them. Now it seems that this solicitation to evil itself can be derived only from an evil principle, thus that the assumption of such an essence is still unavoidable; one is also quite correct to see in this the interpretation of Platonic matter according to which it is an essence originally resisting God, and therefore in itself evil. As long as this part of Platonic doctrine lies in darkness as it has thus far,[23] a definite judgment on this point is indeed impossible. However, from the previous considerations it is clear in what sense it could be said of the irrational principle that it resists the understanding, or unity and order, without therefore assuming it to be an *evil* principle. In this manner, too, we might well explain the Platonic saying that evil comes *from the old nature*. For all evil strives to return to chaos, i.e., to that state in which the initial center was not yet subordinated to light; it is an upsurging of the centers of yet unintelligent longing. However, we have proven once and for all that evil, as such, can

23. Would that this be elucidated someday by some excellent interpreter of Plato, or still sooner by the quick-minded Böckh, who has already given us highest hopes for this with his comments made in the context of his depiction of Platonic harmony, and with the announcement of his edition of the *Timaeus*.

arise only in the creature, since only here light and darkness, or the two principles, can be united in a divisible manner. The initial principle can never be evil in itself, since there is no duality of principles in it. Nor can we presuppose, for instance, a created spirit, which, itself fallen, solicited man to fall; for how evil first arose in the creature is precisely the question here. Hence we are given nothing for the explanation of evil but the two principles in God. God as spirit (the eternal bond of both [principles]) is purest love, but in love there can never be a will to evil, and in the ideal principle just as little. But God himself requires a ground in order that he can be; however, it is not outside him, but within him. And God has a *nature* within himself, which, though belonging to himself, still is different from him. The will of love and the will of the ground are two different wills, each of which is for itself; but the will of love cannot oppose, nor can it annul the will of the ground, since it would then have to strive against itself. For the ground must act in order that love can be, and the ground must act independently of love, in order that love exist in reality. Were love to desire to crush the will of the ground, it would fight against itself, be at odds with itself, and would no longer be love. This allowing of the ground's action is the only thinkable concept of permission, but in its usual reference to man it is entirely inadmissible. Likewise, of course, the will of the ground cannot crush love, nor does it desire to do so, though this often appears to be the case. For it must be a particular will of its own, turned away from love, so that when love breaks through it as light through darkness, love may appear in its omnipotence. The ground is only a will to revelation, but in order that the latter be, the ground must give rise to ownhood and opposition. The will of love and the will of the ground thus become one precisely by being divided and by each acting for itself from the very beginning. Thus the will of the ground arouses the self-will of the creature right in the first creation, so that when spirit then arises as the will of love, it may find something resistant in which it can realize itself.

The sight of all nature convinces us that this arousal has occurred through which all life first achieved the final degree of sharpness and definition. The irrational and accidental, which appears combined with the necessary in the formation of beings, particularly of organic beings, proves that it is not merely a geometrical necessity that was at work here, but that freedom, spirit, and self-will also played a part. Indeed, wherever there is appetite and desire, there is already a kind of freedom inherent, and no one will believe that the desire constituting the ground of this particular natural life, and the drive to survive not just generally but in this determined existence, were attributes given to the creature already created — but rather that they themselves did the creating. The concept of the basis discovered by empiricism, which is to assume a significant role in all of natural science, must, if given proper scientific consideration, also lead to the concepts of selfhood and I-hood. But there are accidental determinations in nature that can be explained only in terms of an arousal, occurring right in the first creation, of the creature's irrational or dark principle, i.e., only in terms of activated selfhood. Whence in nature the unmistakable portents of evil alongside preformed moral relationships, if the power of evil was first aroused by man? Whence the appearances that, even disregarding their dangerousness for man, still arouse general abhorrence?[24] Certainly it cannot appear as an original necessity that all organic beings are heading for dissolution. The bond of forces that constitutes life could just as well be indissoluble in nature; and if anything, a creature that restores what has become faulty within itself through its own forces seems destined to be a *perpetuum mobile*. At the same time, evil announces itself in nature only through its effects; evil itself can break forth in its immediate appearance only at the goal of nature. For as the dark principle had to be in the first creation (which is nothing other than the birth of light) as a ground so that light could be raised from the ground (as from mere potential to act), so there must be another ground for the birth of the spirit, and hence a second principle of darkness, which must be as much above [the first] as spirit is above light. This principle is the very spirit of evil

---

24. Thus the close connection which the imagination of all peoples, especially all fables and religions of the Orient, makes between the serpent and evil is certainly not without reason. For the perfect development of auxiliary organs, which has progressed to the highest stage in man, already indicates the independence of the will from the desires, or a relationship of center to the periphery, which alone is really healthy — where the former has stepped back to its freedom and circumspection and has divided itself from what is merely instrumental (periphal). On the other hand, where the auxiliary organs are not developed or are utterly deficient, there the center has stepped into the periphery, or it is the circle without a center in the passage cited above (in the note) from Franz Baader.

awakened by the arousal of the dark ground of nature; i.e., the spirit of the *disunion* of light and darkness, which the spirit of love, a higher ideality, now opposes, as previously light opposed the ruleless movement of initial nature. For as the selfhood in evil appropriated light or the word, and for this very reason appears as a higher ground of darkness, so the word spoken into the world in opposition to evil must assume humanity or selfhood and itself become personal. This occurs only through revelation, in the most definite sense of the word, which must have the same stages as the first manifestation in nature, namely so that here, too, the highest pinnacle of revelation is man: archetypal, divine man, however, he who in the beginning was with God, and in whom all other things and man himself are created. The birth of spirit is the realm of history, as the birth of light is the realm of nature. The same periods of creation found in the latter are also in the former, and the one is the likeness and explanation of the other. The same principle that was the ground in the first creation is here again the germ and seed, but in a higher form, from which a higher world is developed. For evil is nothing other than the original ground of existence, insofar as it strives towards actualization in created beings, and thus is, in fact, only a higher potential of the ground at work in nature. But just as the latter is eternally only ground and itself has no being, even so evil can never achieve realization, and serves merely as ground, so that the good, developing from it by its own strength, can, by means of its own ground, be independent and divided from God. God has and knows himself in this good, and as such (as something independent) it is in *him*. But as the unseparated power of the initial ground is first known in man as something inward (a basis or center) in the individual, so too in history evil initially remains hidden in the ground, and the age of guilt and sin is preceded by a time of innocence or unconsciousness of sin. For perhaps the initial ground of nature was at work long ago, attempting to make a creation for itself with the divine forces contained within it, but whose creations repeatedly sank back into chaos because the bond of love was missing (as is perhaps indicated by the succession of races that perished before the present creation and did not return), until the word of love went forth, and with it enduring creation began. In the same manner, the spirit of love did not reveal itself at once in history; but because God felt the will of the ground to be the will to his revelation, and recognized according to his providence that there must be a ground independent of him (as spirit) for his existence, he allowed the ground to act in its independence, or, in other words, God himself moved only according to his nature, and not according to his heart or to love. Because the ground, too, now contained within itself all of the divine being, but not as a unity, individual beings alone could have presided in this self-action of the ground. This primeval time thus began with the golden age, of which a faint memory has remained for the present human race only in legends, a time of blessed indecision when there was neither good nor evil. It was followed by the age of the rule of gods and heroes, or of the omnipotence of nature, when the ground showed what it could do by itself. At that time understanding and wisdom came to men only from the depths; the power of oracles welling up from the earth guided and formed their lives; all divine forces of the ground reigned on earth and sat as mighty princes on secure thrones. The age of the highest glorification of nature appeared in the visible beauty of the gods and in all the splendor of art and ingenious science, until the principle acting in the ground finally stepped forth as a world-conquering principle in order to subjugate all things to itself, and to ground a firm and lasting worldly realm. However, because the essence of the ground can never engender true and perfect unity by itself, the time comes when all this glory dissolves, the beautiful body of the previous world decays as from a terrible disease, and finally chaos enters again. But even earlier, before total decay is at hand, the powers presiding in the whole assume the nature of evil spirits, just as the same forces that were beneficent guardian spirits in the time of health become of a more evil and venomous nature with the encroaching dissolution. Belief in the gods disappears, and false magic, along with incantations and theurgic formulas, strives to call back the fleeing spirits and to appease the evil ones. The ground's attraction becomes increasingly apparent: anticipating the coming light, it releases all forces from indecision in order to meet the light in full opposition. As the thunderstorm is mediately stirred up by the sun, but immediately by a counteracting force of the earth, so the spirit of evil (whose meteoric nature we explained earlier) is aroused by the approach of the good, not by means of the impartation, but rather the dispersion of forces. Hence only with the decisive emergence of the good does evil, too, step forth with complete decisiveness *as* evil (not as though it were first emerging, but because only now the opposition is given in which it can appear entirely and as such). Likewise, the very moment at which the earth becomes without form and void for the second time—becomes the moment of the birth of the higher light of the spirit which was from the beginning of the world, but was not comprehended by the darkness acting for itself, and was within still closed and restricted revelation. Indeed, in order to counter personal and spiritual evil, the light of spirit appears likewise in personal, human form and as a mediator, in order to restore the rapport between creation and God to the highest level. For only the personal can heal the personal, and God must become man so that man may return to God. Only with the restored relation of the ground to God is the possibility of healing (of salvation) again given. It begins with the state of clairvoyance that befalls individual men (as organs chosen for this purpose) according to divine fate, a time of signs and wonders when divine forces counteract demonic forces breaking forth all around, and calming unity opposes the dispersion of forces. Finally the crisis results in the *turba gentium*, who stream across the land of the ancient world as in the beginning the waters again covered the creations of primeval time in order to make possible a second creation. A new division of peoples and tongues results, a new realm in which the living word, as a firm and constant center, enters into battle against chaos, and a declared conflict begins between good and evil, which lasts until the end of the present time, and in which God reveals himself as spirit, i.e., as real *actu*.[25]

Thus there is a *general* evil which, even if not present in the very beginning, did begin in God's revelation, having been awakened by the reaction of the ground. While this evil never comes to actualization, it continually strives to do so. This general evil must first be recognized before it is possible to comprehend good and evil in man as well. If in fact evil was already aroused in the first creation, and was finally developed into a general principle by the ground as it acted for itself, then man's natural tendency towards evil seems explicable simply because once the disorder of forces has entered

---

25. Compare this entire section with the author's *Lectures on the Methods of Academic Study*, VIII: "Lecture on the Historical Construction of Christianity."

creation through the awakening of self-will, it is already imparted to man at birth. Yet the ground continues to act unceasingly in the individual man as well, and arouses ownhood and particular will precisely in order that the will of love emerge in opposition to it. God's will is to universalize all, to raise all to unity with the light or to preserve it there; but the will of the ground is to particularize all or to make it creaturely. It wants inequality alone, this in order that equality may become sensitive to itself and to the will of the ground. Therefore it necessarily reacts against freedom as against the super-creaturely, and awakens in the creature an appetite for the creaturely, just as a mysterious voice seemingly calls a man seized by dizziness on a high and precipitous pinnacle to plunge down, or as in the ancient myth the irresistible song of the sirens rang out from the depths in order to draw mariners sailing through down into the whirlpool. The combination of a general will with a particular will in man seems to be an inherent contradiction which would be difficult if not impossible to unite. The fear of life itself drives man out of the center in which he was created; for this center is, as the purest essence of all will, a consuming fire for every particular will; in order to be able to live in it man must be mortified in all his ownhood, for which reason he must almost necessarily attempt to step out of it and into the periphery, in order to seek rest there for his selfhood. Hence the general necessity of sin and death as the actual mortification of ownhood, through which all human will must pass as through a fire in order to be purified. Despite this general necessity, evil always remains man's own choice; the ground cannot produce evil as such, and every creature falls by its own guilt. But just how the decision for evil or good comes about in the individual man, is still shrouded in utter darkness, and seems to call for a special investigation.

Up to now we have examined the formal essence of freedom less closely, although it seems that gaining an insight into it will be no less difficult than was explaining the real concept of freedom.

According to the usual concept, freedom is posited in an entirely undetermined capability for willing one of two contradictory opposites without any determining grounds except that this is wanted, purely and simply. While this concept of freedom has the idea of the original indecision of human essence to its credit, it leads to the greatest incongruities when applied to individual action. To be able to decide for A or − A without any motivating grounds would, to tell the truth, be but the prerogative to act entirely irrationally, and certainly would not distinguish man outstandingly from Buridan's famous beast, which, according to the opinion held by the defenders of this concept of volition, would have to starve between two equidistant haystacks of equal size and kind (because it does not have this prerogative of volition). The only proof for this concept consists in an appeal to the fact that, for example, it lies in everyone's power to retract or extend his arm with no further ground for so doing: for if someone says he is extending his arm to prove his volition, he could do this just as well by retracting it; his interest in proving the statement can determine only that he do one of these two; thus there is obviously an equilibrium here, etc. This sort of proof is poor in every respect, since it infers the non-existence of a determining ground from the ignorance of it; but it could be applied here the other way round, for precisely where ignorance enters, there determination is all the more certain to take place. The main issue is that this concept introduces the entirely accidental nature of individual actions and in this regard has quite correctly been compared to the concept in Epicurus' physics of the accidental swerving of atoms, which he invented with the same intention, namely to escape fate. But accident is impossible and conflicts with reason as with the necessary unity of the whole; and if freedom is to be saved only by the complete accidentalness of actions, then there is no saving it at all. Determinism (or, according to Kant, predeterminism) opposes this system of the equilibrium of volition, indeed with every justification, by asserting the empirical necessity of all actions on the grounds that each of them is determined by representations or other causes lying in the past which are no longer in our control at the time of the action itself. Both systems represent the same standpoint, except that if there were no higher standpoint, determinism would undeniably deserve preference. Both know nothing of that higher necessity equally remote from accident and from compulsion or external determination, which rather is an inner necessity welling up from the essence of the agent itself. And all the improvements one might seek to make on determinism—for example, the Leibnitzian revision that motivating causes only incline the will, but do not determine it—are of no help whatever in the main issue.

It was idealism which first raised the doctrine of freedom to that one region in which it is understandable. The intelligible essence of all things, and especially of man, is, according to idealism, beyond all causal connection, and beyond or above all time as well. Hence it can never be determined by anything preceding it, since it itself rather precedes all else that is or becomes within it, not according to time, but according to the concept, as an absolute unity that must ever exist wholly and perfectly in order that the individual action or determination be possible in it. In fact we are expressing the Kantian concept—not, indeed, exactly in his words, but in the manner in which we believe it must be expressed in order to be understood. But if this concept is assumed, then it seems the following has been correctly inferred as well. Free action follows immediately from the intelligible in man. But this is necessarily a determined action, one that is, for example (to mention what is closest at hand), either good or evil. However, there is no transition from the absolutely undetermined to the determined. The statement that intelligible essence should determine itself from pure, utter indetermination without any basis, leads back to the above-mentioned system of the impartiality of volition. In order for intelligible essence to be able to determine itself, it would have to be already determined in itself, not from outside, of course, since this contradicts its nature, nor from within by some merely accidental or empirical necessity, since all this (the psychological as well as the physical) lies beneath it; but it itself, as its essence, i.e., as its own nature, would have to be its determination. This is no indefinite generality, but is definitely the intelligible essence of this man. In no sense does the saying, *determinatio est negatio*, hold true for this kind of determinacy, since the latter is one with the position and the concept of essence, thus actually is the essence within the essence. Hence intelligible essence can act only in accordance with its own inner nature just as certainly as it acts completely freely and absolutely; or the action can proceed from within itself only according to the law of identity and with absolute necessity, which alone is also absolute freedom. For that is free which acts only in accordance with the laws of its own essence, and is determined by nothing else either within or outside it.

By presenting the matter in this manner at least one thing is gained: the incongruity of the accidental nature of individual actions is removed. It must be established in every higher view as well that the individual action results from an inner necessity of free essence, and accordingly is itself necessary. But this necessity must not be mistaken, as still happens, for empirical necessity based on compulsion (itself only disguised accidentalness). But what is this inner necessity of essence itself? Here is the point at which necessity and freedom must be united, if they can be united at all. If this essence were dead being and with respect to man something merely given to him, then since the act can proceed from him only by necessity, responsibility and all freedom would be annulled. But precisely this inner necessity is itself freedom; man's essence is essentially *his own deed*; necessity and freedom are interrelated as one being which appears as the one or the other only when viewed from different aspects: in itself it is freedom, formally it is necessity. The I says Fichte, is its own deed. Consciousness is the positing of self; however the I is nothing different, but is itself this very self-positing. This consciousness, however, insofar as it is thought of merely as apprehending the self or knowing the I, does not come first, but presupposes true being, as does all mere knowledge. But this being presumed to be prior to knowledge is not being, though it is not knowledge either; it is real self-positing; it is original, basic willing that makes itself into something and is the ground and basis of all essence.

But in a sense much more definite than this general one, these truths have immediate pertinence for man. As has been shown, man is an undifferentiated being in original creation (which can be presented mythically as a state of innocence and initial blessedness prior to this life); only he can differentiate himself. But this differentiation cannot occur in time; it occurs outside all time and hence is concurrent with the first creation (though as an act distinct from it). Although man is born in time, he is created in the beginning of creation (the center). The act by which his life in time is determined does not itself belong to time, but to eternity, nor does it precede time, but moves through time (untouched by it) as an act by its nature eternal. Through this act man's life extends to the beginning of creation; thus through it he is beyond creation as well, free and himself eternal beginning. As incomprehensible as this idea might seem to common thought, yet there is in every man a feeling that is in accord with it: as if he had been what he is from all eternity and had by no means only become so in time. Hence despite the undeniable necessity of all actions, and although every man must admit, if he is mindful of himself, that he is by no means accidentally or voluntarily evil or good, yet the evil man, for instance, seems to himself anything but compelled (since compulsion can be felt only in becoming, not in being), but acts willfully, not against his will. That Judas became a traitor to Christ, neither he nor any creature could alter; and yet he betrayed Christ not under compulsion, but willingly and with full freedom.[26] The same holds for the good man: he is neither accidentally nor voluntarily good, and yet is so little compelled that rather no compulsion, indeed not even the gates of hell, would be able to prevail against his disposition. However, this free act which becomes necessity cannot occur in the consciousness insofar as this is mere apprehension of self and only ideal. For this act is prior to consciousness, as well as to being, and first *produces* it. But it is not therefore an act of which man is not conscious, as the man who, perhaps to excuse his unjust action, says, "That's just the way I am," and yet is quite conscious that he is the way he is through fault of his own, however right he also is that it was impossible for him to act otherwise. How often it happens that from childhood on, from a time when, from an empirical point of view, we can scarcely credit someone with freedom and deliberation, a person shows a tendency towards evil from which can be foreseen that he will never yield to discipline and teaching, and who subsequently actually brings forth the bad fruit we foresaw in the bud. And yet no one doubts his responsibility; everyone is as convinced of this person's guilt as would be possible only if each individual action had been in his control. This general judgment of a tendency towards evil which in its origin is entirely unconscious and even irresistible as being an act of freedom, points to a deed and thus to a life prior to this life — except that it is not thought of as preceding in time, since the intelligible is outside of time altogether. There is greatest harmony in creation, and nothing is as separate and successive as we must portray it to be, but in the prior the subsequent, too, is already coacting, and everything happens at once in one magical

---

26. Thus Luther asserts in his tract, *De servo arbitrio*, and does so rightly, even if he did not correctly comprehend the union of this sort of infallible necessity with the freedom of actions.

stroke. Thus man, who now appears determined and definite, apprehended himself in the first creation in a determined form, and is born as the one he is from eternity, since by this deed even the nature and constitution of his corporealization are determined. The assumed accidentalness of human actions in relation to the unity of the universe designed beforehand in the divine understanding has ever been the greatest offence for the doctrine of freedom. Hence predestination was assumed, since neither the prescience of God nor true providence could be sacrificed. The authors of this doctrine felt that man's actions must have been determined from eternity; but they sought this determination not in that eternal action contemporaneous with creation which constitutes man's being itself, but in an absolute, i.e., completely groundless, decree of God by which this person was predestined to damnation and that one to blessedness; and thereby the root of freedom was abolished. We, too, assert predestination, but in a completely different sense, namely the following: as man acts now, so he has acted from eternity and even in the beginning of creation. His action does not *become*, as he himself as a moral being does not *become*; rather it is eternal by nature. With this that oft-heard, tormenting question ceases to be: why is this particular man determined to act evilly and wickedly, whereas someone else acts piously and justly? For the question presupposes that in the beginning man is not action and deed, and that as a spiritual being he has being prior to and independent of his will, which, as was shown, is impossible.

Once evil had been generally aroused by the ground's reaction to revelation, man apprehended himself from all eternity in ownhood and selfishness, and all who are born are born with the dark principle of evil clinging to them, even though this evil is first raised to their self-consciousness by the entrance of its opposite. As man now is, the good as light can be developed by divine transmutation only out of this dark principle. This original evil in man—which can be denied only by him who has become but superficially acquainted with man as he is within and outside himself—although entirely independent of freedom with respect to present empirical life, is nevertheless in its origin man's own deed, and is for this reason alone original sin. This cannot be said of that disorder of forces, certainly likewise undeniable, which spread like a contagion once anarchy had entered. For it is not the passions in themselves that are

evil, nor do we fight against flesh and blood alone, but against an
evil within and outside us which is spirit. Thus only that evil which
was contracted by one's own deed—but this from birth—can be
called radical evil. It is noteworthy how Kant, who in his theory did
not rise to a transcendental act determining all of man's being, was
led in later investigations by mere faithful observation of the phenomena of moral judgment to the recognition of (as he expressed it)
a subjective ground of human actions preceding all acts in the domain of the senses, which itself had to be, in turn, an act of freedom. Fichte, however, who in his speculation had grasped the concept of such an act, again relapsed into the philanthropism then
prevalent in his doctrine or morals, and purported to find the evil
preceding all empirical activity only in the inertia of human nature.

There seems to be only one ground that could be put forward
against this view, namely, that it cuts off all of man's conversions
from evil to good and vice versa, at least for this life. But if it should
be that human or divine aid—for man is always in need of aid—
determines him for conversion to the good, then the fact that he
allows the good spirit this influence and does not positively shut
himself off from it, likewise is due to that initial action by which he
is this man and no other. Hence in the man in whom this transmutation has not yet occurred, but in whom the good principle is not
completely dead either, the inner voice of his own and better (with
respect to how he now is) essence, never ceases to exhort him to
change. For only through an actual and decisive conversion does he
find peace within his own self and reconciliation with his guardian
spirit, as if only now the idea that was in the beginning had been
given satisfaction. It is true by strictest understanding that however
man is constituted, it is not he himself who acts, but the good or
evil spirit within him. And yet this does no harm to freedom. For
this very allowing of the good or evil principle to act within him is
the consequence of the intelligible deed by which his being and life
are determined.

Now that we have presented the beginning and the emergence of
evil up to its actualization in the individual man, there seems to be
nothing left but the description of its appearance in man.

The general possibility of evil consists, as has been shown, in the
fact that instead of making his selfhood the basis or organ, man can
rather strive to raise it to domination and to universal will, and, on

the other hand, to make the spiritual within him a means. If in man the dark principle of selfhood and self-will is completely penetrated with light and is one with it, then God as eternal love, or as he who actually exists, is the bond of the forces in him. If both of these principles are in discord, however, then another spirit assumes the position in which God should be, namely, the inverted god: that being aroused to actualization by the revelation of God which never attains to act from potential, which indeed never is, but always wants to be, thus which, like matter in the minds of the ancients, cannot be apprehended as actual (actualized) by the perfect under-standing, but only by false imagination (*logismōi nothōi*)[27]—which is sin. Thus it borrows its appearance from true being—since it itself has no being—by means of mirrored representations, as the serpent borrows color from the light; and it strives to bring man to sense-lessness in which it alone can be accepted and comprehended by him. Hence it is rightly represented not only as an enemy of all creatures (since they persist only through the bond of love) and especially of man, but also as man's tempter, enticing him to false appetites and to the acceptance of non-being into his imagination. There it is supported by evil inclinations of man's own, whose eye, being incapable of fixing its gaze upon the glory of the divine and of truth, constantly looks over to non-being. Thus the beginning of sin consists in man's move from genuine being to non-being, from truth to lying, from light to darkness, in order to become himself the creating ground and to rule over all things with the power of the center within him. For the feeling remains even in the man who has moved out of the center that he has been all things, that he was in and with God. For this reason he strives to return there, but by himself and not in God, in whom he could be there. Hence the hunger of selfishness arises, and to the extent that it dissociates itself from the whole and from unity, it becomes increasingly needy and poor, and for this very reason increasingly desirous, hungry, and poisonous. There is a self-consuming, ever destructive contra-diction in evil: it strives to become creaturely precisely while des-troying the bond of creatureliness, and out of its pride to be all things it falls to non-being. Furthermore, manifest sin fills us not

27. The Platonic expression in the *Timaeus*, p. 349, Vol, IX of the Zweibrücken edition; previously in *Tim. Locr. de an. mundi*, ibid., p. 5.

with regret, as do mere weakness and inability, but with fear and horror, a feeling that can be explained only by reason of sin's striving to break the word, to touch the ground of creation and profane the mystery. Yet even this is to become manifest, for only in opposition to sin is the innermost bond of the dependency of things revealed, as well as the essence of God, which is as though *before* all existence (not yet mitigated by it), and therefore terrible. For God himself cloaks this principle in creation and covers it with love by making it the ground and the bearer, as it were, of beings. Whoever now provokes it by abusing the self-will that was raised to self-being, for him — and against him — it will become actual. For since God cannot be disturbed — and even less annulled — in his existence, so, too, according to the necessary correspondence between God and his basis, that very spark of life which also shines in the depths of darkness in each individual man is kindled to a consuming fire in the sinner. Likewise as soon as the individual member or system in a living organism moves out of the whole, it feels the unity and cooperation themselves to which it is opposed, as fire (= fever) and is inflamed with inner heat.

We have seen how through false imagination and through knowledge directed towards non-being man's spirit opens itself to the spirit of lying and falsehood, and, soon fascinated by it, loses its initial freedom. From this follows conversely that true good can be effected only by divine magic, namely, by the immediate presence of being in consciousness and knowledge. Voluntary good is as impossible as voluntary evil. True freedom is in accord with a holy necessity, the likes of which we feel in essential knowledge, where spirit and heart, bound only by their own law, freely affirm what is necessary. If evil consists in discord between the two principles, then the good can consist only in their perfect concord, and the bond uniting both must be divine, since they are one not in a conditional but in a perfect and unconditional way. The relationship between them thus cannot be represented as an arbitrary morality or one proceeding from self-determination. The latter concept presupposes that the two principles are not inherently one; but how are they to become one, if they are not? Moreover, this concept leads back to the incongruous system of the equilibrium of volition. The relationship of both principles consists in the dark principle (selfhood) being bound to the light. Permit us to express this as religiosity in the original sense of the word. We do not understand this word to mean what a sickly generation means by it: idle brooding, affectedly pious presentiments of—or wishing to feel—the divine. For God is the clear knowledge or the spiritual light itself within us. In it all else first becomes clear—far from being unclear itself. And this knowledge does not allow the man in whom it is to be idle or to loaf. Where it is, it is something much more substantial than our philosophers of sensitivity think. We understand religiosity in the original, practical sense of the word. It is conscientiousness, or acting according to one's knowledge and not contradicting the light of knowledge with one's actions. One calls the man religious, conscientious in the highest sense of the word, for whom this contradiction is impossible, not humanly, physically, or psychologically, but in a divine way. He is not conscientious, who in a given case must first hold the law of duty before himself in order to decide, out of his respect for it, to do right. Even by its very meaning, religiosity admits of no choice between opposites, no *aequilibrium arbitrii* (the plague of all morality), but only of supreme decisiveness for the right without any choice. Conscientiousness does not necessarily and always appear as enthusiasm or extraordinary self-elevation, but once the arrogance of arbitrary morality is cast down, another and even worse spirit of pride would gladly make it so. Conscientiousness can have a completely formal appearance in the strict fulfillment of duty, where even a harsh and acerbic character is added, as in the soul of M. Cato, to whom one ancient ascribed this inner, almost divine necessity of action when he said that Cato was most virtuous in that he never acted rightly in order to act so (out of respect for the law), but because he could not have acted otherwise. This severity of disposition is, as the severity of life in nature, the seed from which true grace and divinity first blossom forth; but the supposedly more distinguished morality, of the opinion that it may despise this seed, is like a sterile blossom which bears no fruit.[28] What is highest is not, just because it is highest, always universally valid: and whoever has become acquainted with the race of spiritual voluptuaries, who must appropriate what is highest in science and feeling in order to indulge in the most abandoned indecencies of the spirit and to

28. Some entirely correct comments on the moral geniality of this age are included in the oft-cited review by Mr. Friedrich Schlegel in the *Heidelberg Annals*, p. 154.

elevate themselves above so-called common duty, will think twice before he speaks of the highest in these terms. We can already foresee that when everyone would rather be a beautiful soul than a rational one, and would rather be called noble than be just, morality will come to be derived from the general concept of *taste*, according to which vice will consist merely in bad or corrupt taste.[29] When the divine principle of morality as such breaks through in the serious disposition, then virtue appears as enthusiasm; as heroism (in the battle against evil), as the lovely, free courage of a man to act as God instructs him, and in his actions not to fall from what he has recognized in knowledge; and as belief, not in the sense of holding something for true which might be considered meritorious, or which lacks what certitude requires—a meaning which has been appended to this word in its use for common things—but in its original meaning as trust, confidence in the divine, which excludes all choice. If finally a ray of divine love descends in the unswervingly earnest disposition (which is always presupposed), then the moral life is supremely transfigured into grace and divine beauty.

We have now investigated as far as is possible the emergence of the opposition between good and evil, and how both interact with each other. But still the greatest question of this whole investigation remains. Until now God has been viewed simply as a self-revealing being. But how is he related to this revelation as a moral being? Is revelation an action that proceeds from blind and unconscious necessity, or is it a free and conscious deed? And if it is the latter, how is God as a moral being related to evil, the possibility and actuality of which depends on his self-revelation? In willing self-revelation, has he also willed evil, and how is this willing to be made congruous with the holiness and highest perfection within him, or, as it is commonly expressed, how is God to be justified in the face of evil?

The preliminary question regarding God's freedom in self-revelation appears to have been decided, to be sure, by the foregoing. Were God a mere logical abstraction to us, then everything would

29. Such a grounding of morality in aesthetics has already been announced by a young man, who probably is talking aesthetic nonsense, being, as many others today, too proud to walk the honest ways of Kant, and yet incapable of rising to anything better. In light of such progress perhaps something serious will still come of the Kantian jest that Euclid could be considered a somewhat ponderous introduction to drawing.

have to proceed from him with logical necessity; he himself would be like the highest law from which all things emanate, but would lack all personality or consciousness of revelation. But we have explained God as the living unity of forces, and if personality according to our earlier explanation lies in the combination of an autonomous being with a basis independent of it, so that both interpenetrate each other and are but one being, then God is, by the combination of the ideal principle within him with the independent (relative to the ideal principle) ground — since basis and existence are necessarily united in him in one absolute existence — the highest personality. And if the living unity of both is spirit, then God, as their absolute bond, is spirit understood in the eminent and absolute sense. It is just as certain that God's personality is grounded only in his bond with nature, since conversely the God of pure idealism as well as the God of pure realism is necessarily an impersonal being, of which Fichte's and Spinoza's concepts are the clearest evidence. But because there is an independent ground of reality in God, and consequently there are two equally eternal beginnings of self-revelation, then God, too, must be viewed in relation to both according to his freedom. The first beginning of creation is the longing of the One to give birth to itself, or it is the will of the ground. The second is the will of love, through which the word is spoken in nature, and through which God first makes himself personal. The will of the ground thus cannot be free in the same sense the will of love is free. It is not a will that is conscious or connected with reflection, but neither is it entirely unconscious, moving according to blind mechanical necessity. It is rather of an intermediate nature such as desire or appetite, and is most comparable to the lovely urge of a nature in the process of becoming which strives to unfold itself, and whose inner movements are involuntary (cannot be neglected), yet are made with no feeling of compulsion. However it is the will of love, precisely because it is this, which is utterly free and conscious will; the revelation proceeding from it is action and deed. All of nature tells us that it by no means exists by virtue of mere geometrical necessity; not pure, utter reason, but personality and spirit are in nature (just as we differentiate between the rational and the ingenious author). Otherwise geometrical understanding, which has dominated for so long, would have long since penetrated nature, and its idol of universal and eternal laws of nature would have been verified to a far greater extent than has occurred up to now, since it rather must increasingly acknowledge the irrational relationship between nature and itself. Creation is not an event, but an act. There are no results of universal laws; rather God, i.e., the person of God, is the universal law, and everything that happens, happens by virtue of God's personality and not according to an abstract necessity that *we* would not tolerate in our actions, to say nothing of God. One of the most pleasing aspects of Leibnitzian philosophy, which is all too dominated by the spirit of abstraction, is its recognition that the laws of nature are morally, but not geometrically necessary, yet are just as little arbitrary. "I have found," says Leibnitz, "that the laws that can actually be proven in nature are not absolutely demonstrable, nor is this necessary. They can indeed be proven in various ways, but there must always be something presupposed which is not a geometrical necessity. Hence these laws are the proof of a supreme, intelligent, and free being, and oppose the system of absolute necessity. They are neither entirely necessary (in the abstract sense) nor entirely arbitrary, but stand in between as laws originating from a wisdom perfected over all things."[30] The highest aim of the dynamic explanation is none other than this reduction of the laws of nature to mind, spirit, and will.

However, general recognition of freedom in creation is not sufficient to determine the relationship of God as a moral being to the world; moreover, one must ask whether the act of self-revelation was free in the sense that all its consequences were foreseen in God. But this, too, must necessarily be affirmed; for the will to revelation itself would not be alive if it were not opposed by another will originating from within his being. But in this keeping-to-himself there emerges a reflexive image of all that is contained in his being; in this image God actualizes himself ideally, which is to say, he recognizes himself in his actualization in advance. Thus, since there is a tendency within God counteracting the will to revelation, love and goodness, or the *communicativum sui*, must preponderate in order that there be revelation; and this—this decision—first truly perfects the concept of revelation as a conscious, morally free act.

---

30. *Tentam. theod.* Opp. T. I, pp. 365, 366.

Regardless of this concept, and although the act of revelation in God is only morally necessary, or necessary in relation to goodness and love, the notion of a consultation of God with himself or of a choice between several possible worlds remains unfounded and untenable. On the contrary, as soon as one adds but a closer definition of moral necessity, the statement is completely undeniable that all things follow from divine nature with absolute necessity, that all things possible by virtue of the divine nature must also be actual, and what is not actual must also be morally impossible. Spinozism is by no means mistaken in asserting such an inviolable necessity in God, but rather in assuming it to be lifeless and impersonal. For since this system comprehends only one side of the absolute—namely, the real side, or the extent to which God acts in the ground alone—these statements of course lead to blind, unintelligent necessity. But if God is essentially love and goodness, then what is morally necessary within him also follows with truly metaphysical necessity. If perfect freedom in God required choice in the most proper sense, then we would have to go still further. For there would be perfect freedom of choice only if God had also been able to create a less perfect world than was possible in accordance with all the conditions. Nothing is so incongruous that it has not been put forward once, and people have indeed maintained, some of them actually in earnest—and not merely as the Castilian King Alphonso, whose well-known utterance applied only to the then prevailing Ptolemaic system—that God could have made a world better than this one, had he wanted to do so. Thus the grounds against the unity of possibility and actuality in God derive from the completely formal concept of possibility, that everything is possible which does not contradict itself; as, for example, in the well-known contradiction that all novels intelligibly conceived must, then, be actual events. Even Spinoza had no such merely formal concept: for him all possibility pertains only to divine perfection. And Leibnitz clearly assumed this concept only in order to emphasize a choice in God, and thereby to remove himself as far as possible from Spinoza. "God chooses between possibilities," he says, "and thus chooses freely, without necessitation; only if there were but one possibility would there be no choice, no freedom." If freedom is lacking nothing more than such an empty possibility, then it can be conceded that formally, or without regard for divine essentiality, there was and still is infinite possibility. But this means that we wish to assert divine freedom by means of an inherently false concept possible merely in our understanding, but not in God, who cannot very well be thought to disregard his essence or his perfections. As concerns the plurality of possible worlds, infinite possibility certainly seems to be offered by matter, which is in itself ruleless (such as the original movement of the ground in our explanation), that is still unformed, but receptive to all forms, And if the possibility of several worlds is perhaps to be based on this, then we would need only note that no such possibility would result with regard to God, since the ground is not to be called God, and since according to his perfection God can will only one thing. However, this rulelessness is also not to be thought of as though the prototype of the only world possible according to God's essence were not contained in the ground, the world which in actual creation is raised from potential to act only through the division and regulation of forces, and the exclusion of the ruleless matter hindering or obscuring God. But in the divine understanding itself, as in primordial wisdom in which God actualizes himself ideally or archetypically, there is only one possible world, even as there is only one God.

In the divine understanding there is a system; however, God himself is not a system, but a life, and therein alone lies the answer to the question concerning the possibility of evil with reference to God, for the sake of which the above was offered as an introduction. All existence requires a condition in order for it to become actual, i.e., personal, existence. God's existence, too, could not be personal without such a condition, except that he has this condition *within* himself, not outside himself. He cannot annul this condition, for in that case he would have to annul himself; he can only overpower it through love and subordinate it to himself for his glorification. In God, too, there would be a ground of darkness if he did not integrate the condition into *himself*, combining himself with it as one, in absolute personality. Man never obtains control of this condition, although in evil he strives to do so; it is only loaned to him, is independent of him; thus his personality and selfhood can never rise to perfect act. This is the sadness clinging to all finite life, and if in God, too, there is a condition which is at least relatively independent, then within him there is a well of sadness, which, however, never comes to actuality, but serves only for the eternal joy of overcoming. Hence the veil of despondency spread over all of nature, the deep, indestructible melancholy of all life. Joy must have sorrow, sorrow must be transfigured into joy. Hence whatever comes from this mere condition or from the ground does not come from God, even though it is necessary for his existence. Neither can it be said that evil comes from the ground, or that the will of the ground is its originator. For evil can arise only in the innermost will of one's own heart, and is never accomplished without one's own deed. The solicitation of the ground or the reaction to the super-creaturely awakens the appetite for the creaturely, that is, one's own will, but it awakens this will only so that an independent ground exist for the good, and so that it be overpowered and penetrated by the good. For aroused selfhood in itself is not evil, but only insofar as it has torn itself entirely free of its opposite, light or the universal will. But this very dissociation from the good alone is sin. Activated selfhood is necessary for the sharpness of life; without it there would be complete death, the good would slumber; for where there is no battle, there is no life. Thus the awakening of life alone is the will of the ground, not immediate evil in itself. If man's will encloses activated selfhood in love and subordinates it to light as to the general will, then actual goodness first arises thereby, having become sensitive through the sharpness within him. Thus in the good the reaction of the ground works for the good; in evil it works for evil, as Scripture says: in the pious you are pious; in the perverse, perverse. The good which is without effective selfhood is itself ineffective good. The same thing that becomes evil by the creature's will (when it tears itself free in order to be for itself), is in itself the good as long as it remains swallowed up in the good and in the ground. Only selfhood overcome, and thus retrieved from activity to potentiality, is the good; and as potential, having been overpowered by the good, it also remains in the good forever. If there were not a root of coldness in the body, warmth could not be felt. It is impossible to think of an attractive or a repellent force by itself: for upon what is the repelling force to act, if the attracting force does not make an object for it; or upon what is the attracting force to act if it does not have a repelling force within itself at the same time? Hence it is entirely correct to say dialectically that good and evil are the same thing, but viewed from different aspects; or evil in itself, i.e., viewed in the root of its identity, is the good, as, on the other hand, the good, viewed in its disunion or non-identity, is evil. For this reason the saying is also entirely correct that whoever has neither the material nor the forces for evil within himself is also incapable of the good—of which we have seen sufficient examples in our times. The passions against which our negative morality makes war are forces, each of which has a common root with its corresponding virtue. The soul of all hatred is love, and one sees in the most violent rage only the stillness that has been affected and provoked in its innermost center. In proper measure and in organic equilibrium these forces are the strength of virtue itself and its immediate instruments. "If passions are the members of dishonor," says the excellent J.G. Hamann, "do they therefore cease to be weapons of manliness? Do you under-stand the letter of reason more shrewdly than that allegorizing chamberlain of the Alexandrian Church did the letter of Scripture, who castrated himself for the sake of the heavenly kingdom? The prince of this age makes the greatest self-violaters his favorites—his (the devil's) court jesters are the most wicked enemies of beautiful nature, which indeed has the Corybants and Galli as gormandizing ministers, but strong spirits as its true worshippers."[31] But then let those whose philosophy is better suited for the gynaeceum than for the academy or the palaestra of the lyceum not present these dialec-tical statements to the public, which misunderstands them as they themselves do and sees therein an annulment of all difference be-tween right and wrong, good and evil, and before which these statements are as little appropriate as those were of the ancient dialecticians, of Zeno and the other Eleatics, before the forum of languishing belletrists.

The arousal of the self-will occurs only so that the love within man finds a material or opposite in which it can actualize itself. To the extent that selfhood in its dissociation is the principle of evil, the ground indeed arouses the principle of evil as a possibility, but not evil itself, nor for the sake of evil. But even this arousal does not occur according to God's free will, as he does not move in the ground according to this, or to his heart, but only according to his attributes.

Thus whoever asserted that God himself willed evil would have to

31. *Cloverleaf of Hellenistic Letters*, II, p. 196.

seek the ground of this assertion in the act of self-revelation as creation, even as it has often been supposed that he who willed the world also had to will evil. However, in that God brought the disorderly births of chaos into order and spoke his eternal unity into nature, he much rather acted against darkness, and opposed the ruleless movement of the unintelligent principle with the word as a constant center and eternal lamp. The will to creation was thus immediately but a will to give birth to light, and thereby to the good. But evil came into consideration for this will neither as a means, nor even, as Leibnitz says, as a *conditio sine qua non* of the greatest possible perfection of the world.[32] It was neither the object of divine decree, nor even less of permission. But the question why God did not prefer to forgo self-revelation altogether, since he necessarily foresaw that evil would result, at least attendantly, indeed does not deserve a reply. For this would amount to saying in order that there be no opposition to love, love itself should not be, i.e., the absolutely positive should be sacrificed for what has existence only as an opposite, and the eternal should be sacrificed for the merely temporal. We have already explained that self-revelation in God must be viewed not as an unconditional, voluntary act, but as a morally necessary act in which love and goodness have overcome absolute inwardness. Thus if God had not revealed himself for the sake of evil, evil would have triumphed over the good and love. The Leibnitzian concept of evil as a *conditio sine qua non* can be applied only to the ground, so that it arouses the creaturely will (the principle of evil as possibility) as the condition under which the will of love alone can be actualized. Furthermore, we have already shown why God does not resist the will of the ground or annul it. This would amount to God annulling the condition of his existence, i.e., annulling his own personality. Thus in order for there to be no evil, there would have to be no God.

---

32. *Tentam. theod.*, p. 139: 'Ex his concludendum est, Deum *antecedenter* velle omne *bonum* in se, velle *consequenter* optimum tanquam finem; indifferens et malum physicum tanquam *medium*; sed velle tantum *permittere* malum morale, tanquam *conditionem, sine qua non* obtineretur optimum, ita nimirum, ut malum nonnisi titulo necessitatis hypotheticae, id ipsum cum optimo connectentis, admittatur." Ibid., p. 292: "Quod ad vitium attinet, superius ostensum est, illud non esse objectum decreti divini, *tanquam medium*, sed tamquam *conditionem sine qua non*—et ideo duntaxat *permitti*." These two passages contain the kernel of the entire Leibnitzian theodicy.

Another objection that has bearing not only on this view, but on all metaphysics, is the following: even if God did not will evil, he still continues to act in the sinner and gives him the strength to accomplish evil. And with the proper distinction, this is to be wholly and utterly conceded. The original ground of existence continues to act even in evil, as health continues to act in sickness, and even the most ruined, falsified life still remains and moves in God, insofar as he is the ground of existence. But such a life feels God to be consuming wrath, and through the attraction of the ground itself, it is placed in ever higher tension against unity, until it comes to self-annihilation and final crisis.

After all this the question still remains: does evil come to an end, and how? Does creation have a final intent at all, and if so, why is it not achieved immediately; why is the perfect not there from the beginning? There is no answer to this except the one already given: because God is a life, not merely a being. But all life has a fate and is subject to suffering and becoming. To this, too, God has subjugated himself freely, ever since he separated the world of light from the world of darkness in order to become personal. Being becomes sensitive to itself only in becoming. In being there is no becoming, to be sure; rather being itself is posited as eternity in becoming; but in actualization through opposition there is necessarily a becoming. Without the concept of a humanly suffering God, which is common to all the mysteries and spiritual religions of ancient times, all of history remains incomprehensible; even Scripture distinguishes periods of revelation, and posits a time in the distant future when God will be all in all, i.e., when he will be entirely actualized. The first period of creation is, as has been shown earlier, the birth of light. Light or the ideal principle is, as an eternal opposite of the dark principle, the creating word which redeems the life hidden in the ground from non-being, raising it from potential to act. Spirit rises above the word, and spirit is the first being which unites the worlds of darkness and light, subjugating both principles to itself for the sake of actualization and personality. The ground, however, reacts against this unity and asserts the initial duality, but only towards ever heightening intensification and the final division of good and evil. The will of the ground must remain in its freedom until all has been fulfilled, all has become actual. If it were subjugated before this, then good and evil together would remain hidden within it.

However, the good shall be raised from darkness to actuality to dwell immortally with God; but evil shall be separated from the good to be cast out eternally into non-being. For this is the final intent of creation: that whatever could not be for itself, should be for itself by being raised from darkness, as from a ground independent of God, into existence. Hence the necessity of birth and death. God yields the ideas, which within him were without autonomous life, to selfhood and non-being, so that by being called forth from this into life, they may be in him again as independent existences.[33] Thus in its freedom the ground effects separation and judgment (*chrisis*), and precisely therein it effects the complete actualization of God. For evil, when it *is* entirely separated from the good, no longer *is* as evil. It had been able to act only through the (abused) good that was in it, itself being unconscious of it. In life it still enjoyed the forces of external nature with which it attempted to create, and it still participated mediately in God's goodness. But in death it is divided from all that is good, and while it remains as desire, as eternal hunger and thirst for actuality, it can never step out of potentiality. Thus its state is one of non-being, a state in which its activity, or what strives within it to be active, is constantly being consumed. Thus the restitution of evil to the good (the restoration of all things) is in nowise required for the realization of the idea of a final, comprehensive perfection, for evil is evil only insofar as it goes beyond potentiality, but when reduced to non-being, or to the state of potential, it is what it always should be: a basis, subjugated, and as such no longer in contradiction to God's holiness or love. Thus the end of revelation is the expulsion of evil from the good, the explanation of evil as complete unreality. On the other hand, the good that was raised from the ground is combined with original good in eternal unity; those born out of darkness into light join the ideal principle as limbs of its body in which is the perfectly actualized and now completely personal being. As long as the initial duality lasted, the creating word dominated in the ground, and this period of creation endures throughout all until the end. But when the duality is annihilated by division, the word or the ideal principle subjugates itself, together with the real that has become one with it, to spirit, and the latter, as divine consciousness, lives in like manner

33. *Philosophy and Religion* (Tübingen, 1804), p. 73.

in both principles. As the Scripture says of Christ: he must rule until he brings all his enemies under his feet. The last enemy to be abolished is death (for death was necessary only for division: the good must die in order to divide itself from evil, and evil in order to divide itself from the good). But when all has been made subject to him, then the son himself will be made subject to him who has subjected all things to the son, so that God may be all in all. For even spirit is not the highest; it is but spirit, or the breath of love. Love, however, is the highest. Love is what existed before the ground and before existing beings (as separated) were, but what was not yet as love, but rather—how shall we designate it?

Here we finally reach the highest point of the entire investigation. For a long time we have been hearing this question: what purpose is served by that first distinction between the being insofar as it is the ground, and insofar as it exists? For either there is no common midpoint for these two—then we must declare ourselves for absolute dualism; or there is such a midpoint—and then in the final analysis the two coincide again. In this case we have one being for all opposites, an absolute identity of light and darkness, good and evil, and all the incongruous consequences which must befall every rational system, and which were detected in this system, too, some time ago.

We have already explained what we assume in the first respect: there must be a being *before* all ground and before all existence, thus before any duality at all; how can we call this anything but the original ground, or rather the *unground*? Since it precedes all opposites, these cannot be differentiated within it or be in any way present within it. Thus it cannot be designated as the identity of opposites, but only as their absolute *indifference*. Most people, when they come to the point where they must recognize a disappearance of all opposites, forget that these now have actually disappeared, and they repredicate the opposites, as such, of the indifference that had arisen precisely through their complete cessation. Indifference is not a product of opposites, nor are they contained in it *implicite*; rather it is a being of its own, separated from all opposition, on which all opposites are broken, which is nothing other than their very non-being, and which therefore has no predicate except predicatelessness, without therefore being a nothing or an absurdity. Thus either they actually posit indifference in the unground preceding all ground, in which case they have neither good nor evil (for we will ignore, for the time being, that to elevate the opposition of good and evil to this viewpoint is inadmissible in the first place), and can predicate neither the one nor the other nor both at once of the unground; or they posit good and evil, in which case they at once posit duality as well, and thus no longer posit the unground or indifference. Let the following commentary be made on what was just said: real and ideal, darkness and light, or however else we wish to designate the two principles, can never be predicated of the unground *as opposites*. But nothing hinders their being predicated of it as non-opposites, i.e., in disjunction and each *for itself*; whereby, however, this very duality (the actual twofoldness of the principles) is posited. In the unground itself there is nothing that would hinder this. For precisely because the unground is related to both as total indifference, it is impartial to them. If it were the absolute identity of both, then it could only be both *simultaneously*, i.e., both would have to be predicated of it as *opposites*, and would themselves thereby be one again. Thus from this neither-nor, or from this indifference, duality (which is something entirely different from opposition, even if we should have used both previously as synonyms, since we had not yet arrived at this point in the investigation) immediately breaks forth, and *without* indifference, i.e., *without* an unground, there would be no twofoldness of the principles. Instead of annulling the differentiation as was supposed, the unground much rather posits and confirms it. Far from the differentiation between the ground and the existent being merely a logical one, or one called in only as a stopgap and then found to be a sham again in the end, it rather showed itself to be a very real differentiation which was first rightly proven and fully comprehended from the highest standpoint.

Following this dialectical discussion we thus can most definitely explain ourselves in the following manner: the essence of the ground, as that of the existent, can be only that which precedes all ground, thus the absolute viewed purely and simply, the unground. However it can be this (as has been proven) in no other way than by separating into two equally eternal beginnings, not that it is both *simultaneously*, but that it is in both *in like manner*, thus being the whole or its own essence in both. But the unground separates itself into the two equally eternal beginnings only in order that the two that could not be simultaneous or one in the unground as such, become one through love, i.e., it separates itself only in order that life and love may be, and personal existence. For there is love neither in indifference nor where opposites are combined which require combination in order to be, but rather (to repeat a word already spoken) this is the mystery of love, that it combines what could be by itself and yet is not and cannot be without the other.[34] Therefore, as duality comes to be in the unground, there, too, the love that combines the existent (the ideal) with the ground of existent comes to be. But the ground remains free and independent of the word until the final, total division. Then it dissolves, as initial longing dissolves in man when he moves to clarity and grounds himself as an enduring essence, and all truth and goodness within longing is raised to luminous consciousness, but all else, namely the false and impure, is eternally locked in darkness, in order to remain as the eternally dark ground of selfhood, as the *caput mortuum* of its life process, and as potential which can never proceed to act. Then all is subjugated to spirit: in spirit the existent is one with the ground of existence; in it both are actually simultaneous, or it is the absolute identity of both. But above spirit is the initial unground which is no longer indifference (impartiality) and yet is not the identity of both principles, but rather the general unity, the same towards all and yet affected by nothing. It is beneficence, free from all, yet pervading all — in a word, it is love, which is all in all.

Thus whoever would wish to say (as before) that in this system there is one principle for everything, one and the same essence presiding in the dark ground of nature and in eternal clarity, one and the same effecting the harshness and isolation of things as well as unity and gentleness; the same ruling with the will of love in the good and with the will of wrath in evil — while he might be quite correct in saying this, he should not forget that the one essence actually divides itself in two essences in its two manners of action, that in the one it is *only* a ground of existence, and in the other only essence (and therefore is only ideal); nor that only God as spirit is the absolute identity of both principles, but only because and insofar as both are *subjugated* to his personality. But whoever should find an absolute identity of good and evil in this very highest point

34. "Aphorisms on the Philosophy of Nature," in the *Annuals of Medicine as a Science*, Vol. 1, No. 1, aphorisms 162, 163.

of view shows his complete ignorance, since evil and good by no means form an original opposition, and least of all a duality. There is duality where two essences actually oppose each other. Evil, however, is not a being, but a non-essence which is a reality only in opposition, but not in itself. And for this very reason absolute identity, the spirit of love, is prior to evil, because evil can appear only in opposition to it. Hence it also cannot be comprehended in absolute identity, but is eternally excluded and expelled from it.[35]

Finally, whoever would wish to call this system pantheism since all opposites disappear in relation to the absolute viewed as such, he should be granted this, too.[36] We gladly allow everyone his own manner of making the age and what is in it intelligible to himself. The name means nothing; the issue is what counts. The vanity of a polemic consisting of mere general concepts of philosophical systems employed against a particular one that may well have some points of contact in common with them and thus is already con-

35. From this it is clear how strange it is to demand that the opposition of good and evil be explained at once in the first principles. In this manner, indeed, those must speak who consider good and evil to be an actual duality, and dualism to be the most perfect system.

36. No one can be more in accord than the author with the wish expressed by Mr. Friedrich Schlegel in the *Heidelberg Annuals*, No. 2, p. 242, that the unmanly, pantheistic hoax in Germany might cease, especially since Mr. Schlegel includes aesthetic reveries and presumptions, and insofar as we may also count the opinion concerning the exclusive rationalism of Spinozism to that hoax. It is indeed very easy to stir up a false opinion or even a hoax in Germany, where a philosophical system becomes an object of the literary industry, and so many feel called to join in the philosophizing whom nature has denied understanding even for mundane matters. One can at least be comforted in knowing that one has never personally promoted or encouraged this hoax with one's own helpful support, but rather being able to say with Erasmus (however little one may otherwise have in common with him): *semper solus esse volui nihilque peius odi quam iuratos et factiosos*. The author has never wished, by founding a new sect, to rob others, least of all himself, of the freedom of investigation, in which he has always declared himself and probably always will declare himself to be engaged. In the future he will also follow the course taken in the present treatise, whereby everything arises as in a conversation, even if the external form of the conversation is lacking. Much could have been more sharply defined here and not treated so casually, much could have been more explicitly guarded from misinterpretation. The author neglected to do this in part intentionally. Whoever cannot or will not take it from him as it is, let him take nothing from him at all, let him seek other sources. But perhaps unappointed disciples and opponents will grant this treatise the same respect they showed the earlier, related text, *Philosophy and Religion*, by completely ignoring it, having certainly been prompted to do so less by the threats in the foreword or the manner of presentation than by the content itself.

founded with all of them, but which has its peculiar definitions for each individual point—the vanity of such a polemic has been touched upon already in our introduction to this treatise. Thus it takes but a moment to say that a system teaches the immanence of all things in God; and yet with respect to us, for example, nothing would have been said, even if it could not be called an outright untruth. For we have sufficiently demonstrated that all natural beings have mere being in the ground, or in the initial longing which has not yet achieved unity with the understanding, so that they are mere peripheral beings in relation to God. Only man is in God, and through this very being-in-God, he is capable of freedom. He alone is a central essence, and therefore should also remain in the center. In him all things are created, just as it is only through man that God assumes nature and combines it with himself. Nature is the first or old testament, since things are still outside the center and thus under the law. Man is the beginning of the new covenant; through him as mediator, since man himself is combined with God, God (after the last division) also assumes nature and integrates it *into himself.* Thus man is the redeemer of nature, and all its prototypes point towards him. The word fulfilled in man is a dark, prophetic (not fully expressed) word in nature. Hence the omens that have no interpretation in nature, and are first explained by man. Hence the general finality of causes, which likewise becomes intelligible only from this standpoint. Now whoever omits or ignores these intermediate definitions can easily make refutations. Certainly strictly historical criticism is an easy matter. One need not invest anything of oneself, of one's own resources, and can observe the saying, *Caute per Deos! incende, latet ignis sub cinere doloso*, in fine style. But arbitrary and unproved presuppositions are thereby unavoidable. It would require no less than the whole might of a profoundly conceived and thoroughly developed philosophy to prove that there are only two ways of explaining evil—the dualistic method, according to which an evil principle, regardless of its modifications, is assumed beneath or alongside the good principle; and the cabbalistic method, which explains evil in terms of emanation and departure—and that therefore all other systems must annul the distinction between good and evil. Within the system each concept has its own specific place in which it alone is valid, and which also determines its meaning as well as its limitation. How is he to judge the whole rightly who does not consider the interior, but rather lifts only the most general concepts out of their context? We have shown the particular point in the system at which indifference is the only possible concept of the absolute. If this concept now is taken as a generality, then the whole is distorted, with the consequence that this system annuls the personality of the highest being. Up to now we have been silent with respect to this oft-heard reproach as well as several others, but believe that in this treatise we have established the first clear concept of personality. Certainly there is no personality in the unground or in indifference; but is the starting point the whole? Now we challenge those who have made this reproach so lightly to put forward even the least bit of something intelligible on this concept. Instead we find them forever declaring God's personality to be incomprehensible and by no means to be made intelligible. They are also quite right in doing this, since they consider those abstract systems in which personality is entirely impossible to be the only rational ones, which presumably is also the reason why they are ready to attribute such systems to everyone who does not despise science and reason. We, on the contrary, are of the opinion that clear, rational insight must be possible even into the highest concepts, since only thereby can they actually become our own, taken up and eternally grounded in ourselves. Yes, we go even further, and with Lessing we consider the development of revealed truths to rational truths to be utterly necessary if the human race is to be helped thereby.[37] We are equally convinced that the reason is completely sufficient for exposing every possible error (in truly spiritual matters), and that the inquisitorial mien assumed in judging philosophical systems is quite dispensable.[38] According to an absolute dualism of good and evil either the one or the other principle predominates in all manifestations and works of the human spirit, and there are only two systems and two religions, one absolutely good, the other utterly evil; moreover, this dualism holds that all things began with purity and simplicity, and all later developments (which were necessary in order that the partial aspects contained within the first unity be revealed, and thereby the unity itself be perfectly revealed) were but corruptions and falsifications. While this view

37. *Education of the Human Race*, §76.
38. Especially if those on the other side want to speak only of *opinions* when they should be speaking of the truths which alone effect salvation.

serves as a mighty sword of Alexander, forever effortlessly slashing the Gordian knot in two, to project it onto history introduces a thoroughly illiberal and highly limiting viewpoint. There was a time preceding this division, and there was a world view and religion which, although opposed to the absolute one, sprang forth from its own ground and not from a falsification of the first. Historically speaking, the sacred shrine is as original as Christianity, and even though it is but the ground and basis of the higher form, nevertheless it is not derivative.

These considerations lead us back to our starting point. A system that contradicts the most sacred feelings, the mind, and moral consciousness can, at least with respect to this attribute, never be called a system of reason, but only one of unreason. On the other hand, a system in which reason actually knows itself would have to unite all the demands of spirit as of the heart, of the most moral feelings as of the strictest understanding. The polemic against reason and science does, of course, allow a certain distinguished generality that avoids precise concepts, so that we can more easily guess its intentions than its specific meaning. Meanwhile, we fear that even if we did probe into its ground, we would be met with nothing extraordinary. For however highly we may value reason, we still do not believe, for example, that someone can be virtuous, or a hero, or a great man at all, by means of pure reason, nor even that the human race, as the well-known saying goes, will be propagated by it. Only in personality is there life; and all personality rests upon a dark ground, which, to be sure, must also be the ground of knowledge. But it is the understanding alone that develops what is hidden in the ground, contained there as mere potential, and raises it to act. This can occur only through division, i.e., through science and dialectics, and we are convinced that these alone will arrest and bring to eternal knowledge that system which was present more often than we might think but again and again escaped, which hovered before all of us, and yet was entirely apprehended by no one. As in life we give our real trust only to the vigorous understanding and we are in want of every true feeling of tenderness, especially from those who are always making a show of their feelings to us; so, too, where truth and knowledge are concerned, selfhood, having come only as far as feeling, can win nothing of our trust. Feeling is glorious when it remains in the ground, but not when it becomes conspicuous, wishing to make itself a being and to rule. If, according to Franz Baader's excellent views, the drive for knowledge is most analogous to the drive for procreation,[39] then in knowledge there is also something analogous to decency and shame, and conversely to indecency and shamelessness as well, a sort of faun-like appetite which tastes of everything without earnestness, without love to form or shape anything. The bond of our personality is spirit, and if the active combination of both principles alone can become creative and generative, then inspiration in its proper sense is the effective principle of every generative or formative art or science. All inspiration expresses itself in a definite manner; thus there is also the sort that expresses itself through a dialectical artistic drive, a truly scientific inspiration. For this reason there is also a dialectical philosophy which, as science, is specifically separated from poetry and religion, for example, and subsists entirely for itself. But it is not one with all possibilities in succession, as those maintain who take pains now to mix everything with everything in so many texts. It is said that reflection is hostile to idea; but the highest triumph of truth is that it steps forth victoriously even from division and separation. Reason is in man what, according to the mystics, is in God the *primum passivum* or the original wisdom in which all things are together and yet isolated, one and yet each free in its own way. It is not activity, as spirit is, nor the absolute identity of both principles of knowledge, but rather indifference, the measure and the general locus, as it were, of truth, the quiet place in which original wisdom is conceived, according to which the understanding is to form as if looking to an archetype. Philosophy has its name on the one hand from love, as the generally inspiring principle, and on the other from this original wisdom, which is its true goal.

If the dialectical principle, i.e., the isolating, but thereby organically ordering and shaping understanding, as well as the archetype towards which it is directed are removed from philosophy so that it has neither measure nor rule within itself any longer, then it has no other alternative but to seek a historical orientation and to take *tradition* as its source and guideline. Then comes the time to seek a historical norm and foundation for philosophy, just as one thought

39. See his treatise on this matter in the *Annuals for Medicine*, Vol. III, No. 1, p. 113.

to ground our poetry through the knowledge of the literature of all nations. We have the greatest respect for the profundity of historical investigations, and believe to have shown that the *almost* universal opinion that man only gradually arose from the dullness of animal instinct to rationality is not our own. Yet we believe the truth lies closer to us, and that we should first look for solutions to the problems stirred up in our day at home, on our own soil, before we wander to such distant sources. The time of mere historical faith is past when the possibility of immediate knowledge is given. We have an older revelation than all written ones — nature. It contains prototypes that no man has yet interpreted, whereas those of written revelations have long since received their fulfillment and interpretation. If the understanding of this unwritten revelation were disclosed, the only true system of religion and science would appear, not in shabby attire pieced together out of a few philosophical and critical concepts, but rather at once in the full splendor of truth and of nature. This is not the time to reawaken old oppositions, but rather to seek what lies above and beyond all opposition.

The present treatise will be followed by a series of others in which the whole of the ideal portion of philosophy will gradually be presented.

Translated by Priscilla Hayden-Roy